AF780651

Cybercurrency Law

Cybercurrency Law

A Guide to Digital Asset Regulation Around the World

Edward J. Swan

Wolters Kluwer

Published by:
Kluwer Law International B.V.
PO Box 316
2400 AH Alphen aan den Rijn
The Netherlands
E-mail: lrs-sales@wolterskluwer.com
Website: www.wolterskluwer.com/en/solutions/kluwerlawinternational

Sold and distributed by:
Wolters Kluwer Legal & Regulatory U.S.
920 Links Avenue
Landisville, PA 17538
United States of America
E-mail: customer.service@wolterskluwer.com

ISBN 978-94-035-4306-2

e-Book: ISBN 978-94-035-4386-4
web-PDF: ISBN 978-94-035-4396-3

© 2023 Edward J. Swan

All rights reserved. No part of this publication may be reproduced, stored in a retrieval system, or transmitted in any form or by any means, electronic, mechanical, photocopying, recording, or otherwise, without written permission from the publisher.

Permission to use this content must be obtained from the copyright owner. More information can be found at: www.wolterskluwer.com/en/solutions/legal-regulatory/permissions-reprints-and-licensing

About the Author

Dr. Swan has been one of the world's leading lawyers advising major international financial businesses, international organizations, national governments, banks, exchanges, clearinghouses, markets, and tech companies.

He was Partner and Counsel in major international law firms, including Skadden Arps, Brown Rudnick, Cameron McKenna (CMCK), and Simmons and Simmons.

Professor Swan has been Visiting Professor of Law at University College London and the Catholic University in Lille and Paris, France, and the IESEG School of Management in Lille and Paris. He has been Member of the Board of the Institute of Advanced Legal Studies at the University of London.

Dr. Swan has published many law books and dozens of articles, including three law books for Oxford University Press and five for Kluwer Law International.

Dr. Swan attended Rocky Mountain College, Montana and Harvard University, United States and has a Juris Doctor degree from New York University and a Ph.D. in Law from the University of London.

Table of Contents

Acknowledgments

I thank all the friends, colleagues, clients, opponents, judges, professors and acquaintances who, over many years, taught me how to be a thoughtful, effective analyst and problem solver.

I must also thank my dear friend Vanna Fadda. Without her support and encouragement my books would not have been possible.

Introduction: Digital Assets Are Regulated

THE ELECTRONIC RUSH FOR MONEY

The creation of computers, the spread of ownership of this tool throughout the population and their interaction with the Internet have certainly stimulated the world's financial imagination. A huge level of brain power has been applied to the question of how to make money using computing power and the Internet.

The respected economist Milton Friedman said in 1999:

> The one thing that's missing, but will soon be developed, is reliable E-cash. A method whereby, on the Internet, you can transfer funds from A to B, without A knowing B or B knowing A. The way in which I can take a $20 bill and hand it over to you and there's no record of where it came from and you may get that without knowing who I am. That kind of thing will develop on the Internet.[1]

It took a while for that prediction to come true. There were various attempts during the 1990s to establish usable, and hopefully, popular e-currency, but none really caught on with a wider public.[2]

Finally, around 2009, a difficult-to-identify digital expert called Satoshi Nakamoto introduced Bitcoin, which became a successful, and now leading, cryptocurrency.

DANGEROUS THINKING ABOUT REGULATION OF CRYPTO ASSETS

There is a popular view, sometimes even expressed by lawyers, that "digital assets" (a general term which is often used to cover digital objects of value that are variously known as "cyber/crypto currencies," "tokens" and "non-fungible tokens (NFTs)") are "unregulated."

That is not true.

1. https://www.youtube.com/watch?v=onn34J74dnU http:youtu.be/mlwxdyLnMXM.
2. For a look at some of the earlier attempts, *see* Halaburda and Sarvary, Beyond Bitcoin: The Economics of Digital Currencies (Palgrave Macmillan, New York, 2016), section 4.3.

Throughout the world, digital assets are increasingly becoming subjects of government and international regulatory scrutiny and are increasingly being declared subject to regulation as follows:

- Taxable property.
- Securities.
- Currency.
- Commodities.
- Derivatives.
- Intellectual property.
- Proceeds of crimes.

The way in which digital assets are regulated varies from jurisdiction to jurisdiction around the world and depends on how those digital assets are marketed and used, but it is certainly the case that regulation of digital assets is expanding nearly as fast as the growth of digital assets as objects of commerce.

The purpose of this book is to give an overview of how the digital asset markets are expanding, how governments are responding to them, and how they are increasingly being affected by regulations around the world.

Because digital assets are by nature "digital," they are inevitably international and able to easily cross borders via electronic communication. It is not the intention of this book to provide a detailed explanation of all the ways in which digital assets are used and regulated throughout the world.

NOT LEGAL ADVICE

This book is not legal advice. It would be foolish, and probably impossible, to try to give a complete explanation of all the different ways that digital assets and their uses are affected by the legal regulation that exists and is growing in the many jurisdictions in which digital assets are owned and used.

The purpose of this book is to provide a general understanding of the issues that participants in the digital asset world need to be aware of as they acquire, own, use and are affected by digital assets.

If anyone or any entity finds it necessary to have legal advice about the regulatory effects of the policy and laws of any particular legal jurisdiction, it will be necessary for them to obtain advice from qualified legal advisors in that jurisdiction or jurisdictions.

THE CRYPTO EXPLOSION

At the end of July 2022, the total value of the cryptocurrency market was reported to be more than US$ 950 billion.[3]

3. Jennifer Sor, "The Total Value of the Crypto Market has Surged in Recent Weeks as Bears Start to Buy Back in and Bulls 'Hold on for Dear Life'," Markets Insider, online at: markets.businessinsider.com, August 1, 2022, accessed August 10, 2022.

In 2013 there were sixty-six cryptocurrencies in circulation. By November of 2021, the number had grown to over 7,500 cryptocurrencies.[4] This dramatic rise is probably because cryptocurrencies are not too difficult to create. Just about anyone that wants to can make one up. Not all cryptocurrencies are equal. It is estimated that the top twenty cryptocurrencies constitute about 90% of crypto trading worldwide.

Cryptocurrency is perhaps the best-known example of a global trend that began around 2008 to democratize the creation and ownership of valuable assets.[5] This trend revolves around confidence in the effectiveness of "blockchain" technology.

BLOCKCHAIN

Blockchain technology provides an assumed security with respect to the ownership of nonphysical digital assets that exist in the form of computer code.

Briefly, a "blockchain" is a digital "open electronic ledger" (Ledger) that stores data about purchases and sales of digital assets, allegedly permanently and securely.[6] Essentially, it allows anyone to record a transaction in the Ledger. The existence of this digital record provides proof of the history of the asset from its creation to the present. Supposedly, this prevents a party from pretending that they have the right to possess or dispose of an asset recorded in the Ledger because the Ledger provides a supposedly immutable chain of transaction history that shows who has had ownership rights in an asset from the time of its creation until the present. Blockchains are difficult to hack because they are public Ledgers which are constantly reviewed by users.

A certain level of confidence in the security of blockchain Ledgers is justified, but because of the popularity of cryptocurrency and the use of blockchains, there have been recent reports that highly skilled hackers are working hard to find innovative ways to hack blockchain Ledgers.[7] One hacking technique that is reported to be relatively successful is the so-called 51% attack.

The 51% Attack?

It is difficult and expensive to have the resources to get access to the assets which a blockchain is created to protect. However, as with most things created by humans, despite the apparent difficulty of getting illegitimate access to a blockchain and the assets it intends to protect, it is not impossible to do so.

4. Raynor de Best, "Quantity of Cryptocurrencies as of November 3, 2021," Statista, online, December 17, 2021.
5. "How Crypto is Rewriting the Rules of Digital Ownership: In an Age of Pervasive Digitization, Cryptocurrency is Changing How People Think About Everything from Ownership to the Future of the Internet," nytimes.com, online, Ledger, Paid Post, accessed January 7, 2022.
6. World Bank Group (H. Natarajan, S. Krause, and H. Gradstein), "Distributed Ledger Terminology and Blockchain," 2017, FinTech note, no. 1. Washington D.C., online at: documents.worldbank.org.
7. Pawan Nahar, "What Are 51% Attacks on Cryptocurrencies," The Economic Times, online, August 31, 2021.

It is reported that they can be vulnerable to what is called "a 51% attack" if they use "proof of work" (*see* explanation below) to legitimize asset production.

The attack consists of a hacker getting control of more than 50% of the "hashing power" of a blockchain, which allows the hacker to manipulate the data in the blockchain.[8] "Hashing power" is the total computational power of a cryptocurrency network, or the power of a cryptocurrency mining operation. The larger the chain, as is the case with the most popular cryptos like Bitcoin, the more difficult it is to make a successful 51% attack. However, as mentioned above, there reportedly have been created over 10,000 kinds of cryptocurrencies. Some of the blockchains are smaller unless and not very decentralized. The advantage to the hacker is that a successful attack allows them to duplicate digital token files and thus use them or sell them more than once.

Other hacking methods that affect cryptocurrency include: attacking poorly coded smart contracts that hackers can manipulate to reroute transfers of crypto, or cracking the "private key" to a crypto account which allows the hacker to steal the crypto in the account. It seems that the last one would be vulnerable to the computing power of the recently created quantum computer systems. These are exponentially more powerful than the "classic" computers currently on the market and may be able to find digital passwords and keys much more quickly than they can be discovered today by the computers currently available.

Apparently, there have been a number of 51% attacks involving popular cryptocurrencies, including Bitcoin, Ethereum and Bitcoin Gold and other less well-known cryptos. Attacks are reported to affect the value of the cryptos in question when they become publicly known.

It is reported that Bitcoin suffered from such an attack in August of 2021, and this caused a 5% decline in its value at the time. Bitcoin Gold suffered from a similar attack in 2019. Ethereum has reportedly suffered from several 51% attacks starting in about 2016.[9]

Proof of Work

"Proof of Work" (PoW) is a process that has become an important way of verifying the legitimacy of particular cryptocurrencies, most famously Bitcoin and Ethereum.

PoW is defined as: "a protocol designed to make digital transactions secure without having to rely on the third party."[10]

It is said that the concept behind PoW originated in a paper by Cynthia Dwork and Moni Naor published in 1993 entitled "Pricing via Processing or Combatting Junk Mail."[11]

This paper explored the possibilities of providing an electronic method for restricting access to a desirable resource.

8. *Ibid.*, August 31, 2021.
9. *Ibid.*
10. *Ibid.*
11. *Ibid.*

Specifically, the authors were exploring the possibility of restricting access to email inboxes which they noticed were being filled with unsolicited electronic junk mail. Sadly, their suggested solutions do not seem to have been universally applied to the email junk mail problem so that most of the world's possessors of email addresses continue to receive many unsolicited emails a day. As Dwork and Naor pointed out, this is probably due to the fact that possible email restrictors pose problems that could substantially reduce the benefits of email:

> We do not want a system in which to send a letter or note between friends should have a cost similar to that of a postage stamp; Similarly, we do not wish to charge a high fee to transmit long files between professional collaborators. Such an approach could lead to *underutilization* of the electronic medium.[12]

They suggest that various electronic "gateways" could be imposed between someone wishing to access a desirable electronic asset and the asset itself. These gateways could consist of requiring the access seeker to perform certain electronic functions. The interposed functions could be described as either easy, moderate, or hard. An example they give of a "hard" function would be something like "factoring a 1024 bit product of two large primes."[13]

The term "Proof of Work" was actually coined a few years later in a paper entitled "Proofs of Work and Bread Pudding Protocols" by Marcus Jacobson and Ari Juels, published in 1999.[14] Their paper explored the concept further.

Crypto Mining

With respect to cryptocurrency mining, the purpose of PoW is to produce a complicated calculation that can add a "block" to a blockchain in a computer-accessible "Ledger" that consists of a record of transactions. Each transaction is referred to as a "block." If a "crypto miner" is successful in adding a block to a blockchain, he is rewarded by receiving a crypto coin and a transaction fee. To find the correct calculation solution that will add a block to a blockchain, a crypto miner needs to use expensive, high-powered computational equipment to find the correct calculation before competitors do. The correct calculation is very hard to find because, for example, with Bitcoin, the solution always contains 64 characters. This obviously presents a huge number of possible calculation results, but only one will be correct and permit an addition of a new block to a blockchain.

In 2008, Satoshi Nakamoto published his famous Bitcoin white paper entitled "Bitcoin: A Peer-to-Peer Electronic Cash System." In this paper, he described a way to apply the PoW concept to cryptocurrency.[15]

12. Cynthia Dwork and Moni Naor, "Pricing via Processing or Combatting Junk Mail," published in 1993, available for download online at: dwork.seas.harvard.edu, p. 1, accessed September 16, 2022.
13. *Ibid.*
14. Nick Lindsay, "Proof of Work (PoW): What Is It and How Does It Work," 09 November 2018, BLOCKLR, online at: blocklr.com, accessed September 16, 2022.
15. *Ibid.*

This method of preventing unauthorized access to particular valuable assets is gaining a great deal of interest with respect to other computational activities that seek access to valuable assets which may not be crypto coins. Depending on the value of the asset, the computations required to add a block to the relevant blockchain (the gateway) can be made more or less difficult.

HOW SAFE ARE DIGITAL ASSETS?

So, how "safe" a cryptocurrency or other digital asset investment? Not very safe, according to an article in *The Times*:[16]

> Cryptocurrency-based crime hit a record high last year with criminals pocketing $14 billion worth of bitcoin, ethereum and other digital currencies from scams, ransomware and thefts.

During the last year, cryptocurrency theft has grown enormously. In 2021 there was over a 500% increase in cryptocurrency theft from 2020.[17]

Unlike other investments, there is no organized protection or reimbursement available for cryptocurrency owners who lose or lose access to their cryptocurrency because of illegal activity.

There are a number of different ways to lose money with respect to cryptocurrency, in addition to declines in the market value of a particular cryptocurrency.

According to an organization named "Payback" that claims to "work to get your money back,"[18] there are a number of different ways the cryptocurrency can be stolen. These reportedly can include the following "scams" relating to purchase and sale of cryptocurrency. Payback advises using one of the better-known crypto exchanges, and lists Coinbase, Bitstamp, Kraken, Binance and Bittrex as such. However, one is advised to do due diligence before choosing an exchange.[19]

Some Scams

There are bit mining scams. These are scams that invite people to invest in projects to produce or "mine" cryptocurrency. In these scams, promoters simply take the invested funds and disappear without completing the mining promised.

Then there are "bit wallet" scams which either try to persuade people to place their purchased cryptocurrencies in insecure crypto storage facilities known as "wallets," or persuade crypto owners using legitimate crypto storage wallets to reveal their passwords or "keys" to their wallets.

16. "Cryptocurrency Thieves Make off with a Record $14 Billion," The Times, online, January 8, 2022.
17. *Ibid.*
18. The author has no experience with this organization's recovery efforts. Payback-ltd.com, online, accessed January 10, 2022.
19. *Ibid.*

There are "pump and dump" scams that try to persuade as many people as possible to invest in cryptocurrencies which the promoters have previously bought at a low price prior to the promotion. When enough people have been persuaded to invest in the cryptos in question so that their price rises, the scamming promoters will then liquidate their position making a profit for themselves but causing the value of the cryptocurrency to decline, causing investors to lose money.

There are "pyramid" scams whereby promoters try to persuade people to purchase a particular crypto product (which may be worthless), promising spectacular returns from rises in the product's value and urging purchasers to bring other investors, promising shares of the money these others invest. In pyramid scams, the promoters will steal most of the money invested, without making any of the promised crypto purchases. They will pay early investors a portion of the money put in by later investors, claiming these payments are "dividends" or "profits" from the investing they have done on the investors' behalf. The scam collapses when it runs out of new investors. This type of scam is also called a "Ponzi" scheme,[20] recently made more famous by the scheme run by Bernard Madoff until his arrest in 2008 that took in an estimated US$ 64 billion.[21]

There have been many allegations that cryptocurrencies can be used to construct Ponzi schemes. The U.S. Securities and Exchange Commission (SEC) has published an "Investor Alert" entitled "Ponzi Schemes Using Virtual Currencies."[22]

At the beginning of 2022, an online publication called "NextAdvisor" published a detailed description of cryptocurrency scams and a statement of warnings about investing in cryptocurrency.[23] The article pointed out that about US$ 14 billion had been stolen by crypto-scams in 2021, about double the amount stolen in 2020. Reviewing this article is a useful exercise for anyone considering purchasing or accepting cryptocurrency. Perhaps the most important thing in this review to keep in mind is the following statement:

> Unlike bank accounts for federally regulated currency, there is no such thing as fraud protection or FDIC insurance on the blockchain. When your money gets stolen on blockchain, the only way to get it back is for the recipient to pay you back directly. On a decentralized exchange, that's highly unlikely. And while mainstream crypto exchanges have better fraud and security measures than lesser-known exchanges, there's still no guarantee for investors to recoup stolen crypto.[24]

It should be noted that this lack of guaranteed protection against theft and fraud is not only true for cryptocurrency transactions in the United States (US) but also usually the case throughout the world.

20. Named for Carlo Ponzi, a Boston, Massachusetts, USA, con man operating such a scheme in the 1920s.
21. *See* Wikipedia, "Bernie Madoff," online, accessed January 19, 2022.
22. SEC, online, accessed January 19, 2022.
23. For more detail on the types of crypto-scams, *see*, Megan DeMatteo, "Scammers Stole $14 Billion in Crypto in 2021. Here's How Investors Can Protect Their Coins," Next Advisor: In Partnership with TIME, online, January 6, 2022.
24. *Ibid.*

Another disconcerting development in the world of cryptocurrency is the number of reported "disappearances" of founders of crypto coin exchanges who vanish taking billions in cryptocurrency with them.

The Crypto Queen

In November of 2019, the BBC reported that Ruja Ignatova, creator of the cryptocurrency OneCoin, and known as "The Crypto Queen," "scammed the world, then vanished."[25] She is a good example of how crypto scammers have gone from being a problem in the cryptocurrency market to becoming some of the world's biggest crime problems. Ignatova disappeared in 2017 but not before OneCoin had become so popular that it attracted billions of dollars from investors.

Ignatova was an Oxford-educated businesswoman whose presentation lent significant credibility to a project that she claimed had resulted in the creation of a cryptocurrency that was "a Bitcoin killer." In June of 2016, she told a cheering crowd of loyal fans at Wembley Arena that OneCoin would become the world's most popular cryptocurrency "for everyone to make payments everywhere."

At that time, Bitcoin was becoming well known as an investment that could rise in value dramatically, making fortunes for its early investors. People who had seen this were looking for another opportunity to get into a popular crypto early and make their fortune from their early discovery of a hot investment. OneCoin was purportedly offering that opportunity, and many people wanted to be a part of it. The BBC reported that they had seen evidence that people in Britain invested about € 30 million in OneCoin during the first six months of 2016. By March of 2017, more than € 4 billion had been invested in OneCoin around the world. The Chinese were the biggest investors in this crypto, with Germans, British and Americans being second, third and fourth.[26]

When Ignatova vanished in 2017, U.S. law enforcement authorities were among the first to charge her with fraud and money laundering offenses. However, she has not been found. The Federal Bureau of Investigation (FBI) in the US has designated her as one of the FBI's ten most wanted fugitives. This may or may not help the investors from whom billions have been stolen, but it certainly establishes the Crypto Queen as one of the world's most important financial criminals.

This also moves crypto coin transactions into the arena of being one of the financial markets' most dangerous criminal activities.

A major problem with cryptocurrency is that Bitcoins were first introduced as being the product of a certain amount of computer "work." The crypto world has changed so that thousands of cryptocurrencies have appeared that do not seem to have any production labor involved in their creation. Creators claim that they are offering a cryptocurrency that customers should regard as a product that will increase in value.

25. *BBC*, "Cryptoqueen: How This Woman Scammed the World, Then Vanished," online, November 24, 2019.
26. Jamie Bartlett, "How This Woman Scammed the World, Then Vanished" *BBC News*, online, November 24, 2019.

This gives effective salespeople such as Ignatova opportunities to attract enormous amounts of money into businesses that may offer no returns whatsoever and that may indeed steal the money invested in them. Whether the Crypto Queen will ever be caught remains to be seen. The most recent reports connect her with Dubai, which is one of the countries that she is most associated with.

A legal claim on behalf of those defrauded by OneCoin has been lodged in court at the British Indian Ocean territory which is apparently a jurisdiction that has been used by OneCoin. It remains to be seen whether that action or legal proceedings in any other jurisdiction connected with OneCoin will lead to any compensation being paid to those that were allegedly defrauded. But there was little question that this is one of the biggest scams in history and demonstrates the power of cryptocurrency to extract money from people all around the world. Ignatova may still have over 250,000 Bitcoins, and is thought to be moving around using high-quality, fake, identity documents. In fact, she may be the largest single holder of Bitcoins.[27]

Disappearance in Turkey

In April of 2021, it was reported that the founder of a cryptocurrency exchange in Turkey disappeared with US$ 2 billion worth of client cryptocurrency.[28]

Disappearance in South Africa

In June of 2021, it was reported that Ameer and Raees Cajee, the founders of a South African-based cryptocurrency investment site, had vanished with over US$ 2 billion worth of bitcoin belonging to their customers.[29]

GROWTH OF CRYPTO EXCHANGES

Most cryptocurrency is traded on "cryptocurrency exchanges." This is another area that has experienced explosive growth since cryptocurrencies first came onto the scene in about 2008. The largest exchange is Binance. Over US$ 30 billion worth of cryptocurrencies works changed on Binance in November of 2021.

The next largest is called the Mandala Exchange which traded over 28 billion dollars in cryptocurrencies in that same time period. These two are by far the largest exchanges. There are over 100 other cryptocurrency exchanges in operation.[30]

27. Jane Bartlett and Rob Byrne, "Missing Cryptoqueen: Is Dr Ruja Ignatova the Biggest Bitcoin Holder?" *BBC News*, online July 2, 2022.
28. Anton Shilov, "Crypto Exchange Founder Disappears with $2 Billion," tom'sHARDWARE, online, April 24, 2021.
29. Emily Mason, "South African Brother Disappear, Along With $2.2 Billion Worth of Bitcoin," Forbes, online, June, 23 2021.
30. Raynor de Best, "The 100 Biggest Cryptocurrency Exchanges in the World on November 22, 2021," "Statista," online, December 17, 2021.

The market cap of the two most popular cryptocurrencies is reported to be more than USD 1.2 trillion.[31]

However, the bankruptcy of the FTX exchange (and resulting criminal charges) in late 2022 has caused crypto traders to be less certain about the solidity of exchanges such as Binance.[32]

EXTENSIVE INTERNATIONAL REGULATORY COOPERATION NEEDED

The world Gross Domestic Product (GDP) for 2020 was reported to be more than US$ 84 trillion. It is not difficult to see that a trade in which the two largest exchanges contributed more than US$ 1.2 trillion is likely to have a significant effect on the world economy. In other words, cryptocurrency trading has grown to a size where it can impact on financial stability worldwide.

This puts significant pressure on governments and regulators around the world regardless of the participation of their own citizens in crypto asset transactions. However, regardless of whether regulators have decided to restrict or even ban the ownership and use of crypto in their own economies, it will not be easy to avoid the impact on their economies from the use and trading of cryptocurrency in other countries. World trade is global. The actions of one country and the economic status of other countries affect all participants in global trade. Consequently, governments and regulators will need to think very carefully about how they treat cryptocurrency domestically, and they will also need to consider participating in important international treaties and conventions about how cryptocurrency and other digital assets and their effects will be regulated.

Since the first appearance of cybercurrency, there has been considerable confusion on the part of regulators, courts and governments as to whether these should be considered currencies, commodities or investments. Depending on which it is, the legal and regulatory status of cybercurrencies would be different. This points out the need for international cooperation when it comes to regulating cybercurrencies because it would be very confusing if their status was different from jurisdiction to jurisdiction although they were being traded internationally.

Again, this points up the dilemma of the Internet. Although those using it may be located in a discreet jurisdiction, their activities have an impact throughout the world. Although there has been a considerable amount of cooperation between countries in formulating international conventions and treaties relating to the Internet,[33] the job is far from over with respect to cybercurrencies and other digital assets. These present difficulties make it clear that much more international work still needs to be done in this area.

31. "Today's Cryptocurrency Prices by Market Cap," CoinMarketCap, online, December 17, 2021.
32. Joshua Oliver and Scott Chipolina, "Binance Suffers $1bn Outflow in One Day as Crypto Jitters Spread," The Financial Times, online, December 13, 2022.
33. *See*, Edward J. Swan, Internet Law: A Concise Guide to Regulation Worldwide (Kluwer Law International, 2022).

CHAPTER 1

Cybercurrency

§1.01 WHAT IS CURRENCY?

It is a good question as to when currency first came into existence. Earliest records that we have of trade are cuneiform contracts written to record agreements to buy and sell various items desired by the parties to those contracts.

Earliest examples of those do not describe the exchanges being made for anything that might be considered currency. Usually, they are promises to exchange amount of one commodity for another. An example would be an exchange of roof tiles for a certain amount of a particular kind of grain.[34]

These are very direct exchanges which were free of the intermediation of something we could call currency.

Webster's Dictionary describes "currency" as something in circulation "as a medium of exchange." The key term in this definition is "medium," which indicates something which stands between the object to be purchased and the purchaser which is accepted by both parties and satisfying their understanding of value.

Currency or "money" is something which may have no intrinsic value (depending on the material which is identified as money) but which is assigned a value to allow it to be used to pay for goods and services. In other words, currency is something that receives its value from a belief system of the people using it who give it value by having faith that the issuer of the currency will arrange to protect the value of the "currency" either by putting their reputation for integrity behind the currency, by holding in reserve materials (such as precious metals) equal to the value of the issued currency, or by providing an independent system that prevents manipulation or debasement of the issued currency (such as physical structure to prevent copying or electronically locking it in place with a system such as "blockchain").

34. Edward J. Swan, Building the Global Market: A 4000 Year History of Derivatives (London, Kluwer Law International, 2000), Chapter 2.

Traditionally, for currency to exist and be generally accepted as having value, two conditions are needed: first, a currency must be issued by someone who is accepted as having the authority to create it, and second, those who use the currency must believe that it has a particular value.

Historically, the first condition has been the most important. Generally, it has been difficult or impossible to create currency unless one is accepted as the political ruler of the jurisdiction where the currency is being used.

However, the legal status of manufacturing money is not entirely clear and differs from jurisdiction to jurisdiction. In some countries, there are specific laws against it, in others not. This, of course, is a key issue in determining the legal status of cryptocurrency. In fact, the manufacturers of cryptocurrency do not seem to be completely clear about whether their cryptocurrency is "money," an "investment" or both. In the following chapters, dealing with the laws of particular countries or legal jurisdictions, there are discussions of the currency manufacturing laws and restrictions of particular jurisdictions.

It is usually illegal, punishable by severe penalties, to copy an official currency or to issue something which purports to be in competition with official currency. It is generally accepted that efforts to do those things constitute the criminal offense of counterfeiting.

US law forbids the counterfeiting or alteration of any foreign obligations, securities, or currencies within the United States.

Within the European Union (EU), there are numerous laws and regulations against the counterfeiting of euro notes and coins. A special program, called the Pericles 2020 program, has been set up to aid the members of the EU in their efforts to protect against the counterfeiting of EU currency.[35]

Under European law, the fraudulent making or altering of currency, or making counterfeits or the distribution of counterfeit currency, or the making and possessing of counterfeiting equipment are all punishable as criminal conduct.[36]

So where does cybercurrency fit on this spectrum between being recognized as "medium of exchange" and the copying of national currencies?

It appears that the law on this issue is not completely settled with different countries or international groups of countries. They can take different positions on the legal status of cryptocurrency within their jurisdictions.

The production of cybercurrency does not really fit the standard definition of counterfeiting which is "made in imitation of something else with intent to deceive."[37] From this definition, it appears that in order to be "counterfeit," an item must be: (1) made in imitation and (2) with intent to deceive.

---

35. Regulation (EU) No 331/2014 of the European Parliament and of the Council of March 11, 2014, establishing an exchange assistance and training program for the protection of the euro against counterfeiting (the 'Pericles 2020' program) and repealing Council Decisions 2001/923/EC, 2001/924/EC, 2006/75/EC, 2006/76/EC, 2006/849/EC and 2006/850 EC.
36. Directive 2014/62/EU entered into force on May 22, 2014.
37. Merriam-Webster's Collegiate Dictionary, 11th Edition (Merriam-Webster, Incorporated, Springfield, MA, 2012).

It appears that crossing the line into illegality depends to a significant extent on how the cybercurrency is marketed to potential recipients.

Cybercurrency appears, in some respects, to meet the definition of "currency." It is often described as or understood to be a "medium of exchange" in the sense that it is expected to be used as a medium for purchasing goods and services either immediately or in the future.

However, its ability to act as an effective medium of exchange depends not only on the person offering cybercurrency in exchange for goods or services but also on the belief of the seller of goods or services that they are receiving adequate value for the things they are supplying in exchange for the cybercurrency.

The required confidence in cybercurrency is far less easy to obtain than a medium of exchange that is issued by a national government and reportedly backed by the assets of that government. National governments not only offer their backing to the currencies they issue but also usually require that those within their jurisdiction accept the national currency as "legal tender" for goods and services bought and sold within their jurisdiction. There is usually no such compulsory force behind any of the privately created cyber currencies.[38] Their viability is usually dependent on the belief of individuals that these currencies are valuable now or will be in the future and that they can be exchanged for certain goods and services.

That will change if cybercurrencies are adopted by national governments or if national governments decide to issue their own cybercurrencies.

The electronic nature of cybercurrencies is a modern characteristic made possible by the almost universal availability of computers and access to the Internet. This electronic nature or "cyber" nature is a neutral characteristic. What puts these electronic items into the arena of money is belief in their value and/or the force of law.

Another issue that will affect the legal status of cybercurrencies is the perception that they are "competing" with national currencies in the arena of money. To the extent that they come to be seen as alternatives to national currency, they make national currency less desirable and, therefore, less valuable. This is a dangerous effect. To pay for goods, services and infrastructure that they need to function as governments, countries need to benefit from protecting the maximum value of their national currencies in the minds of those they need to pay, including, of course, the providers of instruments for their national defense.

If the number of people that are happy to accept national currency for their work or products declines because they insist on receiving privately issued cyber currency instead, this threatens the security and stability of a nation. Reviewing the responses of various jurisdictions to the existence and market penetration of cyber currencies so far, it seems that some countries have grasped this principle more quickly than others and have fashioned their legal responses to reflect their concerns about this issue.

38. However, there are some exceptions. For example, El Salvador has reportedly accepted Bitcoins as legal tender in that country. *See* detailed discussion in following chapter.

§1.02 CYBERCURRENCY

Privately issued digital money, popularly known as "cybercurrency" or "cryptocurrency," is a decentralized peer-to-peer payment system that was created to operate separately from national governments and their central banks.

The best-known, and perhaps the most popular, cybercurrency is Bitcoin (BTC). It is intended to be a discreet international medium of exchange.

[A] Bitcoin

Bitcoin was first introduced about 2008.[39] It was apparently originally created by someone called "Satoshi Nakamoto" who was said to be a software developer.

This is how Bitcoin announced the launch of its "cash" in a 2008 "white paper":[40]

> Bitcoin: A Peer-to-Peer Electronic Cash System
>
> Satoshi Nakamoto satoshin@gmx.com www.bitcoin.org
>
> *Abstract.* A purely peer-to-peer version of electronic cash would allow online payments to be sent directly from one party to another without going through a financial institution.

However, it has never been established for certain who originated Bitcoin, and there is still some controversy being fought out in court over who is the actual creator of Bitcoin. There has been a law case in Florida in which claims were being made by two claimants who insist that they are the real inventors of Bitcoin. One is an Australian computer scientist named Craig Wright; the other claimant is the estate of Dave Kleinman who died in 2013. Mr. Kleinman's relatives claim that creation of Bitcoin under the name of Satoshi Nakamoto was a joint venture and that they are entitled to an equal share in a stash of 1.1 million Bitcoins that are now worth in the region of US$ 50 billion dollars.[41]

In that case, the jury rejected the claim that there was a partnership between Wright and Kleinman. However, they did find that Kleinman should receive compensation of US$ 100 million because of the way Wright used some of the Bitcoins for his own purposes.[42]

Wright and his supporters claim that the decision in that case established that Wright is "the sole creator of Bitcoin." However, there are still those that disagree, and the question of who invented cryptocurrency has still not been clearly resolved.[43]

---

39. Simon Duke, Ben Martin, "Does Omicron Panic Show that Cryptocurrency Has Got Serious," The Times, online, December 8, 2021.
40. www.bitcoin.org.
41. "Court Decides that Australian Is Bitcoin Creator," The Times, online, December 9, 2021.
42. Paul Vigna, "Jury in Bitcoin Creator Satoshi Nakamoto Suit Finds No Evidence of Partnership to Create Cryptocurrency," The Wall Street Journal, online, December 6, 2021.
43. Danny Fortson, "Did Craig Wright Invent Bitcoin—or Is He a Crypto Fraud?," The Sunday Times, online, December 12, 2021.

Despite the claims of Mr. Wright and Mr. Kleinman, and the evidence that has been presented on their behalf, there still appear to be major questions as to who invented Bitcoin and who Satoshi Nakamoto is.

About a month after the resolution of the Florida civil case described above, no less a figure than Elon Musk went public with his very different belief as to the identity of Satoshi Nakamoto. Musk stated in an interview on the podcast of artificial intelligence researcher Lex Fridman:[44]

> Obviously I don't know who created Bitcoin for practical purposes, but ... the evolution of ideas is pretty clear before that, it seems as though Nick Szabo is probably more than anyone else responsible for the evolution of those ideas.

According to an *IFLS* report, Nick Szabo is a secretive person who many people believe is the "real" Satoshi Nakamoto. This speculation has been supported by what are believed to be similarities between the language of Szabo's writing and writing that is purported to be that of Satoshi Nakamoto. Szabo is reported to have invented another cryptocurrency called "bitgold" about ten years before Bitcoin appeared.[45]

However, Szabo has consistently denied that he is Satoshi Nakamoto. Musk does not appear to be claiming definitively that he is. What Musk appears to be saying is that Szabo's work significantly contributed to the evolution of cryptocurrency.[46] Mush is quoted as saying:[47]

> "You can look at the evolution of ideas before the launch of Bitcoin and see who wrote about those ideas," Musk said. "He [Szabo] claims not to be Nakamoto, but ... that's neither here nor there. He seems to be the one more responsible for the ideas behind Bitcoin than anyone else."

So how close are we to accurately identifying Satoshi Nakamoto? Musk does not seem very bothered by this, saying:

> "What is the name anyway? ... A name attached to an idea. What does it even mean, really?"[48]
>
> This may have been partially resolved in August 2022 when Craig Wright won a UK libel case against a blogger who reportedly alleged that Wright was a fraud. The court ruled that the defendant's allegations caused "serious harm" to Wright's reputation. Defendant allegedly claimed in podcasts that "Craig Wright is not Satoshi" and was "a fraud."[49]

---

44. Katie Spalding, "Who is Satoshi Nakamoto? Elon Musk Has An Answer—And It Might Not Be What You Expect," IFL Science (IFLS), online, December 31, 2021.
45. Katie Spalding, December 31, 2021.
46. *Ibid.*
47. *Ibid.*
48. *Ibid.*
49. Padraic Flanagan, "Bitcoin Inventor Craig Wright Awarded £1 Damages in Libel Case," The Times, online, August 2, 2022.

The Times article reported that:

> In 2016 Wright claimed to be Nakamoto, author of a 2008 paper describing a digital currency outside official control.[50]

As of this writing, on Bitcoin's website at "bitcoin.com," they say:

> "Bitcoin.com
>
> "Your gateway to Bitcoin & beyond"

The parent organization of Bitcoin is reported to be a company named "Saint Bitts LLC." This company is reported to have offices in Tel Aviv, Israel, and in Yamanashi, Kai, Japan. It is reported to have over 100 employees and is one of thirty-eight cryptocurrency companies in Israel.[51]

It was reported that, in 2018, Israeli tax authorities ruled that Bitcoin was classed as a "taxable asset" that attracted a capital gains tax of 25% on each profitable sale.[52] People who mine or trade Bitcoin or other cyber currencies in Israel are treated as businesses subject to corporate tax and Value Added Tax (VAT).

However, under Israel's financial services regulation law, those who are providing services in "financial assets" are required to obtain a license from the Supervisor of Financial Services. Currencies such as Bitcoin and others are defined as "financial assets."

However, in 2022, the head of the Israeli Securities Authority said that crypto tokens should be considered securities rather than simply as "financial assets." The chairwoman of the Authority, Anat Guetta, is quoted as saying:

> I think that, in the end, securities regulators should adopt crypto as a security regardless of its format without going into details.[53]

[B] Ethereum (ETH)

Ethereum describes itself as a product that is "decentralized, open-source blockchain with smart contract functionality." Its goal was to be digital currency, a method of international payments, and to be useful in other financial applications. It was initially offered in July of 2015. It has the second largest market capitalization of any cryptocurrency after Bitcoin.[54]

To manage an Ethereum account, one needs an application that is called a "wallet."

---

50. *Ibid.*
51. This information is found online at: https://soleadify.com/listings/saint-bitts-llc-4151565?cat=10447&loc=ilta,iljm,ilha,ilz,ilm,ild&tot=38.
52. Kamsi King, "Crypto Tax: Israelis to Disclose Crypto Holdings," Cryptopolitan, online, December 27, 2020.
53. Sandali Handagama, "Israel's Securities Regulatory Chief Lays Out Crypto Plans," CoinDesk, online, February 14, 2022.
54. Ethereum.org, online, accessed January 4, 2022.

[C] Wallets

A crypto wallet is purportedly a digital application where one can, in theory, "securely" keep digital currencies. There are different kinds of wallets, including "hosted wallets," "non-custodial wallets," and "hardware wallets."

Cryptocurrency wallets come from a variety of suppliers. For example, some cryptocurrency dealers, such as Coinbase, provide a wallet if you purchase cryptocurrency through them. Coinbase provides what is described as a "hosted wallet," which is how a third party that holds a cryptocurrency for another party is described. One advantage of a hosted wallet is that one cannot "lose" access to the wallet by forgetting one's password or other wallet keys.

This issue has been a problem for some earlier investors in cryptocurrency where they have set up a wallet to hold their cryptocurrency but later forgot their password and are unable to access what is sometimes a large fortune in cryptocurrency. There have been several depressing stories in the media about investors in crypto that built their holdings to a large fortune and then forgot the password to their crypto wallets, locking them out of crypto fortunes.[55]

Forgetting passwords is just one way that cryptocurrency owners can lose a fortune. It has been reported that in 2013, an IT engineer accidentally threw out a computer hard drive that contained 7,500 Bitcoins that he had bought for a low price years before. Those Bitcoins are now estimated to be worth about US$ 200 million, and the engineer has been desperately trying to persuade the City Council in Newport, England, to permit him to search a landfill site that he thinks might contain the hard drive. The City Council has so far been unwilling because it would be very expensive (estimated to be around £10 million) to undertake such a search, and there is no guarantee that it would be successful.[56]

There is Stephen Thomas, a German computer programmer who is left with two guesses to figure out his wallet password which would allow him to access Bitcoin worth over US$ 200 million. His wallet is a so-called hardware wallet because it exists as a small hard drive called an "IronKey." This hard drive contains the keys to a digital wallet containing over 7,000 Bitcoins. Mr. Thomas lost the paper where he had written down the password to his IronKey. He had ten guesses to find the password, and he has used eight of them without success. Thomas said:

> I would just lay in bed and think about it. Then I would go to the computer with some new strategy, and it wouldn't work, and I would be desperate again.[57]

---

55. Nathan Popper, "Lost Passwords Lock Millionaires Out of Their Bitcoin Fortunes," The New York Times, online, January 14, 2021.
56. Lawrence Sleator, "Engineer's £10m Quest to Fish Lost Bitcoin from the Dump," The Times, online, August 3, 2022.
57. Nathan Popper, January 14, 2021.

It is estimated that around 20% of Bitcoin, worth about US$ 140 billion, is locked away in lost or otherwise inaccessible wallets, according to Chainalysis,[58] a firm that provides data about cryptocurrency.

There is a firm, Wallet Recovery Services, that specializes in trying to help people find lost digital access keys to cryptocurrency wallets. It is reported that they were getting about seventy requests a day from people who have lost access to their crypto, as of January 2021.[59]

§1.03 MINING AND BLOCKCHAINS

Bitcoin is "mined" or earned by using computer power to solve complex mathematical problems over the Internet. Theoretically, anyone can become a Bitcoin miner, but the process is extremely complex and requires sophisticated electronic equipment.[60]

Once earned, the existence and authenticity of a Bitcoin are protected by its entry into a decentralized digital ledger called a "blockchain." Blockchains record the existence and ownership history of digital assets, such as a Bitcoin (or other cybercurrency units). Once entered, the data in a blockchain ledger, theoretically, cannot be changed.

Once created, a unit of cryptocurrency can be transferred into and expressed as a "token." The creation of a token is entered into a separate blockchain ledger. Tokens make transfer and payment of cryptocurrency easier.[61]

§1.04 IMPACT OF CYBERCURRENCY

Bitcoin's popularity has attracted a flood of competitors. As of November 2021, there were over 10,000 cybercurrencies in existence.[62] Ten of the most important cryptocurrencies other than Bitcoin are reported[63] to be:

(1) Ethereum (ETH)
(2) Litecoin (LTC)
(3) Cardano (ADA)
(4) Polkadot (DOT)
(5) Bitcoin Cash (BCH)
(6) Stellar (XLM)
(7) Dogecoin (DOGE)
(8) Binance Coin (BNB)

58. Chainalysis, online at: chainalysis.com.
59. Nathan Popper, January 14, 2021.
60. More details about the process can be found in specialized publications such as Investopedia, online at investopedia.com.
61. Jake Frankenfield, "Crypto Tokens," Investopedia, online, October 8, 2021.
62. Luke Conway, "10 Important Cryptocurrencies Other Than Bitcoin," Investopedia, online, November 19, 2021.
63. *Ibid.*

(9) Tether (USDT)
(10) Monero (XMR).

§1.05 CRYPTO EXCHANGES

Cybercurrencies, once created and owned, can be bought and sold by individuals in private transactions, but crypto "exchanges" have been created for the purchase and sale of cryptocurrencies. An operation called "Binance" claims to be "the world's largest bitcoin exchange."[64]

[A] UK Binance Ban

In June of 2021, the UK Financial Conduct Authority (FCA) banned Binance from engaging in regulated activities because it did not meet the required anti-money-laundering standards. As a result, Binance was forced to leave the important UK Faster Payments system.[65] Faster Payments provides rapid payments of individual and corporate transfers of money ("almost at the touch of button").[66] As mentioned elsewhere, Binance was able to reconnect with that system after entering into an arrangement with Paysafe, a regulated online payments organization.

However, that did not end Binance's regulatory problems. After the tie-up with Paysafe, both were reported to be subject to concerns by the FCA and were reported to be subject to "close ongoing supervision."[67]

Part of the supervisory problem is that Binance claims "it does not have a headquarters." However, it says: "we take our compliance obligations very seriously and work proactively and collaboratively with regulators."[68]

§1.06 CRYPTO PROBLEMS FOR FINANCIAL SYSTEMS

The innovation of Bitcoin and similar cybercurrencies over the last few years has caused some disruption in the world's financial systems.

Over the last few years, cryptocurrencies have become a well-known and immensely popular medium of exchange and investment.

The very existence of digital currencies challenges the traditional monopoly of national central banks to produce currencies that can be used to transfer value in commercial transactions.

A major problem of their existence has been their anonymous creation and the difficulties in identifying who owns them and where they are being transferred.

---

64. www.binance.com, accessed November 30, 2021.
65. Owned and operated by Pay UK.
66. "Benefits of Faster Payments," fasterpayments.org.uk, online, accessed March 10, 2022.
67. Ben Martin, "Financial Conduct Authority Still Worried Over Binance," The Times, online, February 17, 2022.
68. *Ibid.*

This has made them attractive for international criminals to use when perpetrating online crimes such as "ransomware" attacks and even offline crimes (such as kidnapping), where the transfer of money in digital form may be demanded by the criminals.

§1.07 CRYPTO VOLATILITY

Another major problem of digital currencies, and one that affects everyone that invests in or uses them, is their volatility. Taking Bitcoin as an example, its price has fluctuated from about US$ 10 in 2012 to over US$ 20,000 in 2021, with dramatic rises and falls during that period. On June 22, 2021, its price was US$ 2,903,131. On June 23, its price was US$ 3,479,033.[69]

The volatility of Bitcoin does not appear to have lessened significantly. Between November of 2021 and the end of May 2022, the value of Bitcoin was reported to have fallen by about 50%.[70]

In early May of 2022, it was reported that a sell-off of cryptocurrencies was occurring and values were falling significantly. One example: a cryptocurrency known as a "stablecoin" had fallen as much as 45% in a single day. This particular product is formally known as "Terra USD." The USD refers to the fact that this crypto asset is designed to track the value of the U.S. dollar. However, it is unclear what protection this design provides. A "sister token" of Terra USD called "Luna" is reported to have fallen in value by more than 90% in a single day.[71]

The impact of such value changes is significant because Bitcoin reportedly represents about a third of the world cryptocurrency market. Ethereum which is the next biggest cryptocurrency declined by about 10% in value during the first ten days of May 2022.

§1.08 VALUE ISSUES

However, perhaps the most troubling question about cryptocurrencies is what in fact is the basis of their value, if any? This is a question that is frequently discussed in the media and among the public generally. Among those that have expressed strong opinions on this issue are the principal executives of Berkshire Hathaway, an investment vehicle which is considered one of the most successful in the world over the last several decades. When asked in interviews about the wisdom of purchasing any form of cryptocurrency, both Warren Buffett and his colleague Charlie Munger expressed strong skepticism.[72] They point out that its principal weakness is that cryptocurrency

69. Charles Bovaird, "Bitcoin Price Volatility Reached A 14-Month High in June," Forbes, online, July 1, 2021.
70. "Bitcoin Value Drops by 50% Since November Peak," *BBC News*, online, May 9, 2022, referring to Coinbase cryptocurrency exchange valuation.
71. Callum Jones, "Stablecoin TerraUSD on the Slide" The Times, online, May 12, 2022.
72. Yun Li, "Charlie Munger Call Bitcoin 'Disgusting and Contrary to the Interests of Civilization'," CNBC, online, May 4, 2021.

is a "non-productive asset" unlike other assets such as companies, farms or many other assets cryptocurrency produces nothing in addition to its own existence. The only purpose in buying it is a hope that someone else will want to pay more for it in the future, described as the "greater fool theory."

Mr. Buffet describes the current enthusiasm for cryptocurrency as a classic "bubble" that bears comparison to the tulip obsession in Holland in the 17th century. Mr. Munger said, "I hate the Bitcoin success, ... I think I should say modestly that I think the whole damn development is disgusting and contrary to the interests of civilization." To which Mr. Buffet responded, "I'm alright on that one."

Mr. Buffet continued:

> I think that anytime you buy a non-productive asset you are counting on somebody else later on to buy the non-productive asset because they think they can sell it to somebody for more money, and it's been tried with tulips and it's been tried with various things over time and it does come to a bad ending.

Apparently, these two gentlemen consider buying cryptocurrency to be simply a form of gambling.

However, Berkshire Hathaway is reported to invest in companies that do participate in the cryptocurrency market in one way or another. For example, it was reported that the company invested a billion dollars in a digital lender named Nubank. Nubank allows its customers to invest in funds which are traded on crypto exchanges.[73] However, the investment itself does not seem inconsistent with the overall philosophy of Buffett and Munger that they should invest in productive assets. Newbank, as indicated on its website, is a bank offering its customers products such as credit cards and loans for which it does receive interest payments and fees. Therefore, it does earn income in addition to funds received for the purchase of its shares. Consequently, it is clearly a productive asset in line with the Berkshire Hathaway investment philosophy.

Bill Gates, another well-known successful entrepreneur, who was a founder of Microsoft, has expressed a similar view online:

> I like investing in things that have valuable output. The value of companies is based on how they make great products. The value of crypto is just what some other person decides someone else will pay for it so not adding to society like other investments.[74]

Bill Gates has also argued that cryptocurrencies and NFTs are underpinned by nothing more than 'greater fool theory'—the premise that one investor is simply willing to pay more than another.[75]

73. Pawan Nahar, "Why are Bitcoin Critics Buffet & Munger Investing in Crypto-Friendly Companies?" Economic Times, online, February 17, 2022.
74. Rachel Sandler, "Bill Gates Explains Why He Doesn't Own Any Cryptocurrency," Forbes, online, May 19, 2022.
75. Callum Jones, "Cryptocurrencies and NFTs Depend on 'Greater Fool Theory', Says Bill Gates," The Times, online, June 16, 2022.

[A] Tether and the U.S. Dollar

Tether is a cryptocurrency that is reportedly "pegged" to the U.S. dollar. Does this protect it from the kind of volatility that has been seen with respect to other cryptocurrencies? Tether is a cryptocurrency that was created by a company in Hong Kong, Tether Limited. Tether reportedly has a market capitalization of over USD 80 billion. Does that mean that Tether tokens are backed one-to-one with U.S. dollars held by Tether Limited? Apparently not. On its website, Tether Limited has said that Tether Tokens "are backed 100% by Tether's reserves."

Tether's website includes a daily "reserves breakdown." When accessed on April 4, 2022, that reserves breakdown showed the following:

- 5.54% other investments, including digital tokens;
- 4.99% secured loans (none to affiliated entities);
- 5.22% corporate bonds, funds & precious metals;
- 84.25% cash and cash equivalents and other short-term deposits & commercial paper.

There was a further breakdown of what constitutes the item "cash & equivalents & other short-term deposits & commercial paper." That included the following:

- Treasury bills.
- Reverse repo notes.
- Cash and bank deposits.
- Money market funds.

So, what portion Tether Limited reserves that are actually in U.S. dollars or another respected national "Fiat" currency?

In early April of 2022, reports appeared on the Internet and in the print media such as one published by *The Wall Street Journal*, online, April 3, 2022, "Short Sellers Bet Tether Crypto's Central Bank, is Vulnerable to a Run." It was reported that hedge funds were questioning how much risk there was in the investment portfolio backing Tether tokens. At least two investment firms, Fir Tree Partners and Viceroy Research LLC. "have placed substantial bets in recent months that the price of Tether will fall, according to people familiar with the matter."[76]

There have been other articles questioning Tether.[77]

In February of 2022, the following report appeared online:

> Tether has been in hot water with several different authorities. Last year the New York Attorney General's office said it had lied about its assets and it paid $18.5 million in fines. The CFTC[78] has also fined it $41 million, and Bloomberg reports the Department of Justice may pursue criminal proceedings. ... [P]eople are

76. Peter Rudegeair, *supra*, The Wall Street Journal, online, April 3, 2022.
77. For example: Jacob Silverman, "Is Tether Just a Scam to Enrich Bitcoin Investors," TNR (The New Republic) Soapbox, online January 13, 2021, accessed April 5, 2022.
78. The U.S. Commodity Futures Trading Commission.

concerned Tether doesn't have enough cash in reserve to support all the tokens it has issued.[79]

In February of 2021, Bitfinex and Tether were fined US$ 85 million by the New York Attorney General, and required to cease trading with New Yorkers. The New York Attorney General said that "Tether's claims that its virtual currency was fully backed by U.S. dollars at all times was 'a lie.'"[80]

Tether's problems with the New York Attorney General were not its only regulatory difficulties. In October of 2021, the U.S. Commodity Futures Trading Commission (CFTC) ordered Tether (including a number of Tether affiliates) to pay a penalty of US$ 40 million "for making untrue or misleading statements and omissions of material fact in connection with the U.S. dollar Tether token (USDT) stablecoin."

At the same time, the CFTC issued a separate order requiring Bitfinex (including affiliated companies, which reportedly includes Tether Limited) to pay a US$ 1.5 million civil penalty for engaging in "illegal, off-exchange retail commodity transactions in digital assets with U.S. persons on the Bitfinex trading platform and [operating] as a futures commission merchant (FCM) without registering as required."[81]

Tether has now reportedly modified the claim it reportedly made until March of 2019 that it was backed one-to-one by U.S. dollar reserves.[82]

[B] Other Stablecoins

In addition to Tether, there have been offered a number of other cryptocurrencies that claim to be "pegged" to U.S. dollars, other Fiat currencies or other independent assets such as gold.

As the case brought by the New York Attorney General makes clear, it may be a mistake to take the promotions of any "stablecoin" at face value.

To understand the extent to which any cyber currency is in fact "pegged" to any other asset requires careful inquiries and careful examination of any reports about the cyber currency or any documentation related to the cyber currency to determine what the real connection is between any cybercurrency and any other assets to which it claims to be "backed."

General asset classifications such as "precious metals," "commercial paper," "cash and bank deposits" need to be queried to determine exactly what things are included in those categories, the quantities in which they are held, and the legal and contractual conditions under which they may be accessed by the crypto promoter and/or any other owners of that cryptocurrency.

---

79. Emma Newbery, "Can USDC Overtake Tether in 2022," the Ascent, online, February 23, 2022.
80. Avi Salzman, "Key Crypto Company Tether Settles With New York State. How That Could Affect Bitcoin," Barron's, online February 23, 2022.
81. CFTC, online at cftc.gov, October 15, 2021.
82. Nicholas Gans, "Tether (Finally) Releases Breakdown of Its $42 Billion in Crypto Reserves," Forbes, online, May 13, 2021, accessed April 5, 2022.

There is a danger that cryptocurrency purchasers who I think they are being cautious by purchasing "stablecoins" may not fully understand how those cryptocurrencies are supported.

Stablecoins have had a complex, if short, history.

[C] TerraUSA

Surprisingly, it was reported at the beginning of June 2022 that the British government was making plans to have the Bank of England deal with the collapse in value of "stablecoins." The role of the Bank of England would be to set up a "special administration" in the event of a collapse of a major stablecoin issuer in order to prevent that event from damaging the wider UK economy.[83]

Apparently, the concern with the potential impact of changes in stablecoin prices was triggered by the dramatic fall in the value of a stablecoin called "TerraUSD."

TerraUSD was developed in South Korea but was reportedly pegged to the value of the U.S. dollar.[84] When the price fell dramatically in mid-2022, this stablecoin disconnected from the U.S. dollar for a period of time.

Reports of the dramatic fall of the value of this stablecoin first began to appear in early May of 2022:

> TerraUSD, known as a stablecoin, has fallen precipitously after substantial withdrawals. It was down by 45% on the day at $0.49 yesterday and has been as low as 26 cents.[85]

This crash was considered to be somewhat surprising because apparently many in the crypto coin market believed that stablecoins, because of their relationship to well-known government-backed fiat currencies, "were not prone to volatile gyrations in their value."[86] However, terraUSD showed that this was not always the case, and a related digital asset called "Luna" was reported to have fallen by more than 90% in a single day.[87]

It is reported that the collapse in the value of this stablecoin caused concern because:

> It is said that the failure of a systemic firm that operates a stablecoin could threaten the "continuity of service is critical to the operation of the economy and access of individuals to their funds or assets."[88]

83. Ben Martin, "Bank of England to Take Rescue Role if Stablecoin Collapses," The Times, online, June 1, 2022.
84. Krisztian Sandor, "A Guide to the Terra Ecosystem," Coindesk, online at coindesk.com May 10, 2022.
85. Callum Jones, "Stablecoin TerraUSD on the Slide," The Times, online, May 12, 2022.
86. *Ibid.*
87. *Ibid.*
88. Martin, *supra*.

§1.09 NATIONAL REACTIONS TO CRYPTO

Despite the objections to crypto's use and existence, governments are beginning to recognize that cybercurrency or "cryptocurrency" is here to stay and in this increasingly Internet-centric world may be useful to national governments.

Consequently, there have been several discussions within and between national central banks about creating their own digital currencies or adopting one of the existing ones, such as Bitcoin.

It is reported that China, the UK and the US are among the countries that have been considering creating their own cryptocurrencies, tied to the value of their existing currencies: the yuan, the pound and the dollar.[89]

89. *See* Chapters 3, 5 and 6, following.

CHAPTER 2

International Law

By the beginning of 2022, the value of the cryptocurrency market had risen to more than US$ 2.5 trillion. Its rapid growth had become a concern around the world that cryptocurrency presented a risk to global economic stability.

However, despite the growth of the cryptocurrency and digital asset markets during the last decade or so, there had not yet been extensive efforts to develop international agreements on how to deal with, control and regulate these clearly international phenomena.

This is not to say that there had been no thought given to it or no international activity to respond to the growing crypto markets, but more effort will probably need to be made in the future.

Thus far, significant international efforts have been proposed by: the G20 Financial Stability Board (FSB), the EU, the World Economic Forum (WEF), the International Monetary Fund (IMF) and the US's Proposed Framework for International Engagement on Digital assets. A summary of those efforts is given below in this chapter, and more detail about the EU's regulatory stance is found in the following Chapter 4.

§2.01 FINANCIAL STABILITY BOARD

One group that is tasked with worrying about global economic stability is the Financial Stability Board (FSB) that coordinates rules for the economies of the developed nations that constitute the G20.

The G20 is a group of large developed and emerging economies that seeks to encourage economic growth and provide worldwide economic prosperity.[90]

FSB expressed the following concern:[91]

90. "About the G20," online, G20.org.
91. "Rise of cryptocurrencies Poses Risk to Global Financial Stability Warns Financial Stability Board," The Times, online, February 17, 2022.

> Crypto assets markets could reach a point where they represent a threat to global financial stability due to their scale, structural vulnerabilities, and interconnectedness with the traditional financial system.
>
> Although the extent and nature of use of crypto assets varies across jurisdictions, financial stability risks could rapidly escalate underscoring the need for timely and preemptive evaluation of possible policy responses.[92]

According to the FSB, one area that needs particular attention is the fact that banks, hedge funds and other investing institutions are increasingly becoming involved in the crypto markets and the number of crypto-related derivatives was also increasing. This meant that the opportunities for investing in highly volatile virtual assets were increasing dramatically and growing participation in these kinds of assets risked a financial collapse comparative to that of 2007/2008. This is because financial institutions may be assuming more risk than they will be able to deal with if the value of these crypto-related assets declines significantly. That is what happened to many financial institutions, the liquidity of which was tied to the value of subprime, mortgage-backed securities in 2007/2008.[93]

The Bank of England has warned financial institutions to be "cautious and prudent" about crypto assets because the regulators have not yet created comprehensive rules about how they will be regulated.

The FSB is based in Switzerland, but it has no powers to impose rules on the members of the G20.[94]

A significant problem in regulating crypto assets and in judging the level of risk they represent is created by the fact that they have been unregulated in some jurisdictions, and trade across borders, which means that it is hard to know how many there are, who owns them, and where they are located. They usually have no physical existence, existing only digitally and on the Internet that is their principal home.

There are certain principal crypto exchanges where these assets are bought, sold and traded. The FSB has pointed out that this is likely to concentrate risks and lead to conflicts of interest.

The Chairman of the FSB, Klaas Knot, has said that the virtual nature of cryptocurrency will make it difficult to control any actions that nations may wish to take with respect to financial sanctions such as those against Iran or Russia, etc.[95]

§2.02 THE EUROPEAN UNION

In the EU Electronic Money Directive (EMD), the EU does provide direction for the regulation of electronic money (E-money).[96]

92. *Ibid.*
93. *Ibid.*
94. *Ibid.*
95. *Ibid.*
96. Directive 2009/110/EC of the European Parliament and of the Council of September 16, 2009, on the taking up, pursuit and prudential supervision of the business of electronic money institutions amending Directives 2005/60/EC and 2006/48/EC and repealing Directive 2000/46/EC.

The EMD outlines the regulatory standards relating to E-money to be adopted by national financial regulators in EU Member States.

Member States did adopt regulations on electronic money in response. For example, the UK (then a member of the EU) promulgated The Electronic Money Regulations (EMRs) 2011, which provide detailed regulations on the issuance and distribution of electronic money.[97]

Given that cybercurrency is digital in creation and existence, a question arises as to whether cybercurrency and other digital assets are E-money for the purposes of regulations under the EMD, and consequently already subject to detailed Member State regulations.

The European Central Bank (ECB) defines E-money as:

> Electronic money (e-money) is broadly defined as an electronic store of monetary value on a technical device that may be widely used for making payments to entities other than the e-money issuer. The device acts as a prepaid bearer instrument which does not necessarily involve bank accounts in transactions.[98]

This does rather sound like a description of cybercurrency.

[A] Is Cybercurrency E-Money?

Taking as an example Bitcoin which is the best-known and probably the most widely traded cybercurrency, the creator and issuer of Bitcoin, who used the name Satoshi Nakamoto, wrote in his famous "White Paper" that Bitcoin would be:

> A purely peer-to-peer version of electronic cash [that] would allow online payments to be sent directly from one party to another without going through a financial institution.[99]

Something described as "electronic cash" certainly seems to fall within the regulatory definition of E-money.

But, apparently, it does not. On April 1, 2022, the European Parliament published a report online that stated, "crypto assets are currently out of the scope of EU legislation."[100]

An online publication called Investopedia says that E-money is different from cryptocurrency because: "Electronic money is backed by fiat currency, which distinguishes it from cryptocurrency."[101]

In response to what the EU Parliament called the "substantial risks" presented by digital assets, the EU has developed a set of new rules, for markets in Crypto assets,

97. The EMRs, online at legislation.gov.uk, accessed November 2, 2022.
98. ECB, "Electronic Money," online, December 19, 2021.
99. Satoshi Nakamoto, "Bitcoin: A Peer-to-Peer Electronic Cash System," Bitcoin.org, online, December 20, 2021.
100. European Parliament, "Cryptocurrency Dangers and the Benefits of EU Legislation," online at europarl.europa.eu, April 1, 2022, updated October 11, 2022.
101. Andrew Bloomenthal, Investopedia, "Electronic Money," online at Investopedia.com, May 21, 2020.

proposed by the European Commissioners in June of 2022 for approval by the Parliament and the Member States.[102]

Markets in Crypto Assets Regulation (MiCA) will be in effect in 2023. *See* Chapter 4 herein for more information.

§2.03 THE WORLD ECONOMIC FORUM

The WEF identifies itself as an international organization for public-private cooperation. It strives to engage business, political, and cultural leaders to formulate political and business agendas to have an international impact. It is a not-for-profit foundation headquartered in Geneva, Switzerland.

In March of 2022, the WEF published an online article on the state of cryptocurrency regulation.[103]

The article gave some startling statistics about the cryptocurrency market:

> Today, there are 18,142 cryptocurrencies, 460 crypto exchanges and the market cap of cryptocurrencies amounts to $1.7 trillion. Every 24 hours, $91 billion worth of cryptos are traded, most of them Bitcoin or Etherium.

They point out that the traditional financial system is increasingly coming into contact with cryptocurrency transactions, and the interaction between them could affect the stability of financial systems worldwide. Substantial impacts may already be apparent. Data published by the IMF in early 2022 shows a correlation between Bitcoin price movements and the S&P 500.

The view of the WEF is that international regulation of digital assets is essential:

> Given the size of the industry and the impending regulatory push, it is worth now taking stock of the current state of regulation. In doing so, it will become clear that a globally coordinated approach to regulation is necessary.

In their review of the current state of cryptocurrency regulation, there is a significant amount of positive reaction to U.S. President Biden's executive order on cryptocurrencies issued in March of 2022. In an online article dated March 11, 2022,[104] the WEF says:

> On Wednesday President Biden issued a much anticipated executive order on cryptocurrencies. The first-of-its-kind order advances a 'whole-of-government' approach to regulating the sector, instructing federal agencies to coordinate efforts at drafting policy and regulation on digital assets.

The WEF points out that computer technology is a tool that enables cross-border transactions without the need for any intermediaries. The effectiveness of crypto's communication ability in combination with new digital financial products and methods

102. *Ibid*. For more detail, *see* Chapter 4, following.
103. Kathryn White, Arushi Goel and Sandra Waliczek, "Cryptocurrency Regulation: Where Are We Now, and Where Are We Going?," WEF, online at weforum.org, March 28, 2022.
104. Aideen Slavin, "Five Things You Need to Know About Biden's Executive Order on Cryptocurrency," WEF, online at weforum.org, March 11, 2022.

such as tokens, decentralized finance and NFTs, has allowed decentralized independent organizations to change and bypass traditional understandings of who is a "person," what is a "value" and how these persons can transact in relation to these "values."

These new financial models can create conflict with existing regulations on such things as cross-border data transfers, intellectual property rights and financial controls. They can also cause taxation problems and problems with many other regulatory policy concerns.[105]

The potential implications for global financial stability make it important that urgent regulatory discussions and decisions at national and international levels are necessary.

The WEF says that as of March 2022 there was "no internationally coordinated regulation of cryptocurrencies."[106]

Central banks and financial regulators throughout the world are aware of these problems and are considering the regulatory options. The WEF says that they all have similar objectives: protection of consumers, prevention of illegal financing activity, protection of the integrity of financial markets and the encouragement of financial and technical innovation.

Different approaches have been tried. Some countries have amended their existing laws. Other jurisdictions such as the EU and the UAE have proposed creating new regulations for the digital asset industry. However, the absence of common regulatory standards and different technologies offers unfortunate "jurisdictional arbitrage opportunities," which allow circumvention of national laws and create complexities that burden legitimate financial businesses operating across borders:

> For a truly global coordinated approach, countries and international organizations must work together, leveraging best practices and learnings from each other. As well as risk assessments and establishing common standards, there is also a pressing need to leverage the technology itself to develop fit for purpose and inclusive solutions, through public-private collaboration.[107]

And the WEF emphasizes that a truly internationally coordinated regulatory solution for crypto assets will be the best way to encourage the development of these new financial methods while also protecting consumers and preventing the crypto asset markets from becoming forums for illegal activity.

To achieve this end, the WEF has organized a Digital Currency Governance Consortium of 80 organizations from different business sectors and countries to focus on the economic impacts of digital assets and propose appropriate regulatory approaches. Their activities also consider the continued development of these new financial models and the best way to employ cryptocurrencies, including central bank-issued cryptocurrencies and other digital assets.

---

105. Kathryn White, Arushi Goel and Sandra Waliczek, *supra*, WEF, March 28, 2022.
106. *Ibid.*
107. *Ibid.*

Hopefully, the efforts of this Consortium will produce regulatory proposals useful for the regulatory agencies of jurisdictions throughout the world. Future reports of the work of this Consortium will certainly be of interest to both the digital asset industry and its regulators.

§2.04 INTERNATIONAL MONETARY FUND

In early 2022, the IMF published a chart showing a correlation between the prices of Bitcoin and U.S. stocks during the pandemic. This correlation is one reason why the IMF has concluded that the growth of transactions in crypto assets raises "financial stability concerns."[108]

In December of 2021, the IMF published a statement on the uses of cryptos and the risks crypto assets posed to financial systems:

> "These include, for example, operational and financial integrity risks from crypto asset exchanges and wallets, investor protection, and inadequate reserves and we didn't see accurate disclosure from some stable coins. Moreover, in emerging markets and developing economies, the advent of crypto can accelerate what we have called 'cryptoization'—when these assets replace domestic currency and circumvent exchange restrictions and capital account management measures."
>
> "Such risks underscore why we now need comprehensive international standards that more fully address risks to the financial system from crypto assets, their associated ecosystem, and their related transactions, while allowing for an enabling environment for useful crypto asset products and applications."

In September of 2022, the IMF published proposals for regulating cryptocurrency.[109]

Their proposals express the strong view that global regulation of what they call "crypto assets" is the best way forward:

> A global regulatory framework will bring order to the markets, help instill consumer confidence, lay out the limits of what is permissible, and provide a safe space for useful innovation to continue.[110]

This recommendation is based on the fact that although crypto assets have been around for more than a decade, they have only recently begun to have a significant impact on the traditional regulated financial markets.

The rapid evolution of the crypto market has left regulators struggling to keep pace with the rapid developments and volatility of the crypto asset markets. Regulators do not always have the knowledge to be able to understand how these markets are operating. Monitoring the markets is difficult because accurate data is not always available. The markets are not currently subject to consistent disclosure or reporting regulations.

---

108. Tobias Adrian, Tara Lyer, Mahvash S. Qureshi, "Crypto Prices Move More in Sync With Stocks, Posing New Risks," International Monetary Fund, online at imf.org, January 11, 2022.
109. Aditya Marain, Marina Moretti, "Regulating Crypto," IMF, online at imf.org, September 2022.
110. *Ibid.*

Also, the terminology used to describe the products and processes in the crypto asset markets is not globally consistent. This makes it difficult to exchange transaction or market information across borders.

The participants in the crypto asset markets are not easily covered by traditional financial regulation because their activities (such as mining or blockchain operation) do not fit the traditional definitions of regulated entities. Regulators may also not understand all of the functions that crypto exchanges perform in connection with crypto assets, and the conflicts of interest that may arise as a result of their many functions.

There are also unexpected public policy issues that have arisen in the crypto asset markets which have not played a role in traditional financial markets such as the amount of electricity needed to operate crypto mining operations.

There has also been a lack of clarity as to whether and how crypto assets are "backed" by physical assets such as fiat currencies or precious metals.

There is as yet no organized international regulatory code for crypto assets. Some nations have put regulation in place, others are in the process of drafting regulations and others are only considering what regulation may be necessary. Some countries have prohibited transactions in crypto assets, others have sought to attract the business they represent, and a minority of others have adopted cryptocurrency as legal tender.

Although applauding the efforts of some international organizations such as the Financial Action Task Force (FATF) and the International Organization of Securities Commissions (IOSCO) to offer proposed international regulatory frameworks for aspects of the crypto asset business, the IMF states that much more needs to be done.

The IMF's report states that:

> The regulatory fabric is being woven, and a pattern is expected to emerge. But the worry is that the longer this takes, the more national authorities will get locked into differing regulatory frameworks. This is why the IMF is calling for a global response that is (1) coordinated, so it can fill the regulatory gaps that arise from inherently cross-sector and cross-border issuance and ensure a level playing field; (2) consistent, so it aligns with mainstream regulatory approaches across the activity and risk spectrum; and (3) comprehensive, so it covers all actors and all aspects of the crypto ecosystem.[111]

§2.05 US PRESIDENT'S EXECUTIVE ORDER ON ENSURING RESPONSIBLE DEVELOPMENT OF DIGITAL ASSETS

On March 9, 2022, U.S. President Joe Biden issued an Executive Order (Order) intended to promote the responsible development of digital assets.

The key points emphasized in the Order are:

- Digital assets have a future in the United States to contribute to the expansion of financial services to more people, and the expansion of financial innovation.

111. *Ibid*.

- Federal regulatory agencies are directed to be more cooperative in communicating together about their work involving digital assets.
- Digital assets development will play a role in helping to maintain the US as the dominant power in the international financial markets.
- The US will need to pay attention to the consideration being given in over 100 countries as to whether to adopt a central bank digital currency (CBDC).
- The expansion of the availability of digital markets may help to democratize the financial system.
- The principal focus of the order is, of course, what the response of U.S. regulatory agencies should be with respect to development and use of digital assets within the United States, but Section 8 of the Order also provides detailed instructions about U.S. policy with respect to international cooperation in creating consistent digital asset regulation across the globe.

Section 1 of the Order says that expansion of the digital assets business-connected technologies have had a significant impact on a number of important policy areas, including the following:

- Consumer protection.
- Data privacy and security.
- Financial stability and systemic risk.
- Crime.
- National security.
- Human rights.
- Financial inclusion and equity.
- Energy demand and climate change.

It points out that CBDCs are being considered in many countries and being introduced in some.

It says that although existing laws cover many aspects of digital asset transactions, the US will have to evolve and align its overall government approach to the regulation of digital assets. No specific regulations are proposed, but it says the US must take "strong steps" to reduce the risks that digital assets can pose in the policy areas listed above.

Section 2 sets out the objectives of U.S. policy with respect to digital assets. The important areas are the responsible development of digital assets in a way that protects consumers and market participants. It is also important to protect financial stability and lessen systemic risk. Illegal finance, and national security risks such as those posed by money laundering, cybercrime and terrorism. Those risks need to be limited as much as possible, but US leadership in financial services and technology needs to be protected.

Section 3 requires implementation of steps to secure the cooperation and participation in the development of digital asset policies of all major federal regulatory agencies.

Section 4 emphasizes that fiat currency ("sovereign money") is the key to a stable financial system. However, it is urgent to research and consider development of a potential U.S. cyber currency. A report is to be submitted to the President on these efforts within 180 days after the publication of the Order.

Section 5 requires key federal regulatory agencies to submit a report to the President within 180 days of the Order discussing measures to protect consumers, investors and businesses in the digital asset markets.

Section 6 requires that within 210 days the Secretary of the Treasury in conjunction with the Financial Stability Oversight Council needs to submit a report outlining actions to promote financial stability, mitigate systemic risk and strengthen market integrity.

Section 7 describes the necessity of taking action to limit illegal finance and other national security risks posed by the digital asset markets.

Section 8 outlines the U.S. policy for fostering international cooperation with respect to digital assets and financial innovation without reducing U.S. competitiveness:

> Technology-driven financial innovation is frequently cross-border and therefore requires international cooperation among public authorities. This cooperation is critical to maintaining high regulatory standards and a level playing field. Uneven regulation supervision and compliance across jurisdictions creates opportunities for arbitrage and raises risks to financial stability and the protection of consumers, investors, businesses and markets. Inadequate ... regulation, supervision and enforcement by other countries challenges the ability of the United States to investigate illicit digital asset transaction flows that frequently jump overseas, as is often the case in ransomware payments and other cybercrime and related money laundering. There must also be cooperation to reduce inefficiencies in international funds transfer and payment systems.

This section provides considerable additional detail about how the US has cooperated internationally in financial regulation in the past and how it proposes to do so with respect to the regulation of digital assets.

Section 9 includes a number of definitions for terms used in the Order relating to the digital asset markets, including the statement that:

> Regardless of the label used, a digital asset may be, among other things, a security, a commodity, a derivative, or other financial product. Digital assets may be exchanged across digital asset trading platforms, including centralized and decentralized financial platforms or through peer-to-peer technologies.

§2.06 THE FUTURE OF INTERNATIONAL COOPERATION

This chapter shows that there is a great deal of thought being given and effort made to evolve effective international cooperation in the regulation of the digital asset businesses around the world. However, with the possible exception of the new regulations to be adopted by all Member States within the EU, these efforts have yielded a patchwork of different results that will not provide cooperative and consistent regulation around the globe. As shown by the statements discussed above, these results are simply not good enough, and many financial market commentators and regulators are acutely aware of the inadequacies that currently exist with respect to international cyber asset regulation. There seems little doubt that over time many of these inadequacies will be corrected and that global regulation will become more effective. However, it is unclear how long this will take or what damage will be done to financial markets or participants in the cyber asset markets in the meantime.

Some major market jurisdictions have introduced a significant amount of regulation and taken strong steps against those they believe have misbehaved in the cyber asset markets. These major markets and their actions are discussed in the following chapters. The fact that major market jurisdictions try to provide a level of protection to their financial systems and market participants against the risks of crypto assets brings some relief and may protect a large proportion of the participants in the markets, but how complete that protection can be when dealing with financial transactions that can easily cross borders and maybe poorly understood by regulators in many countries, is likely to remain a problem for some time.

CHAPTER 3
U.S. Law

About 20% of the approximately 295 million cryptocurrency users throughout the world were located in the United States at the beginning of November 2022.[112]

§3.01 US EFFORTS TO REGULATE CRYPTOCURRENCY

It is certainly true that digital assets have become more widely known and more popular; the U.S. Congress has shown increasing interest in regulating digital assets. It is reported that by the beginning of 2022 more than twenty bills had been introduced in the U.S. Congress relating to digital assets including cryptocurrencies.[113]

In the U.S. regulatory scheme, as it pertains to digital assets such as cryptocurrency and other digital assets, there are at least five levels of regulatory oversight and jurisdiction to be aware of. These include the following:

- The Internal Revenue Service (IRS) imposes capital gains tax on digital asset transactions.
- The Treasury Department and FinCEN, the Financial Crimes Enforcement Network of the U.S. Treasury, oversees digital asset transactions to prevent and detect financial crimes such as money laundering and terrorist finance.
- The SEC regulates investment activities that may include the marketing and transactions in digital assets (including cryptocurrencies, tokens, coins, and NFTs) that are being offered as "investments."

112. Farran Powell, "10 Best Crypto Exchanges of 2022," Forbes Avisor, online at forbes.com, November 2, 2022.
113. Bloomberg Law, "Cryptocurrency Laws and Regulations by State," online at pro.bloomberglaw.com, March 30, 2022.

- The CFTC regulates transactions in commodities. Since 2014, the CFTC has classified cryptocurrencies as "commodities" subject to CFTC regulation under the U.S. Commodity Exchange Act (CEA).[114]
- State banking regulation can apply to both US and foreign currency exchanges where cryptocurrency and other digital assets are traded. One particular group of state laws that can apply to transactions in digital assets are state money transfer laws.

For some years, the situation in the United States has been that cryptocurrencies are regulated by a variety of state regulations, and some evolving federal regulations. But until 2021, there had been no coordinated effort by the key federal agencies to develop an overall approach to regulate crypto assets.

One difficulty for the U.S. and for any jurisdiction in which cryptocurrency is a factor in its financial markets is the fact that cryptocurrency represents a significant target for criminals and that criminals are becoming increasingly clever about how to access and steal cryptocurrency that does not belong to them.

In early October of 2021, the US took a positive step toward countering this kind of crime by establishing the National Cryptocurrency Enforcement Team (NCET). This was announced by Deputy Attorney General Lisa O. Monaco in a press release that said:

> Under the supervision of Assistant Attorney General Kenneth A. Polite Jr., the NCET will combine the expertise of the Department of Justice Criminal Division's Money Laundering and Asset Recovery Section (AMLARS), Computer Crime and Intellectual Property Section (CCIPS) and other sections in the division with experts detailed from the U.S. Attorneys' Offices. The team will assist in tracing and recovery of assets lost to fraud and extortion, including cryptocurrency payments to ransomware groups.[115]

Prior to that, several federal agencies whose regulatory responsibilities were affected by crypto responded to what they perceived as illegal or otherwise improper financial activity by participants in the new digital asset markets.

In the pages below in this chapter, the regulatory developments in both key federal agencies and state and key U.S. non-state jurisdictions will be discussed.

§3.02 FEDERAL REGULATION

Since at least September of 2021, the Federal Government is moving toward a coordinated policy on digital assets. In September 2021, it was reported that U.S. regulators were making efforts to provide a regulatory framework for cryptocurrency.

114. CFTC, "Testimony of CFTC Chairman Timothy Massad Before the U.S. Senate Committee on Agriculture, Nutrition and Forestry (December 10, 2014)," online at cftc.gov., accessed April 15, 2022.
115. DOJ, Office of Public Affairs, "Deputy Attorney General Lisa O. Monaco Announces National Cryptocurrency Enforcement Team," online, October 6, 2021.

More recently published was President Biden's Executive Order on digital assets issued on March 9, 2022, discussed at the end of the previous chapter.

Federal regulators have become concerned about the large number of business operations that are seeking to adapt their businesses to accommodate payments in digital currencies.[116]

The rise of the interest in digital assets affects the regulatory jurisdictions of a number of U.S. federal agencies and requires them to respond to the growth of these markets. There is no doubt that digital assets including cryptocurrencies, tokens and NFTs are having impact on nearly every sector of the U.S. economy. Consequently, the number of federal government agencies that are affected in one way or another is too numerous to completely catalog in this book. However, the agencies that most commonly will be required to respond to issues created by digital assets are the following:

- The Department of the Treasury (Treasury).
- The Securities and Exchange Commission (SEC).
- The Internal Revenue Service (IRS).
- The Commodity Futures Trading Commission (CFTC).
- The Department of Justice (DOJ).
- The Federal Reserve (Fed).

This chapter will include a summary of some of the more notable responses of these agencies to digital asset issues, but readers should keep in mind that the impact of digital assets is so wide that other government agencies may also feel that they need to take action.

In contrast to the Chinese crackdown on cryptocurrencies,[117] U.S. Government agencies have not indicated any general regulatory interest in banning cryptocurrency or other digital assets.

§3.03 TREASURY

In the US, the Department of the Treasury is tasked with the role of encouraging a strong economy, including creating economic and job opportunities. It aims to promote economic prosperity and financial security of the United States.

Consequently, anything that has a significant impact on the U.S. financial system will attract the attention of the Treasury. There is no question that the impact of the rise of digital assets including cyber currency, digital tokens and NFTs has generated such an impact. This has caused the Treasury to consider the effects of that impact and how, as a major government agency dealing with economic and financial issues, how it should respond.

116. Eric Lipton, Ephrat Livini and Jeanna Smialek, "Regulators Racing Toward First Major Rules on Cryptocurrency," The New York Times, online, September 23, 2021.
117. *See* Chapter on Chinese regulation, below.

That response, as is the case with any financial regulator around the world, has not come all at once, and it is still in the process of being fully formulated. Nevertheless, the Treasury has made it clear that it has an important role in regulating digital assets and will continue to expand that role as interest in digital assets grows and their uses become more varied.[118]

[A] FinCEN

The United States Treasury set up a Financial Crimes Enforcement Network (FinCEN) in 1990 to protect the financial system from illicit activities, fight money laundering and other crimes, prevent terrorism, and promote national security.

Over time it has become clear that FinCEN is very concerned about the impact of cryptocurrency. Their particular focus, as is shown in the very large number of crypto-related reports, speeches, and articles on their website, is the prevention of financial crime through the use of cryptocurrency. The cryptocurrency misuse that they consider to be a problem includes money laundering, the financing of terrorism, the avoidance of sanctions and the financing of cybercrime such as ransomware attacks. The tools FinCEN deploys to fight these things are registration for money service businesses (MSBs) and the reporting of suspicious activity by those businesses exposed to cryptocurrency.

Under FinCEN rules, the following MSBs are subject to suspicious activity reporting (SAR) requirements:[119]

- Money transmitters.
- Money order issuers, sellers and redeemers.
- Travelers check issuers, sellers and redeemers.
- U.S. Postal service.

Regardless of whether any business has been required to register with the U.S. Treasury, the U.S. SEC, the CFTC, or any other regulator, exposure to cyber currency and other crypto assets may impose duties to be aware of and report suspicious crypto-related activity to appropriate regulatory and/or enforcement agencies.[120]

Although that FinCEN press release was focused on crypto activity relating to Russian sanctions,[121] it is also a description of FinCEN policies with respect to all activities that may raise suspicions of being related to cybercrime, money laundering, the financing of terrorist activity, or the avoidance of other sanctions such as those that have been imposed on Iran.

---

118. U.S. Department of the Treasury, home.treasury.gov.
119. FinCEN, "Money Service Business (MSB) Suspicious Activity Reporting," online at fincen.gov, accessed April 11, 2022.
120. *Ibid.*
121. *Ibid.*

The first FinCEN cryptocurrency guidance document issued (FIN-2019-G001)[122] provided interpretations that entities subject to the Bank Secrecy Act (BSA) including MSBs were supposed to regard involving transmissions of cryptocurrency.

The first point raised was that any money transmitters that might be subject to FinCEN's regulations needed to be aware of the characteristics of certain kinds of transactions. Those subject to FinCEN regulation included money services businesses which are defined as person or entity:

> wherever located doing business, whether or not on a regular basis or as an organized or licensed business concern, wholly or in substantial part within the United States, operating directly, or through an agent, agency, branch, or office, who functions, among other things as a "money transmitter.

A money transmitter, or an entity that engages in "money transmission services," is defined as a person or entity that engages in:

> the acceptance of currency, funds, or other value that substitutes for currency from one person and the transmission of currency, funds, or other value that substitutes for currency to another location or person by any means. The term other value that substitutes for currency encompasses situations in which the transmission does not involve currency, or funds, but instead involves something that the parties to a transaction recognize has value that is equivalent to or can substitute for currency.[123]

This is intended by FinCEN to be a very broad definition which they certainly feel embraces cryptocurrency in any form including tokens or even in NFTs or anything else considered by the parties to have value.

However, there is a regulatory distinction between MSBs regulated by FinCEN and financial institutions or financial market participants that are regulated by other regulatory agencies such as the U.S. SEC or the U.S. CFTC, or foreign equivalents to those U.S. agencies.[124]

[B] Money Service Business

Under the BSA, which is administered by the U.S. Treasury, certain financial institutions that are not regulated as banks are required to register as MSBs.[125]

The MSB Registration Rule applies to five types of businesses:

(1) Currency dealers or exchanges.
(2) Check cashers.
(3) Issuers of traveler's checks or money orders.
(4) Sellers or redeemers of traveler's checks, money orders or stored value.

122. FinCEN, "Application of FinCEN's Regulations to Certain Business Models Involving Convertible Virtual Currencies" online at fincen.gov, May 19, 2019.
123. FinCEN, *supra*, in section 1.2.1.
124. *Ibid.*, in section 1.2.2.
125. FinCEN, "Fact Sheet on MSB Registration Rule," online at fincen.gov., accessed April 11, 2022.

(5) Money transmitters.

The provisions of the MSB Rule[126] require that:

- MSBs must register with the Department of the Treasury and renew their registration every two years;
- agents of MSBs are not now required to register regardless of the dollar volume of their money service activities unless they engage in money service activities both on their own behalf and as an agent for others;
- MSBs must maintain a list of their agents and update that list annually;
- the initial registration form had to be filed by December 31, 2001, and the initial agent list prepared by January 1, 2002;
- the term "money service business" does not include a bank or a person registered with and regulated or examined by the SEC or the CFTC;
- the definition of money transmitter clarifies that the activity that makes a person a money transmitter must be carried on as a business, and that generally the acceptance and transmission of funds as an integral part of the execution and settlement of a transaction other than the funds transmission itself (e.g., in connection with a bona fide sale of securities), will not cause a person to be a money transmitter;
- issuers and sellers of stored value are included as MSBs, but they are not required to register at this time;
- treasury also is announcing its intention that SAR requirements for money transmitting and the travelers checks and money order segments of the industry will be forthcoming. In the coming months, Treasury and FinCEN will be working with the industry to develop guidance to assist in identifying suspicious activity;
- to permit effective implementation, Treasury will not begin requiring suspicious transaction reporting until the registration process is complete.[127]

The penalties for failing to comply with the registration or agent list requirements of the MSB rule are stated as follows:

> Any person failing to comply with the registration or agent list requirement may be assessed a civil penalty of $5000 for each violation. Each day during which a violation occurs constitutes a separate violation and can be connected to evasion of sanctions. Any relevant suspicious information should be shared with law enforcement authorities including, US Department of Justice, international partners of the US and any groups that have been established to track and freeze the assets of sanctioned Russian institutions and persons.

126. *Ibid.*
127. *Ibid.*

"Financial institutions that should be on the lookout for suspicious activity include the following:[128]

- Casinos.
- Depository Institutions.
- Insurance Industry Participants.
- Money Services Businesses.
- Mortgage Companies or Brokers.
- Precious Metals and Jewelry Industries.
- Securities and Futures Industries Participants."

[C] Sanctions Avoidance

In March of 2022, FinCEN published a paper on "red flags" that should alert financial institutions to attempts to avoid financial sanctions, such as those that were imposed on Russia as a result of the war in Ukraine or on Iran because of other international violations.[129] They point out that although very large-scale transactions involving cyber currency may not be possible, there may be other, less visible, flows of cyber currency in the form of transactions related to cryptocurrency wallets that may be associated with Russia, Russians or affiliated persons.

In addition, the dangers of Russian ransomware campaigns have not diminished and may increase due to attempts to raise money to help fund Russia's invasion of Ukraine.[130]

To guard against successful sanctions evasions, FinCEN urges all financial institutions who are in a position to observe cryptocurrency or other virtual asset flows to be alert to identify and report suspicious activities which might constitute evasions or attempts at evasions to the Treasury's Financial Crimes Enforcement Network (FinCEN).

[D] Virtual Currency Misuse

In May of 2019, FinCEN issued guidance about regulation of virtual currencies and advice on threats of virtual currency misuse. The purpose of the guidance was to help banks and other financial institutions identify and report suspicious activity such as potential money laundering, evasion of sanctions or other illegal financial activities relating to cryptocurrency. Although this guidance did not introduce new regulations, it affirmed what FinCEN said was its long-standing policy in this area.[131]

128. *Ibid.*
129. FinCEN, "FinCEN Provides Financial Institutions with Red Flags on Potential Russian Sanctions Evasion Attempts," online at fincen.gov, March 7, 2022, accessed April 12, 2022.
130. *Ibid.*
131. FinCEN, "New FinCEN Guidance Affirms its Longstanding Regulatory Framework for Virtual Currencies and a New FinCEN Advisory Warns of Threats Posed by Virtual Currency Misuse," online at fincen.gov, May 19, 2019.

[E] Stablecoins

An early Federal regulatory effort on digital assets involved a cooperative effort by the U.S. Treasury and other Federal agencies to impose a regulatory system on a digital currency product known as "stablecoins."

Stablecoin has that name because it is supposedly indexed on a one-to-one basis with so-called stable assets like the U.S. dollar, or other "stable" assets such as foreign fiat currencies and precious metals.

This concept itself appears to contain a significant fallacy—that assets such as U.S. dollars and gold are stable. Although the value of these things may not fluctuate as often or as dramatically as cryptocurrencies do, the market values of gold, U.S. dollars, etc., do change constantly, not only day to day but also during the days that market transactions for those assets are being concluded.

So, what "stability" stablecoins are meant to have is not clear.

There is also the problem that issuers of stablecoins have not always been clear about how their products are actually being supported.

US regulators are aware of this inherent instability and have become concerned that the adoption and use of so-called stablecoins, such as Tether token, USD coin and PAX dollar, could lead to serious financial losses if their values fluctuated significantly.

As reported in *The New York Times*, the total value of stablecoins in circulation increased from US$ 30 billion to approximately US$ 125 billion between January and mid-September 2021.[132]

In November of 2021, an Interagency Report on Stablecoins was published by the President's Working Group on Financial Markets, the Federal Deposit Insurance corporation, and the Office of the Comptroller of the Currency.[133] It discussed the nature of stablecoins, the risks related to stablecoins and the regulatory gaps that existed with respect to that digital product. It suggested that legislation should be promulgated to:

> limit stablecoin issuance and related activities of redemption and maintenance of reserve assets, to entities that are insured depository institutions. The legislation should prohibit other entities from issuing payment stablecoins. Legislation should also ensure that supervisors have authority to implement standards to promote interoperability among stablecoins.

The U.S. Treasury is leading an effort to provide a sensible framework for regulation of digital currencies like stablecoins.[134]

Jerome Powell, the Chairman of the U.S. Federal Reserve said in early October 2021 that the US did not intend to ban cryptocurrencies. With respect to stablecoins, he is quoted as saying:

---

132. Eric Lipton, Ephrat Livini and Jeanna Smialek, September 23, 2021.
133. Available for download on the Department of the Treasury website: home.treasury.gov.
134. Eric Lipton, Ephrat Livini and Jeanna Smialek, September 23, 2021, citing a statement by Treasury undersecretary Nellie Liang.

> Stablecoins are like money market funds, bank deposits, but they're to some extent outside the regulatory perimeter, and it's appropriate that they be regulated. Same activity, same regulation.[135]

§3.04 TREASURY ENFORCEMENT

The Treasury is not only concerned with policy that effects crypto assets but also concerned with enforcement against misuse of digital assets. The Treasury takes action and joins with other agencies to take action and impose penalties in instances where cryptocurrency transactions may involve money laundering, sanction avoidance or other violations.

[A] OFAC

For example, in October of 2022, the Treasury's Office of Foreign Assets Control (OFAC) joined with the Financial Crimes Enforcement Network (FinCEN) in imposing financial penalties of about US$ 24 million and US$ 29 million on Bittrex (a cybercurrency exchange) because of violations of anti-money laundering regulations, sanctions, and SAR requirements. Bittrex is a "money services business" regulated by FinCEN.[136] This was the largest penalty paid to OFAC until then.

Some other investigative, regulatory and enforcement actions involving the Treasury and relating to digital assets are discussed in this book.

For more information about U.S. Treasury enforcement actions and penalties, the Treasury website includes a detailed section on "Civil Penalties and Enforcement Information," listed by year.[137]

§3.05 THE SECURITIES EXCHANGE COMMISSION

The SEC is a major regulator of the investment business in the US. It is tasked with protecting investors and maintaining fair, orderly, and efficient markets, and facilitating capital formation.

In general terms, the SEC is responsible for regulating the sale and trading of investments (securities). Persons and entities involved in numerous aspects of this business including the purchase and sale of securities, advising on securities, managing securities, trading securities are required to be licensed and regulated by the SEC. This regulation also includes the filing of numerous documents with the SEC about securities and the persons or entities that issue them.

135. Hamza Khalique-Loonat, "Bitcoin jumps 9% after U.S. Federal Reserve Gives Cryptocurrencies the All-clear," The Times, online, October 2, 2021.

136. U.S. Department of the Treasury, Press Releases, "Treasury Announces Two Enforcement Actions for over $24M and $29M Against Virtual Currency Exchange Bittrex, Inc." online at: home.treasury.gov, October 11, 2022.

137. home.treasury.gov.

Consequently, an important issue for the SEC, since the creation of cyber assets, is whether such assets are being marketed or used in ways that bring them within the definition of securities regulated under the securities laws. In many cases, such digital assets have been found to be within the securities laws, and this has caused the SEC to become involved in actions involving crypto investigation, regulation and enforcement. A number of such actions are discussed in the other chapters of this book.

§3.06 REGISTRATION OF EXCHANGES

In September of 2021, the Chairman of the U.S. SEC, Gary Gensler, said that cryptocurrency exchanges should register with the SEC because they deal in tokens "that may be securities." It is reported that there has been a debate for some time going on between Coinbase, and the other cryptocurrency exchanges, with the SEC over whether the cryptocurrency exchanges are dealing in products that could be classed as "securities" that would come within the jurisdiction of the SEC. Indeed, it has been reported that the SEC issued a formal notice to Coinbase saying that the Federal Communications Commission (FCC) would charge Coinbase with a regulatory violation if Coinbase proceeded with a plan to launch a product allowing users to make interest by live lending digital assets.[138]

Top Coinbase executives, in Internet posts, responded that neither cryptocurrencies nor stablecoins were within the definition of securities and should not be regulated by the SEC. Coinbase said that their "lend" product that was the subject of this debate was not and "investment" but was a lending program that did not constitute a security. Reportedly, the SEC has repeatedly asked cryptocurrency companies to come in and "talk" to the SEC. However, Coinbase says it had been trying to have a dialogue with the SEC for over six months, but there had been no substantial response.[139]

[A] BSTX and Share Tokens: An Investing Revolution?

One area in which the SEC has an important regulatory and investigative role is in the licensing and regulation of securities exchanges where securities are bought and sold. In January of 2022, the SEC granted approval to a new, cyber-related stock exchange named BSTX. BSTX is a subsidiary of the BOX Exchange in Boston, Massachusetts. It was announced that stocks and exchange-traded funds will be traded there. What connects this event to cryptocurrency is the fact that BSTX will use blockchain technology.[140]

It is reported that the goal of BSTX is to eventually trade all U.S. stocks and to offer "tokenised securities." Tokenized securities are digital instruments the value of which is pegged to the market value of particular shares. However, rather than

138. Todd Ehret, "SEC Spat with Coinbase Previews Complex Legal Battle Over Crypto," Reuters, online, September 28, 2021.
139. *Ibid.*
140. John Mccrank, "U.S. SEC Approves New U.S. Exchange with Blockchain Feed, Faster Settlement," Reuters, online, January 29, 2022.

representing the full value of the share they would represent fractional values of shares. This presumably would allow more people to participate in changes in values of those shares although to a lesser degree than owning the full share.

The goal is to open the stock market to a wider population of investors who may be unable or unwilling to spend the money necessary to buy full equity shares. Reuters points out that BSTX will be similar "to crypto exchanges such as Coinbase (COIN.O) as opposed to traditional stock and bond exchanges like NASDAQ (NDAQ.O)."[141]

This may help investors who wish to participate in the movements of high-performing equity shares but have been unable or reluctant to do so because of their high market price. For example, the main share price of Berkshire Hathaway (BH), which is headed by the famously successful investment guru, Warren Buffett, has been more than US$ 450,000 a share. In the past, other financial instruments have been offered, pegged to the value of BH shares to give people an opportunity to participate in rises in the value of BH shares. BH responded by issuing Berkshire Hathaway B shares, which have a market value of around US$ 300 per share. With the appearance of BSTX, it may be the case that tokens pegged to the value of BH shares might (if they have the correct approvals) be sold representing even smaller fractional values. Perhaps Berkshire Hathaway may be moved to issue its own tokens.

The offering of tokens related to fractions of share market prices could lead to a watershed change in the equities market and perhaps to markets for bonds, commodities and other financial assets as well. A significant portion of the world's population may become investors in such financial market offerings.

Apparently, this plan occurred to the founders of BSTX at an early stage. Their original proposal to the SEC was to have an exchange called the Boston Security Token Exchange that would trade only securities-related tokens. However, this plan was rejected by the SEC at the end of 2020. However, the world's attitude toward digitalized assets has evolved significantly in the last couple of years, and the indications are that BSTX intends to try to revive this kind of trading in the future.[142]

One important significant difference between BSTX and some other cryptomarkets is that it is an entity regulated by the U.S. government through the Securities Exchange Commission. This should provide a higher degree of security, and perhaps less volatility, than has been the case with privately run cryptocurrencies and crypto markets. If the attraction of that is strong enough to interest a large enough portion of the investing public, cryptocurrencies and tokens issued by private persons may become significantly less attractive to the general public. Most, if not all of the thousands of cryptocurrencies issued may disappear or become interesting only to criminal elements then wished to avoid the scrutiny of government regulatory authorities.

The use of blockchain technology by a government-regulated exchange also significantly increases the credibility of blockchain as a guarantee of transaction security. Although, in theory blockchains are supposed to be impossible to tamper with

141. *Ibid.*
142. *Ibid.*

and to provide a clear picture of the purchase and sale history of assets, a couple of problems have been pointed out. The first is that they are assembled and offered by private operators who may or may not be truthful about how they operate. Another is that some criminal operations have been able to acquire the expertise and computing power to steal cryptocurrency.

[B] SEC Expands Crypto and Cyber Enforcement

In May of 2022, the SEC issued the following press release:

> *Washington DC, May 3, 2022*—the Securities and Exchange Commission today announced the allocation of 20 additional positions to the unit responsible and protecting investors in crypto markets and from crypto-related threats. The newly named Crypto Assets and Cyber Unit (formerly known as the Cyber Unit) in the Division of Enforcement will grow to 50 dedicated positions.[143]

The SEC has been paying close attention to the growth of the crypto and cyber markets. It has been particularly concerned with what its Enforcement Division has perceived to be violations of investment law and regulations in connection with the sale of digital products.

In 2017, the SEC created an enforcement unit to monitor the cyber markets. This also expanded into monitoring of the crypto and digital asset markets. The SEC reports that since 2017:[144]

> The unit has brought more than 80 enforcement actions related to fraudulent and unregistered crypto asset offerings and platforms, resulting in monetary relief totaling more than $2 billion.

These enforcement actions have related to a wide variety of alleged violations including the following:[145]

- Crypto asset offerings.
- Crypto asset exchanges.
- Crypto asset lending products.
- Decentralized finance (DeFi) platforms.
- Non-fungible tokens (NFTs).
- Stablecoins.

The SEC also has brought many other actions against those registered with the SEC and other public companies for having inadequate cyber security controls and for not properly disclosing Internet-related risks and problems.[146]

143. U.S. SEC, Press Release, 2022-78, "SEC Nearly Doubles Size of Enforcement's Crypto Assets and Cyber Unit," online at: sec.gov, May 3, 2022, accessed July 28, 2022.
144. *Ibid.*
145. *Ibid.*
146. *Ibid.*

For example, in February of 2022, the SEC imposed on Block Five Lending LLC (a cryptocurrency company that allowed almost 600,000 people an opportunity to earn interest by lending their holdings to other traders) to pay US$ 100 million fine to settle SEC claims that its business violated investor protection laws. This was the highest fine ever imposed by the SEC on a cryptocurrency company. This was also the SEC's first enforcement action against a crypto lending platform.[147]

In March of 2022, the SEC proposed amendments to its rules to improve and expand disclosures regarding cyber security risk management and requirements relating to incident reporting by public companies.[148] The chairman of the SEC, Gary Gensler, said:

> Over the years, our disclosure regime has evolved to reflect evolving risks and investor needs. Today cybersecurity is an emerging risk with which public issuers increasingly must contend. Investors want to know more about how issuers are managing those growing risks. A lot of issuers already provide cybersecurity disclosure to investors. I think companies and investors alike would benefit if this information were required to make consistent, comparable, and decision-useful manner.[149]

[C] Crypto Assets and Cyber Unit

The Securities Exchange Commission sees itself as a key regulator of the digital asset markets. It has been reported that between 2013 in 2022, the SEC brought more than ninety enforcement actions related to cryptocurrency issues usually involving fraud and/or failure to register securities.[150]

Of these, more than forty involved litigation brought by the SEC and more than thirty involved administrative proceedings. Approximately half of the litigation cases were commenced in the federal courts in New York, which is a principal center of financial business activity in the United States.[151]

The number of crypto-related actions brought by the SEC has rapidly increased over those years with only one brought in 2013 and nineteen brought in the first quarter of 2021.

In 2017 the SEC created its special Cyber Unit within its Division of Enforcement.

---

147. Dave Michaels, "BlockFi to Pay Record Penalty to Settle SEC Probe of Crypto Lending Business," The Wall Street Journal, online, February 14, 2022, accessed 01 August 2022.
148. U.S. SEC, Press Release, 2022-39, "SEC Proposes Rules on Cybersecurity Risk Management, Strategy, Governance, and Incident Disclosure by Public Companies," online at: sec.gov, March 9, 2022, accessed July 28, 2022.
149. *Ibid.*
150. Simona Mola, SEC Cryptocurrency Enforcement, Q3 2013-Q42020, the Tables and Appendices included in the report contain lists and details of the enforcement actions reported, Cornerstone Research, available for review and download on online at: cornerstone.com. Also *see*, Simona Mola, SEC Cryptocurrency Enforcement: Q3 2021 Update. The Tables and Appendices included in the report contain lists and details of the enforcement actions reported, Cornerstone Research, available for review and download online at: cornerstone.com, November 3, 2021, all accessed July 29, 2022.
151. *Ibid.*

The SEC says that, since 2017, it has brought enforcement actions against fraudulent and unregistered crypto asset offerings and platforms which resulted in recovery of more than US$ 2 billion.

As discussed above, in May of 2022, during a time of turmoil in the crypto markets, the SEC announced that it was almost doubling the size of its Cyber Unit and renaming it as the Crypto Assets and Cyber Unit (CACU).

CACU has taken action against SEC registrants and other public companies which have failed to maintain adequate cyber security controls and failed to adequately disclose cyber-related risks and incidents.

It is not possible within this book to give the details of all of the enforcement actions which the SEC has undertaken with respect to crypto and cyber issues in a period these can be reviewed at the SEC website but consulting their list of press releases.[152] However, to give the reader a general understanding of the kinds of matters that the SEC focuses its attention on, a description of number of SEC crypto cases follows.

[D] SEC Crypto Enforcement

[1] Coinbase Insider Trading Case

In July of 2022, the SEC brought insider trading charges against a former Coinbase product manager and two other defendants accusing them of scheming to trade ahead of the offering of crypto assets which were to be made available for trading on the Coinbase platform. The product manager was helping to coordinate Coinbase's announcements about what crypto assets were to be made available for trading. This information was supposed to be confidential, but the manager provided tips to the other defendants about upcoming crypto trading announcements. These crypto assets were often classed as "securities" regulated by the SEC.

The defendants would arrange to purchase them in advance of listing announcements and would sell them at a profit shortly afterward. Their illegal profits added up to over US$ 1 million. The SEC charged the defendants with violating the anti-fraud provisions of the securities laws and sought civil penalties against the defendants, including injunctions, disgorgement of profits with interest and civil penalties. In addition, the U.S. attorney's office for the Southern District of New York also brought criminal charges against the three defendants.[153]

[2] MCC International Corp. Case

On May 6, 2022, the SEC announced fraud charges against MCC international Corp (MCC), its founders and other connected defendants. It is alleged the defendants made

152. U.S. SEC, Press Releases, online at: sec.gov, accessed August 23, 2022.
153. U.S. SEC, Press Release, "SEC Charges Former Coinbase Manager, Two Others in Crypto Asset Insider Trading Action," July 21, 2022, online at: sec.gov.

unregistered offerings and fraudulent sales of investment plans to thousands of investors telling the investors that the investments were for crypto mining and trading projects. In fact, the defendants are alleged to have used the money to fund lavish lifestyles.

The SEC is reportedly seeking to impose penalties of injunctions against future securities law violations, discouragements of the defendants' gains, civil penalties and barring the individual defendants from future participation in regulated activities.[154]

[3] *NVIDIA Corporation* Case

Also, on May 6, 2022, the SEC announced that it had settled charges against NVIDIA corporation relating to inadequate disclosures concerning the impact of crypto mining on the company's gaming business.

NVIDIA had allegedly reported revenue growth of its gaming business which was allegedly due in significant part to crypto mining. The SEC alleged that NVIDIA was required to reveal to its investors that a significant part of its earnings and cash flow was due to a volatile business. Consequently, the SEC alleged that NVIDIA's omissions of this "material information" were misleading and in violation of provisions of the Securities Act of 1933 and the Securities Exchange Act of 1934. NVIDIA agreed to comply with a cease-and-desist order and pay a US$ 5.5 million penalty.[155]

[4] *Barksdale* Case

On March 8, 2022, the SEC charged the siblings John and Jonatina Barksdale with defrauding thousands of retail investors out of more than US$ 124 million using two unregistered fraudulent crypto token securities involving a digital token called "Ormeus Coin."

They offered the Ormeus Coin on a number of crypto trading platforms and also in subscription packages which consisted of an Ormeus coin and an investment in a crypto trading program. They promoted their products with roadshows around the world and also produced social media posts, YouTube videos, press releases and other promotional materials selling their products. They also falsely claim that the Ormeus coin was supported by a large crypto mining operation that was producing up to US$ 8 million a month in mining revenues.

The SEC charge the defendants with violating U.S. security laws and sought injunctive relief, disgorgement of revenues plus interest and other civil penalties. In a parallel action, the U.S. attorney's office for the Southern District of New York brought a criminal complaint against John Barksdale.[156]

---

154. U.S. SEC, Press Release, 2022-81, "SEC Halts Fraudulent Cryptomining and Trading Scheme," May 6, 2022, online at: sec.gov, accessed August 24, 2022.
155. U.S. SEC, Press Release, 2022-79, "SEC Charges NVIDIA Corporation with Inadequate Disclosures about Impact of Cryptomining," 06 May 2022, online at: sec.gov, accessed August 24, 2022.
156. U.S. SEC, Press Release, 2022-37 "SEC Charges Siblings in $124 Million Crypto Fraud Operation that Included Misleading Roadshows, YouTube Videos," March 8, 2022, online at: sec.gov, accessed August 25, 2022.

[5] *BlockFi* Case

On February 22, 2022, the SEC charged BlockFi Lending LLC (BlockFi) with violating the Investment Company Act of 1940 by not registering its offers and sales of retail crypto lending products. BlockFi settled the charges with the SEC by agreeing to pay a US$ 50 million penalty, and to cease its unregistered offers and sales. BlockFi agreed to bring its business into compliance with the Investment Company Act of 1940 within sixty days.

In addition, BlockFi agreed to pay a total of US$ 50 million in fines to thirty-two U.S. states to settle similar charges regarding violation of state regulations.[157]

[6] *Ryan Ginster* Case

On November 18, 2021, the SEC charged Ryan Ginster of Corona, California with conducting two unregistered and fraudulent securities offerings that raised over US$ 3.6 million in cryptocurrency from retail investors.

It is alleged that Ginster used two online platforms that promised astronomical returns to retail investors by promising profits from cryptocurrency trading and advertising arbitrage. Ginster is alleged to have misappropriated at least US$ 1,000,000 of the money he collected to pay personal expenses.

Ginster was charged, under a complaint filed in the U.S. District Court for the Central District of California, with violating the anti-fraud and registration provisions of the Securities Act of 1933 and the Securities Exchange Act of 1930. The SEC sought permanent injunctions, disgorgement of revenue with interest and civil penalties against Ginster. The U.S. attorney's office for the Northern District of California wrought a parallel criminal action against Ginster.[158]

[7] *American CryptoFed Proceedings*

On November 10, 2021, the SEC began proceedings against American CryptoFed DAO LLC, a Wyoming-based organization, halting that company's registration of two digital tokens, the Ducat and Locke tokens, as equity securities.

The SEC alleged that the relevant registration form failed to contain required information about American CryptoFed's business, management and financial condition, including audited financial statements. Consequently, the SEC found the filing to be "materially deficient and misleading."

157. U.S. SEC, Press Release, 2022-26 "BlockFi Agrees to Pay $100 Million in Penalties and Pursue Registration of Its Crypto Lending Product," February 14, 2022, online at: sec.gov, accessed August 25, 2022.
158. U.S. SEC, Press Release, 2021-237 "SEC Charges Promoter with Conducting Cybercurrency Investment Scams," November 18, 2021, online at: sec.gov, accessed August 25, 2022.

The SEC said:

> [I]ssuers attempting to raise money from the public must provide the information necessary for investors to make informed decisions.[159]

[8] John McAfee

John McAfee was a brilliant computer programmer and a pioneer of antiviral software. He was the founder of McAfee Corp., a software company now worth billions of dollars. He sold his interest in the company to Intel in about 1994. He was found dead, apparently from suicide, in a Spanish prison in 2021. McAfee, who had led a controversial life since selling his antivirus software company, was awaiting extradition to the US to face a number of criminal and civil charges, including tax evasion and cryptocurrency fraud.

The cryptocurrency fraud charges related to a "pump and dump" scheme where, representing himself as an impartial, sophisticated investor, McAfee promoted the initial coin offerings (ICOs) of various cryptocurrencies. Following his public statements on the potential value of these cryptocurrencies, a number of people were apparently persuaded to invest in them and the prices rose significantly. Thereafter, McAfee, who had acquired a significant number of these cryptocurrencies before he made his statements and before they were publicly offered, sold his stake in these cryptocurrencies, allegedly making more than US$ 23 million. In October of 2020, McAfee and an associate were charged by the SEC "for promoting investments in initial coin offerings (ICOs) to his Twitter followers without disclosing that he was paid to do so."[160] The complaint also alleged that he made other false and misleading statements in connection with the ICOs including that he claimed to have personally invested in some of the ICOs and that he was advising certain issuers. Kristina Littman, Cyber Unit chief of the SEC, said:

> Potential investors in digital asset securities are entitled to know if promoters were compensated by the issuers of those securities McAfee allegedly leveraged his fame to deceptively tout numerous digital asset securities to his followers without informing investors of his role as a paid promoter.[161]

[9] BitConnect **Case**

On September 1, 2021, the SEC brought an action against BitConnect and related defendants, alleging they defrauded retail investors out of US$ 2 billion by means of worldwide fraudulent and unregistered marketing of investments in digital assets.

159. U.S. SEC, Press Release, 2021-231, "Registration of Two Digital Tokens Halted," November 10, 2021, online at: sec.gov, accessed August 26, 2022.
160. *SEC v. McAfee, et al.*, Case No. 2020-cv-8281, U.S. District Court for the Southern District of New York.
161. U.S. SEC, Press Release, 2020-246 "SEC Charges John McAfee With Fraudulently Touting ICOs," October 5, 2020, online at: sec.gov, accessed December 21, 2022.

The SEC charged the defendants with conducting a fraudulent and unregistered offering and sale of securities in a so-called Lending Program sold by BitConnect. BitConnect claimed that investments in this program would generate extremely high returns. However, the SEC alleged that the defendants misappropriated the funds collected for their personal benefit.[162]

A criminal indictment was also brought against the defendants by the Justice Department.[163]

[10] ***Poloniex*** **Case**

On August 9, 2021, the SEC announced that Poloniex LLC had agreed to pay more than US$ 10 million to settle charges brought against them by the SEC for operating an unregistered online digital asset exchange and operation of a trading platform for buying and selling securities based on digital assets.

The SEC alleged that although Poloniex did operate a genuine exchange, it had not registered it properly as a national security exchange, and it did not operate under any exemption from registration.

These things were alleged to be violations of section 5 of the Exchange Act.

The SEC penalties that Poloniex agreed to accept were the entry of a cease-and-desist order, an agreement to pay a disgorgement penalty of over US$ 8 million, along with interest of over US$ 400,000. In addition, they agreed to pay a civil penalty of US$ 1.5 million. A fund was also established for the benefit of any victims.[164]

[11] ***Crypto Lending Securities Offering*** **Case**

On May 28, 2021, the SEC brought a case, against five individuals for offering and selling unregistered securities, as part of a crypto lending program that advised on the merits of investing in BitConnect's lending program. The SEC said:

> We allege that these defendants unlawfully sold unregistered digital asset securities by actively promoting the BitConnect lending program to retail investors.

The SEC sought injunctive relief and disgorgement plus interest against the defendants and additional civil penalties.[165]

---

162. U.S. SEC, Press Release, 2021-172 "SEC Charges Global Crypto Lending Platform and Top Executives in $2 Billion Fraud," September 1, 2021, online at: sec.gov, accessed August 25, 2022.
163. *See*, "DOJ Selling Cryptocurrency Seized From Bitconnect Worth $56 Million," Bitcoin.com News, online, November 16, 2021.
164. U.S. SEC, Press Release, 2021-147, "SEC Charges Poloniex for Operating Unregistered Digital Asset Exchange," August 9, 2021, online at: sec.gov, accessed August 26, 2022.
165. U.S. SEC, Press Release, 2021-90, "SEC Charges U.S. Promoters of $2 Billion Global Crypto Lending Securities Offering," May 28, 2021, online at: sec.gov, accessed August 26, 2022. *See also*, discussion of BitConnect Case, above.

[12] XRP Digital Currency

In December of 2020, the SEC brought an action against Ripple Labs, Inc. and its Chairman and its CEO, claiming that they illegally sold unregistered securities in the form of Ripple's XRP Digital Currency.[166] The SEC has claimed that Ripple sold XRP to investors to pay for Ripple's operating expenses. Ripple moved to dismiss the SEC's case, on several grounds including that Ripple's right to due process of law had been violated because the SEC had failed to give them due notice that their conduct violated section 5 of the Securities Act of 1933.[167]

In March of 2022, Judge Torres of the U.S. District Court for the Southern District of New York denied the defendant's motion to dismiss the case but granted the defendants the right to assert the defense that they were not given fair notice their activities were in violation of law.[168]

Ripple says that it was founded in 2012 and is a "privately held payments technology company that uses block chain innovation ... To allow money to be sent around the world instantly, reliably and more cheaply than traditional avenues of money transmission."[169]

Ripple says that it holds a large percentage of XRP which it describes as having used as a "bridge currency" and having "other types of currency uses."[170]

Ripple admitted that it traded XRP in exchange for dollars and other currencies. Ripple worked with market makers who bought XRP both "on ledger" and on exchanges where XRP was traded. The proceeds of the sales were used to pay Ripple's operating expenses. However, Ripple claims that it did not sell XRP as an investment and that the holding XRP did not give the holder any ownership interest in Ripple.[171]

XRP currency is issued by XRP II, LLC (XRP II) which is a wholly owned subsidiary of Ripple. XRP II Is registered as a money service business with the FinCEN and is licensed by the New York Department of Financial Services to conduct some virtual currency business transactions.

In June of 2018, the SEC's then-Director of Corporate Finance said that the SEC did not regard Bitcoin or Ether to be securities and that it would ignore the fund-raising that accompanied the creation of Ether and look instead at the present state of Ether.

In 2019 SEC staff met with a digital currency platform that was considering listing XRP. The platform asked the SEC for guidance on whether the SEC considered XRP a security. The SEC did not say that it considered XRP to be a security, and the exchange listed XRP.

However, the SEC has stated publicly at different times that digital assets may be considered securities under certain circumstances.[172]

---

166. *Securities and Exchange Commission v. Ripple Labs Inc., et al.* (USDC SDNY, 20 Civ. 10832 [AT][SN]), Decision of District Judge Analisa Torres, Document 440, filed March 11, 2022.
167. *Ibid.* p. 1.
168. *Ibid.*
169. *Ibid.*
170. *Ibid.* p. 2.
171. *Ibid.*
172. *Ibid.* p. 4.

As of this writing, March 2022, the case goes on. It is hard to imagine a more ironically appropriate title than *SEC v. Ripple.* When this case is finally resolved, its effects will be felt worldwide.

[13] ***Virgil Capital*** **Case**

In late December of 2020, the SEC announced that it had obtained an asset freeze and other emergency relief against Virgil Capital LLC and affiliated companies relating to alleged securities fraud in connection with Virgil's cryptocurrency trading fund, Virgil Sigma Fund LP.

The SEC alleged that the owner of Virgil had been defrauding investors since about 2018 by misrepresenting the cryptocurrency trading fund's strategy, assets, and financial condition. The SEC alleged that defendants told investors their money was being used only for cryptocurrency trading based on a proprietary formula. However, the defendants were using investments by customers for personal purposes or for other high-risk investments. Fraudulent promises were made to lure investors into the fund and to hide his improper use of investor funds.

The SEC sought injunctions, disgorgement of improper revenues with interest and civil penalties.[173]

[14] ***AML Bitcoin*** **Case**

On June 25, 2020, the SEC charged NAC Foundation and related individuals with conducting a fraudulent, unregistered offering of AML Bitcoin, a digital asset security that the defendants claimed was a new and improved version of Bitcoin.

The SEC alleged that NAC Foundation had obtained US$ 5.6 million from over 2,000 investors by selling tokens that supposedly could later be converted into AML Bitcoin.

The defendants had allegedly claimed that AML Bitcoin contained anti-money laundering, anti-terrorism, and theft-resistant technology built into the coin on what they said was in AC's own privately regulated blockchain. The SEC alleged that none of these claims was true.

A number of other false statements were allegedly made in connection with AML Bitcoin. The SEC also alleged that defendants created a market manipulation strategy to increase their tokens trading volume and price, and the CEO of NAC Foundation took over US$ 1,000,000 for his personal use. The SEC sought injunctions, disgorgement and civil penalties against the defendants. One of the defendants, a former political lobbyist, settled with the SEC by accepting injunctions limiting future

173. U.S. SEC, Press Release, 2020-341, "SEC Obtains Emergency Asset Freeze, Charges Crypto Fund Manager with Fraud," December 28, 2020, online at: sec.gov, accessed August 30, 2022. *See also*, discussion of *BitConnect Case*, above.

investment-related activity, paying a disgorgement of US$ 50,000 and interest over US$ 5,000 with the possibility of future civil penalties.[174]

[15] Hvizdzak Cryptocurrency Offering Fraud

On June 19, 2020, the SEC filed an emergency action and obtained a temporary restraining order and asset freeze against two Pennsylvania-based brothers and other defendants to stop offering fraud and misappropriation of customer proceeds. The Hvizdzak brothers were accused of offering securities in a private fund that supposedly invested in digital assets. The brothers misrepresented fund performance, fabricated financial statements and forged audit documents. They were accused of violating the anti-fraud provisions of federal securities laws.[175]

[16] Enigma Tokens as Securities **Case**

On February 19, 2020, the SEC settled charges against blockchain technology start-up Enigma MPC for conducting an unregistered offering of securities in the form of an initial coin offering (ICO). Enigma agreed to return funds to investors, register its tokens (ENG tokens) as securities, file periodic reports with the SEC, and pay a US$ 500,000 penalty. The SEC order found that the ENG tokens are securities under federal securities laws and did not qualify for exemption from registration requirements.[176]

[17] Ackerman Targeting Physicians **Case**

On February 11, 2020, the SEC filed charges against a businessman who allegedly promoted a digital asset scheme that defrauded about 150 investors, many of whom were physicians. The defendant, Michael W. Ackerman along with other defendants raised at least US$ 33 million by claiming that he had developed a proprietary algorithm that allowed him to generate extraordinary profits from trading cryptocurrencies. The SEC complaint filed in federal court in New York charged Ackerman with violations of the anti-fraud provisions of the federal securities law. The SEC sought a permanent injunction, disgorgement plus interest, and a civil penalty. Both the U.S. Attorney's Office for the Southern District of New York and the CFTC also filed charges against Ackerman arising from his conduct.[177]

---

174. U.S. SEC, Press Release, 2020-145, "SEC Charges Issuer, CEO, and Lobbyist with Defrauding Investors in AML Bitcoin," June 25, 2020, online at: sec.gov, accessed September 6, 2022.
175. U.S. SEC, Press Release, 2020-137, "SEC Emergency Action Halts Brother' Cryptocurrency Offering Fraud," June 19, 2020, online at: sec.gov, accessed August 30, 2022.
176. U.S. SEC, Press Release, 2020-37, "ICO Issuer Settles SEC Registration Charges, Agrees to Return Funds and Register Tokens As Securities," June 25, 2020, online at: sec.gov, accessed September 6, 2022.
177. U.S. SEC, Press Release, 2020-32, "SEC Charges Orchestrator of Cryptocurrency Scheme Ensnaring Physicians," February 11, 2020, online at: sec.gov, accessed September 6, 2022.

[18] Block one Unregistered ICO Case

On 30 September 2019, the SEC announced that it had settled charges against a blockchain technology company named Block.one for conducting an unregistered initial coin offering of digital tokens ICO. During the course of a year, Block.one had raised "several billion dollars" with its scheme. The company agreed to settle charges by paying a civil penalty of US$ 24 million. The SEC charged Block.one with failing to register its ICO as a securities offering pursuant to federal securities laws, nor did Block.one qualify for or seek an exemption from the registration requirements.

Stephanie Avakian, Codirector of the SEC Division of Enforcement, said, "Companies that offer or sell securities to U.S. investors must comply with the securities laws, irrespective of the industry they operate in or the labels they place on the investment products they offer."[178]

[19] Bitqyck Unregistered Digital Asset Exchange Case

On August 29, 2019, the SEC charged a Dallas company and its founders with defrauding investors by making an unregistered offering and operating an unregistered digital asset exchange. The defendant, Bitqyck, Inc. and its founders allegedly defrauded investors by offering two digital assets and operated an unregistered exchange where one of the digital assets, a digital token, called Bitqy could be traded. The defendants allegedly raised more than US$ 13 million from investors. The defendants allegedly told investors that they operated a cryptocurrency mining facility powered by "below-market rate electricity." In fact, they had no discounted electricity and did not own or operate a mining facility. The SEC complaint filed in federal court in Texas sought permanent injunctions, return of illegal gains with interest and civil money penalties. Bitqyck and its founders consented to an order requiring them to pay disgorgement, interest, and a civil penalty of over US$ 8 million. The two individual defendants were each required to pay disgorgement, interest, and civil penalties of over US$ 850,000.[179]

[20] Longfin Cryptocurrency Fraud Case

On June 5, 2019, the SEC filed a fraud action against the former Longfin CEO, a consultant, and affiliated defendants. The defendants were charged with illegally trading the proceeds from distributions of Longfin stock. Longfin was a purported cryptocurrency company. The defendants were accused of declaring fake revenues and making misrepresentations to the SEC. The defendants agreed to settle the claims,

178. U.S. SEC, Press Release, 2019-202, "SEC Orders Blockchain Company to Pay $24 Million Penalty for Unregistered ICO," September 30, 2019, online at: sec.gov, accessed September 7, 2022.
179. U.S. SEC, Press Release, 2019-164, "SEC Charges Dallas Company and Its Founders With Defrauding Investors in Unregistered Offering and Operating Unregistered Digital Asset Exchange," August 29, 2019, online at: sec.gov, accessed September 7, 2022.

making significant returns to clients and paying large penalties totaling over US$ 4 million.[180]

[21] Pacheco Fraud Promising Crypto Riches Case

On May 23, 2019, the SEC filed a civil action against Daniel Pacheco and other defendants who allegedly perpetrated a multi-million-dollar pyramid scheme.[181] Defendant Pacheco allegedly conducted a fraudulent unregistered offering of securities. He allegedly raised more than US$ 26 million from investors by selling packages that provided lessons on e-commerce from which the investors received points that allegedly could be converted to a digital asset called PRO Currency in the future. His fraud was based on a fraudulent pyramid scheme called IPro. Pacheco used a significant portion of the money collected to pay personal expenses toward the purchase of a home and a Rolls Royce. The complaint found that the products sold by Pacheco constituted unregistered securities.

[22] Mayweather Celebrity Coin Touting Case

On November 29, 2018, the SEC settled charges against professional boxer Floyd Mayweather, Jr. and music producer Khaled Kahled known as DJ Khaled for failing to disclose payments they received for touting ICOs.

These were the first cases the SEC brought for touting involving ICOs in violation of federal securities laws, but others have now been brought as discussed in other sections of this book.

The SEC alleged that Mayweather failed to disclose promotional payments from three ICO issuers, and Khaled failed to disclose payment from one issuer.

Khaled touted an offering as "a game changer," and Mayweather included the following Twitter message to his followers about an offering:

> starts in a few hours. Get yours before they sell out. I got mine ... .

In settlement of the SEC charges, Mayweather agreed to pay a US$ 300,000 disgorgement plus interest, and Khaled agreed to pay US$ 50,000 in disgorgement, a US$ 100,000 penalty and interest. In addition, Mayweather agreed not to promote any securities, digital or otherwise for three years. Khaled agreed to a ten-year ban. Mayweather also agreed to continue to cooperate with the SEC investigation.[182]

---

180. U.S. SEC, Press Release, 2019-90, "SEC Adds Fraud Against Purported Cryptocurrency Company Longfin, CEO, and Consultant," June 5, 2019, online at: sec.gov, accessed September 7, 2022.
181. U.S. SEC, Press Release, 2019-74, "SEC Sues Perpetrator of Fraudulent Pyramid Scheme Promising Investors Cryptocurrency Riches," May 23, 2019, online at: sec.gov, accessed September 7, 2022.
182. U.S. SEC, Press Release, 2018-268, "Two Celebrities Charged With Unlawfully Touting Coin Offerings," November 29, 2018, online at: sec.gov, accessed September 8, 2022.

The SEC said that Khaled and Mayweather's promotions came to their attention when the SEC issued its *DAO Report* in July of 2017.[183]

[23] Steven Seagal ICO Case

On February 27, 2020, the SEC announced that it had settled charges against the actor Steven Seagal for failing to disclose payments he received for promoting an investment in an initial coin offering (ICO) conducted by Bitcoin2Gen (B2G). The SEC order said that Seagal failed to disclose that he was promised US$ 250,000 in cash and US$ 750,000 worth of B2G tokens in exchange for his promotions which he posted on social media accounts where he encouraged the public "not to miss out" on the offerings. Seagal agreed to pay US$ 157,000 in disgorgement plus interest and an additional US$ 157,000 penalty. Seagal also agreed not to promote any securities, digital or otherwise for a period of three years.[184]

[E] The DAO Report

The *DAO Report* was an SEC investigative report that concluded that offers and sales of digital assets by "virtual" organizations (Decentralized Autonomous Organizations (DAOs)) can be subject to federal securities laws. The SEC said:

> "Such offers and sales, conducted by organizations using distributed ledger or blockchain technology, have been referred to, among other things, as 'initial coin offerings' or 'token sales'. Whether a particular investment transaction involves the offer or sale of a security—regardless of the terminology or technology used—will depend on the facts and circumstances, including the economic realities of the transaction."
>
> "The SEC's report of its investigation found that tokens offered and sold by a 'virtual' organization known as 'the DAO' were securities and therefore subject to the federal securities laws. The report confirms that issuers of distributed ledger or blockchain technology-based securities must register offers and sales of such securities unless a valid exemption applies."
>
> "Those participating in unregistered offerings also may be liable for violations of securities laws. Additionally, securities exchanges providing for trading in these securities must register unless they are exempt."[185]

§3.07 SEC ENFORCEMENT POLICY

[A] Slock Case

As shown by the above cases, over the years, the SEC has brought a number of actions relating to digital assets. The SEC says that its decision to bring those actions focuses on

183. *Ibid.*
184. U.S. SEC, Press Release, 2020-42, "Actor Steven Seagal Charged With Unlawfully Touting Digital Asset Offering," February 27, 2020, online at: sec.gov, accessed September 6, 2022.
185. U.S. SEC, Press Release, 2017-131, "SEC Issues Investigative Report Concluding DAO Tokens, a Digital Asset, Were Securities," July 25, 2017, online at: sec.gov, accessed September 8, 2022.

two important questions. The first is weather a digital asset constitutes "security" under U.S. security laws. The second is that if it is a security what security laws apply?[186]

The SEC has considered the issue of the application of securities laws to digital assets and published a number of statements on this issue.[187] For example, see the 2017 Slock.it UG case. Slock was a German DAO.

However, in that case, the SEC took no action against the German company, Slock, that was the focus of that "report." The result of that action was that the SEC indicated that U.S. securities laws could apply to digital assets.[188] But there remained concern, throughout the financial services industry, that the SEC has not been clear enough about the regulatory status of digital assets such as cybercurrency, digital tokens and NFTs.[189] The chairman of the SEC, Gary Gensler, was harshly criticized by Paul Jossey, an adjunct fellow at the Competitive Enterprise Institute for not providing enough leadership on the issue of regulating digital assets:[190]

> "Crypto insiders lauded Gary Gensler's nomination to chair the Securities and Exchange Commission SEC last February. They thought the Massachusetts Institute of Technology professor who had taught blockchain classes would bring an enlightened approach to crypto compared with the scattershot, perplexed style of his predecessor Jay Clayton."
>
> "But a year in, the professor gets an 'F' in crypto guidance and leadership. He has encouraged the worst bureaucratic instincts of the federal government, deepened regulatory confusion and thwarted any hope of progress during his tenure—while claiming the mantle of little-guy defender and public interest protector."[191]

That criticism may have been a bit harsh. In January of 2022, Mr. Gensler gave an interview in which he said that an activity that seeks to raise money from the public where the public expects to profit from investment in that product is within the U.S. securities laws:

> Because Congress painted with a broad brush, they wanted to protect you the investing public so that you have proper information or what's called full and fair information and protect you against fraud and scammers and the like. It's just the

186. U.S. SEC, "Statement on Digital Asset and Securities Issuance and Trading," online, at sec.gov, November 16, 2028.
187. *See*, for example: SEC, Securities Exchange Act of 1934, Release No. 81207/July 25, 20017, "Report of the Investigation Pursuant to Section 21(a) of the Securities Exchange Act of 1934: The DAO." Online at sec.gov, accessed March 17, 2022.
188. Kevin Aguirre, "Cryptocurrency ICO Issuers on Notice After SEC Seminal DAO Report," Fordham Journal of Corporate and Financial Law, online, January 25, 2019.
189. *See*, for example, Letter of Vincent R. Molinari, CEO of Sustainable Holdings to the SEC, April 12, 2021, "Re: Rulemaking Regarding Non-Fungible Tokens," online at sec.gov, accessed March 17, 2022, requesting the SEC to engage in meaningful discussion on how to regulate FinTech companies and individuals that are creating NFTs that may be deemed digital asset securities and the platforms that facilitate the issuance and trading of NFTs. "We encourage the SEC to publish a concept release on the regulation of NFTs to provide suitable guidance to the industry followed by the adoption of a new regulation on the same."
190. Paul Jossey, "Professor Gensler Gets an F on Crypto," CoinDesk, online at coindesk.com, January 23, 2022.
191. *Ibid.*

> simple basic idea you get to decide whether you want to invest in this security or that security, and if they call themselves a token there's still probably possibility that it's a security. You get to decide but there needs to be some basic disclosures and protection against lies and frauds.[192]

That does not sound like a difficult or confusing explanation. As Gensler went on to say, the U.S. Congress made the definition of regulated activity broad because of the recognition that new ways of investing were coming into the market all the time, and regardless of its format, the public needed to be protected by being provided with the information it would need to decide whether an investment was sensible for them or not. Gensler pointed out that this view of securities activity had not changed since the 1930s, but the ways and means of investing being offered to the public had changed significantly in a number of ways, including the offering of "spacs" [special purpose acquisition companies], over-the-counter derivatives and digital assets such as cryptocurrency NFTs and tokens. However, these were all subject to the same tests of whether they are being offered by those seeking to raise money from the public, and the public in buying them was anticipating profit from their investment.

It is understandable that those promoting digital assets would prefer not to have the SEC find that these were within the securities law. This requires additional regulatory steps such as registration and possibly licenses to be held by the persons making these offers, by the persons trading these digital products and requires significant amounts of specific kinds of information to be made available to the public as part of the promotion of the sale of these new assets. However, Gensler does make a persuasive argument that that is necessary if the fundamental securities tests are met: (1) raising money from the public and (2) the public's expectation of profit from their investment.[193]

These basic tests were articulated by the U.S. Supreme Court in 1946 in the *SEC v. Howey* case when the Supreme Court held that an offer of land sales and a service contract was an "investment" within the U.S. securities law. This decision established the "Howey Test" which determines if an activity is within the Securities Act of 1933, which is that an offering can be an "investment" if it comprises:

> a contract, transaction or scheme whereby a person invests his money in a common enterprise and is led to expect profits solely from the efforts of the promoter or third party.

In *Howey*, it was interests in citrus groves that were being promoted. Although the activity being examined did not fall within the parameters of the usual concepts of what constitutes a security, such as publicly traded shares in companies or bonds, that does not prevent the securities laws from being applied.[194]

---

192. "SEC Chair Gary Gensler on Potential Crypto Regulation: It's Within the Securities Laws," CNBC, online at cnbc.com, January 10, 2022.
193. *Ibid.*
194. *Securities and Exchange Commission v. W.J. Howey Co., et al.*, 328 U.S. 293 (1946).

§3.08 INTERNAL REVENUE SERVICE

Because of its role in the regulation of taxation, the IRS has frequently come into contact with cryptocurrency transactions. As a result, it has encountered many types of illegal activity connected to cryptocurrency, including fraud, money laundering and other types of illegal activity, failure to report taxable income and false reporting of taxable income.

This has led the IRS to create specific regulations relating to transactions in cryptocurrency, to become a regulator of cryptocurrency-related transactions and a prosecutor of various types of illegal activity relating to transactions in cryptocurrency that violate IRS regulations.

In its capacity as both regulator and prosecutor of cryptocurrency-related transactions, the IRS has conducted many investigations and prosecutions relating to cryptocurrency. There have been far too many to give the details of each in this book, but summaries of such cases can be found on the IRS website under the heading "press releases" which give summaries of significant activities of the IRS for each year on a month-by-month basis.[195]

To provide an understanding of the types of actions undertaken by the IRS in connection with cryptocurrency investigations, a summary of some of the recent cases is provided below.

[A] IRS Crypto Policy

The IRS classifies virtual currency as "property." As a result, the IRS says:[196]

> Virtual currency transactions are taxable by law just like transactions in any other property. Taxpayers transacting in virtual currency may have to report those transactions on their tax returns.[197]

The IRS defines "virtual currency" as follows:

> Virtual currency is a digital representation of value that functions as a medium of exchange, a unit of account, and/or a store of value. In some environments, it operates like "real" currency (i.e., coin and paper money of the United States or any other country that is designated as legal tender, circulates, and is customarily used and accepted as a medium of exchange in the country of issuance), but does not have legal tender status in the U.S. Cryptocurrency is a type of virtual currency that utilizes cryptography to validate and secure transactions that are digitally recorded on a distributed ledger, such as a blockchain.
>
> Virtual currency that has an equivalent value in real currency, or that acts as a substitute for real currency, is referred to as "convertible" virtual currency. Bitcoin is one example of a convertible virtual currency. Bitcoin can be traded between

195. Online at: irs.gov
196. U.S. IRS, "Virtual Currencies," online at: irs.gov, accessed August 18, 2022.
197. *Ibid.*

users and purchased for or exchanged into, U.S. dollars, EUR, and other real or virtual currencies.[198]

To further clarify its position on the tax status of virtual currency transactions, the IRS has published an "IRS Virtual Currency Guidance" notice (VCG)[199] on its website. In "Section 4 Frequently Asked Questions,"[200] of the VCG, the IRS says:

> For federal tax purposes, virtual currency is treated as property. General tax principles applicable to property transactions apply to transactions using virtual currency.

A number of other issues and relevant questions are also dealt with in that VCG, but that material is too lengthy to be repeated here and can be found on the website cited.[201]

[B] Compliance

The IRS has taken the issue of taxpayer compliance very seriously with respect to virtual currency-related transactions. In July and August of 2019, the IRS sent more than 10,000 "educational letters" to taxpayers relating to virtual currency transactions that the IRS felt:

> "potentially failed to report income and pay the resulting tax from virtual currency transactions or did not report ... transactions properly."
>
> "The IRS will remain actively engaged in addressing noncompliance related to virtual currency transactions through a variety of efforts ranging from taxpayer education to audits to criminal investigations."[202]

[C] IRS Enforcement

The IRS has made it clear that:

> "Virtual currency is an ongoing focus area for IRS criminal investigation ... ."
>
> "Taxpayers who do not properly report the income tax consequences of virtual currency transactions are, when appropriate, liable for tax, penalties and interest. In some cases, taxpayers could be subject to criminal prosecution."[203]

198. *Ibid.*
199. IRS, Notice 2104-21, IRS Virtual Currency Guidance. Contact information is also provided in section 5. "Drafting Information" about how to contact relevant IRS officials if further information is needed, online at: irs.gov, accessed August 18, 2022.
200. *Ibid.*
201. *Ibid.*
202. IRS, "IRS has begun sending letters to virtual currency owners advising them to pay back taxes, file amended returns; part of the agency's larger efforts," IR-2019-132; July 26, 2019, online at: irs.gov, accessed August 18, 2022.
203. *Ibid.*

The seriousness of the policy of the IRS on these issues is demonstrated by the fact that the IRS has conducted a number of criminal investigations relating to virtual currency transactions. The following are a few examples.

[1] ***Vinnik*** **Case**

On August 5, 2022, the IRS announced that as a result of investigation by the IRS and other law enforcement agencies in the United States and abroad, a person accused of operating an illicit cryptocurrency exchange called BTC to Dash was extradited from Greece to the United states to face charges of operating an illegal exchange and money laundering more than US$ 4 billion of criminal revenue.[204]

The IRS press release said:

> According to the indictment, [Alexander] Vinnik [a Russian citizen] and his co-conspirators owned, operated and administered BTC-e a significant cybercrime and online money laundering entity that allowed its users to trade in bitcoin with high levels of anonymity and developed a customer base heavily reliant on criminal activity.[205]

[2] ***Jayton Gill*** **Case**

On July 12, 2022, the IRS announced that Jayton Gill of Durham, North Carolina, USA, had pled guilty in federal court to operating an unlicensed money-transmitting business and failing to file a tax return.[206]

The press release said:

> "Gill operated an unlicensed money transmitting business involving the exchange of millions of dollars of cash and other monetary instruments for cryptocurrencies such as Bitcoin and Monero ... ."
>
> "Gill further admitted that he failed to file US individual income tax returns for tax years 2015 through 2019, despite earning significant income from his unlicensed money transmitting business and from investing in cryptocurrency."

[3] ***Hvizdzak*** **Case**

On August 10, 2021, the IRS reported that a joint investigation by the IRS and the FBI led to an indictment of two Pennsylvania brothers on charges of conspiracy to commit wire fraud and money laundering in connection with a fraudulent cryptocurrency scheme.[207]

---

204. IRS, Press Release, "Alleged Russian Cryptocurrency Money Launderer Extradited to the United States," August 5, 2022, online at: irs.gov, accessed August 19, 2022.
205. *Ibid.*
206. IRS, Press Release, "Durham, N.C. Man Admits to Operating an Unlicensed Cryptocurrency Business and Related Tax Charges," July 12, 2022, online at: irs.gov, accessed August 19, 2022.
207. IRS, Press Release, "Northwestern Pennsylvania Brothers Indicted in Cryptocurrency Investment Scheme," August 10, 2021, online at: irs.gov, accessed August 19, 2022.

This scheme was conducted by setting up a partnership that claimed to be an investment in cryptocurrency. However, funds collected from investors were not invested as promised but were funneled enter the defendant's personal accounts.[208]

[4] *Cryptocurrency Forfeiture* Case

In early April of 2022, U.S. prosecutors in Florida recovered, through a "forfeiture" complaint, more than US$ 30 million in cryptocurrency relating to Dark Web transactions. A Florida resident was accused of using the Dark Web to conduct over 100,000 illegal transactions. Many of these were for the purposes of money laundering connected to drug trafficking.[209]

[5] *BitClub* Case

On March 24, 2022, a Nevada man pled guilty to laundering funds in connection with a more than US$ 700 million fraudulent cryptocurrencies scheme known as the BitClub Network, and preparation of a false tax return. The BitClub Network solicited money from investors in exchange for shares of what were claimed to be cryptocurrency mining pools.

[6] *Binance Investigation*

In May of 2021, the world's largest cryptocurrency exchange, Binance, was reported to be under investigation by do U.S. IRS, the U.S. DOJ, the U.S. CFTC, and Japanese, British, and Canadian regulators. These regulators are apparently concerned with tax and money laundering issues among other things.[210]

Binance claims it has no established headquarters. It is alleged that this is because Binance is busy moving from country to country to avoid financial regulations. These policies apparently raise questions in the minds of regulators in the US and elsewhere.

[D] State Tax Payments in Crypto

Another tax problem that may affect the U.S. economy and be a headache for both the IRS and the U.S. Treasury is the movement by individual states to allow payment of taxes with cryptocurrency.

208. *Ibid.*
209. IRS, Press Release, "United States Forfeits Million in Cryptocurrency Used to Launder Illicit Dark Web Proceeds," April 4, 2022, online at: irs.gov, accessed August 22, 2022.
210. "Binance under Investigation by Justice Department, IRS—*Bloomberg News*," Reuters, online, 13 May 2021, accessed August 19, 2022.

By the end of February 2022, some states in the United States began to consider allowing their citizens to pay their state taxes in cryptocurrency, in particular in Bitcoin.

Although state officials may have perceived there would be some political benefit in being seen to consider this, or even if they genuinely believed that it would offer some real economic benefit to their state, it is difficult to understand why a state administration would be willing to take this risk.

It is well understood that cryptocurrency, even the better-known types such as Bitcoin, are extremely volatile, going dramatically up and down in price over a relatively short period of time.

There can be really no question that these cryptocurrencies offer anywhere near the price stability that a major national currency, such as the U.S. dollar, can offer to holders of that currency. Consequently, the U.S. dollar is more likely to preserve its value than any cryptocurrency. It clearly entails less risk for U.S. citizens to hold U.S. dollars than to hold any form of cryptocurrency.

In terms of stability, it seems obvious that no cryptocurrency will approach the low volatility of the U.S. dollar before the U.S. government decides that it will support a cryptocurrency with full faith in the credit of the US to the same extent that it supports the U.S. dollar. Whether a currency is digital or in paper is not the key issue. The key issue is whose credit is supporting the value of that currency. If the U.S. government decides to support a digital currency, then the volatility of that currency will be less than those cryptocurrencies that are unsupported by a major nation.

It is reported that two U.S. states that are considering allowing payment of state taxes in cryptocurrency, specifically Bitcoin, are Colorado and Arizona. The governor of Colorado has said publicly:

> In Colorado we've been laying the groundwork to be a center of crypto and blockchain innovation for a number of years. we see it as a critical part of Colorado overall innovation ecosystem.[211]

This seems another example of a politician that is dazzled by the rise of cryptocurrency to the extent that they forget the fundamental principle of Gresham's law, "Bad money drives out good." This is a short way of describing the principle that a wise person prefers to hang on to a more respected currency by paying as many obligations as they can in a less respected currency.

It seems obvious that if state citizens are allowed to pay their taxes in Bitcoin, prior to the decision of the United States government to support Bitcoin to the same extent as it does the U.S. dollar, citizens will overwhelmingly prefer to pay their state taxes in Bitcoin and preserve their U.S. dollars to satisfy other obligations where Bitcoin cannot be used. This may lead to a state government holding a significant excess of Bitcoin. Given the fact that Bitcoin is extremely volatile, this could easily lead to dramatic declines in the value of the currency held by the state government which could severely affect the state government's ability to pay for the services it needs to

211. "Colorado will let citizens pay their tax in bitcoin," The Times, online, February 28, 2022.

provide to its citizens. It is possible, but such a dramatic decline could lead to state government bankruptcy—even in a state as affluent as Colorado or Arizona. This could have a knock-on effect on the U.S. economy generally.

[E] Federal Government Reaction

The only fly in the ointment for this flood of enthusiasm by local politicians is whether the U.S. government is going to remain happy that locally created currencies are competing with U.S. dollars in the purchasing of goods and services, the payment of salaries and perhaps even in the payment of taxes.

It seems a dramatic, publicity-gathering action for the mayors of major cities to insist that they receive their pay in cryptocurrency, some have done, and to suggest that other municipal workers do the same. However, it certainly has not been established that the IRS is going to be willing to accept tax payments from these people in cryptocurrency. That means that people being paid in cryptocurrency will have to convert their crypto to U.S. dollars at some point. During the time said people are receiving their cryptocurrency and paying their federal taxes, they will be speculating on whether cryptocurrency will continue to retain the same value against U.S. dollars that it had at the time they were paid. If the value should fall significantly prior to the tax payment dates, and cryptocurrencies have shown themselves to be very volatile in the past, the crypto employees could be in real trouble.

§3.09 COMMODITY FUTURES TRADING COMMISSION

The CFTC regulates transactions in commodities, certain related derivative instruments, and, since 2014, the CFTC has classified cryptocurrencies as "commodities" subject to CFTC regulation under the U.S. CEA.[212]

On their website, they say:[213]

> These technologies have the potential for significant or even transformational impact on the CFTC regulated markets and the agency itself. One of the most recent marketplace developments driving a lot of interest is the rise in prominence of digital assets.

[A] CFTC Cryptocurrency Actions

Judging from its actions between 2015 and 2021, the CFTC has also shown itself to be an enthusiastic regulator of the cryptocurrency markets. During that time, it brought sixty actions against virtual currency market participants. The actions involved such things as fraudulent schemes and illegal off-exchange commodity transactions. In

212. CFTC, "Testimony of CFTC Chairman Timothy Massad Before the U.S. Senate Committee on Agriculture, Nutrition and Forestry (December 10, 2014)," online at cftc.gov., accessed April 15, 2022.
213. CFTC, "Digital Assets," online at cftc.gov., accessed April 14, 2022.

2021, the fines and restitution imposed relating to these actions totaled more than US$ 765 million.[214]

As a result, the CFTC has assumed an "oversight role" over certain aspects of the digital assets business.[215]

One of the particular concerns that the CFTC has concentrated on is the potential of digital assets to support scams and other forms of criminal activity. Consequently, the CFTC has issued a number of "customer advisories" about how to recognize and avoid such scams. These advisories are available online from the CFTC website and include the following:

- Customer Advisory: Avoid Forex, Precious Metals, and Digital Asset Romance Scams.
- Beware of Fee Scams Targeting Workers Sidelined by COVID-19.
- Watch Out for Fraudulent Digital Asset and "Crypto" Trading Websites.
- There's Nothing to Like about Scammers on Social Media.
- Use Caution When Buying Digital Coins or Tokens.
- Beware Virtual Currency Pump-and-Dump Schemes.
- Beware of "IRS Approved" Virtual Currency IRAs.
- Risks of Virtual Currency Trading.

The CFTC has also made considerable efforts to provide educational materials to the markets and the public about the operation and regulation of digital asset products in their trading. On their website, they have published a number of "Primers/Backgrounders" detailing various aspects of the digital aspects business and on the oversight role of the CFTC. The list includes the following:[216]

- Digital Assets Primer.
- CFTC Backgrounder on Oversight of and Approach to Virtual Currency Futures Markets.
- A CFTC Primer on Virtual Currencies.
- CFTC Backgrounder on Self-Certified Contracts for Bitcoin Products.

The CFTC also provides additional material in the form of "brochures," including the following:[217]

- What is a Bitcoin ETF?
- Bitcoin Basics.
- An Introduction to Virtual Currency.

214. Abe Chernin, Nicole Moran and Mitchell Allen, Trends in CFTC Virtual Currency Enforcement Actions, 2015-2021. The Tables (Figures 1-5) included in the report contain details of the enforcement actions reported, Cornerstone Research, available for review and download online at: cornerstone.com.
215. *Ibid*. List as of April 14, 2022.
216. *Ibid*.
217. *Ibid*.

With respect to any of their publications, including those listed above, the CFTC offers to provide bulk orders to organizations that wish them.[218]

[B] CFTC Oversight of Digital Asset Business

In its *CFTC Backgrounder on Oversight of and Approach to Virtual Currency Futures Markets,* the CFTC describes[219] the nature of U.S. Federal and State oversight of and jurisdiction over cryptocurrency. This includes the CFTC's role in the regulation of crypto and other details of the regulatory landscape that applies to crypto assets.

[C] Regulated "Commodity"

The CFTC's definition of what constitutes a "commodity" within its jurisdiction is broad. It includes, "among other things, all services, rights, and interests in which contracts for future delivery are presently or in the future dealt in."[220]

This broad definition has been recognized by court decisions as appropriate in light of the continuing expansion of products and assets offered for trading.[221] The CFTC says:

> Bitcoin and other virtual currencies are encompassed in the definition and properly defined as commodities and are therefore subject as a commodity to applicable provisions of the [Commodity Exchange] Act and [CFTC] Regulations.[222]

The CFTC identifies its role with respect to cryptocurrencies as not being specific to particular cryptocurrencies but as relating to futures and swap contracts in any commodity. As pointed out, the CFTC does consider "virtual currencies like Bitcoin" to be commodities within the jurisdiction of the CFTC. Being a little more specific, the CFTC does say:

> The CEA [Commodity Exchange Act] defines the term commodity very broadly so that in addition to traditional agricultural commodities, metals, and energy, the CFTC has oversight of derivative contracts related to treasury securities, interest rate indices, stock market indices, currencies, electricity, and heating degree days, to name just a few underlying products. Derivative contracts based on virtual currency represent one area within our responsibility.[223]

---

218. *Ibid.*
219. CFTC, "CFTC Backgrounder on Oversight of and Approach to Virtual Currency Futures Markets," online at cftc.gov, January 4, 2018, as updated, accessed April 14, 2022.
220. 7 U.S.C. section 1a (9). *See,* CFTC, Order Instituting Proceedings Pursuant to sections 6(c) and 6(d) of the CEA, as "Amended, Making Findings and Imposing Remedial Actions," June 2, 2016, CFTC Docket No. 16-19, online at cftc.gov, accessed April 15, 2022.
221. For example, *see* the *Seventh Circuit Court of Appeals opinion in Board of Trade of the City of Chicago v. Securities and Exchange Commission,* 677 F.2d 1137, 1142 (1982).
222. CFTC, *In re BXFNA Inc.* d/b/a Bitfinex, Dkt. No. 16-19 (CFTC June 2, 2016).
223. CFTC, "Testimony of Chairman Timothy Massad Before the U.S. Senate Committee on Agriculture, Nutrition & Forestry," online at cftc.gov, December 10, 2014.

In late May of 2022, CFTC Commissioner Caroline D. Pham discussed crypto regulation and the importance of customer protection in a media interview that provided additional insights into the CFTC's attitude toward the relatively new crypto markets.[224] She said:

> The key question that regulators and lawmakers need to address is whether stablecoins, including the subset of algorithmic stablecoins, are in fact derivatives. The SEC regulates securities, but for everything that is not a security, the CFTC probably has some regulatory touchpoint over it. We have the regulation over derivatives based on commodities, but we also have certain areas where we directly regulate spot [physical commodity] markets. The last time we had something blow up like this the financial crisis [of 2008]—risky, opaque, complex financial products—Congress came up with a solution for that and that was the Dodd Frank [the Wall Street Reform and Consumer Protection Act of 2010] in response to the [2008 financial collapse]. I think what I'm worried about is that without appropriate customer protections in place, and the right disclosures, that people are buying some of these crypto tokens thinking that they're guaranteed to strike it rich.

[D] CFTC Crypto Enforcement

[1] Bitfinex

In 2016, the CFTC brought enforcement proceedings against Bifinex and affiliated entities on the grounds that beginning in 2013 Bitfinex had been operating an exchange platform on which users had been exchanging and trading cryptocurrencies such as Bitcoin.[225] The CFTC found that during the relevant period, Bitfinex did not actually deliver cryptocurrencies to the persons who purchased them but held the cryptocurrencies in "deposit wallets" that Bitfinex owned and controlled. Bitfinex was not registered with the CFTC.[226] The CFTC concluded that:

> Bitfinex engaged in illegal, off-exchange commodity transactions and failed to register as a futures commission merchant, in violation of Sections 4 (a) and 4d of the [Commodity Exchange] Act.[227]

The "remedial sanctions" imposed by the CFTC followed the CFTC's acceptance of an offer of settlement by Bitfinex were that:[228]

- Bitfinex would consent to the CFTC's findings that Bitfinex violated section 4(a) and 4d of the CEA.

224. U.S. CFTC, Press Release Number 8538-22, "ICYMI: CFTC Pham Discusses Crypto Regulation and Customer Protections with CNBC and Yahoo! Finance," online at: cftc.gov, May 31, 2022, accessed August 9, 2022.
225. *Ibid.*
226. CFTC, "CFTC Orders Bitcoin Exchange Bitfinex to Pay $75,000 for Offering Illegal Off-Exchange Financed Retail Commodity Transactions and Failing to Register as a Futures Commission Merchant," Release Number 7380-16, online at cftc.gov, June 2, 2016.
227. 7 U.S.C. Sections 6(a) and 6d.
228. *Supra*, CFTC Order June 2, 2016.

- Bitfinex would cease and desist from such violations.
- Bitfinex would pay a civil monetary penalty of US$ 75,000 plus interest.

[2] Bitfinex 2

However, despite the penalties imposed and the consent of Bitfinex to various conditions imposed by the CFTC, a few years later the CFTC brought a further enforcement action against Bitfinex on the grounds that Bitfinex had not fully complied with the CFTC's 2016 Order. The CFTC's unhappiness with Bitfinex's activities was expressed by requiring Bitfinex to pay a US$ 1.5 million penalty and comply with new conditions.[229] In October of 2021, the CFTC issued an Order against Bitfinex finding that:

> From at least March 1, 2016 through at least December 31, 2018, Bitfinex offered, entered into, executed and confirmed the execution of illegal, off-exchange financed retail commodity transactions with US persons that were not eligible contract participants (ECPs) under the CEA. ... Bitfinex violated the terms of the 2016 order, which had directed Bitfinex to cease and desist from offering, entering into, executing, or confirming the execution of illegal, off exchange financed retail commodity transactions and from accepting orders and receiving funds in connection with retail commodity transactions.

In addition to the US$ 1.5 million fine, Bitfinex was required to:

> comply with certain undertakings by December 31, 2021, including implementing, as necessary, and maintaining systems and procedures reasonably designed to prevent non-ECP U.S. persons from engaging in retail commodity transactions.

Under section 1(a)18 of the CEA,[230] an ECP is an "eligible contract participant" which the CFTC describes in a very long, detailed and complex definition based on financial assets, regulatory status and experience or "other qualifications." It is not possible for this book to repeat the entire definition and explain all of its terms. However, anyone seeking to determine whether a particular person or entity can be considered an ECP will need to make a careful study of the scope of that definition and consult a qualified legal advisor on how the term should be interpreted in a particular situation.

The CFTC Glossary summarizes ECP more succinctly as:

> An entity, such as a financial institution, insurance company, or commodity pool, that is classified by the Commodity Exchange Act as an Eligible Contract Participant based upon its regulated status or amount of assets. This classification permits these persons to engage in transactions (such as trading on a derivatives

229. CFTC, "Bitfinex to Pay $1.5 Million for Illegal Transactions While Operating Bitfinex Cryptocurrency Trading Platform and Violation of Prior CFTC Order," Release Number 8450-21, online at cftc.gov, October 15, 2021.
230. 7 USC [US Code] section 1a(18).

transaction execution facility) not generally available to non-eligible contract participants, i.e, retail customers.

But this Glossary summary does not fully explain all the details of the statutory definition.

[3] Michael Ackerman

In February of 2020, the CFTC filed a civil enforcement action in the U.S. District Court for the Southern District of New York against Michael Ackerman and his companies Q3 holdings LLC and Q3I, LP, charging that they fraudulently solicited over US$ 33 million that they said they would trade and that the defendants misappropriated a substantial portion of that money.[231]

From 2017 through 2019, the defendants are alleged to have solicited funds from customers saying that they would trade digital assets. The CFTC alleges that the defendants claim that the defendants' trading would result in:

> (i) earning customers .5% in daily trading profits and roughly 15% per month, (ii) using algorithms that generated winning traits 75% of the time, and (iii) utilizing security measures that made it impossible for any principal to transfer or withdraw customer funds.[232]

The CFTC further alleged that:

> In reality, the defendants sent only a small portion of the customer's funds to digital asset trading accounts, and did not earn the trading profits they claimed, and misappropriated funds period to conceal the fraud. The defendants provided customers with false accounting statements, newsletters containing false trading returns, and fictitious screenshots reflecting the amount of money under Q3's management.[233]

In separate criminal actions, the U.S. Attorney's Office for the Southern District of New York arrested Ackerman on charges of wire fraud and the SEC filed a multicount complaint against Ackerman and Q3 for securities fraud and misappropriation.[234]

On September 8, 2021, Ackerman pled guilty to the criminal charge of wire fraud. He was facing a maximum sentence of twenty years in jail, but he avoided prison because in February of 2022, the Federal District Judge accepted that Akerman was suffering from a terminal illness and sentenced him to five years of probation, including a year of home confinement.[235]

---

231. CFTC, "CFTC Charges Company and Its Principal in $33 Million Fraudulent Digital Asset Scheme," Release Number 8115-20, online at cftc.gov, February 11, 2020.
232. *Ibid.*
233. *Ibid.*
234. *Ibid.*
235. Rachel Scharf, "Terminally Ill Ex-NYSE Broker Avoids Prison For Crypto Scam," Law360, online, February 15, 2022.

[4] Tether

On October 15, 2021, the CFTC hit Tether with a US$ 41 million fine over Tether's claims that Tether Stablecoin was "fully backed by U.S. dollars."[236] The CFTC said that its actions against Tether-affiliated companies (doing business as "Tether") were:

> for making untrue or misleading statements or omissions of material fact in connection with the US dollar Tether token (USDT) stablecoin. The order requires Tether to pay a civil monetary penalty of $41 million and to cease and desist from any further violations of the Commodity Exchange Act (CEA) and CFTC regulations as charged.

The CFTC accused Tether of claiming that all its USDT stablecoins were 100% backed by fiat currencies such as U.S. dollars or euros deposited in Tether bank accounts. The CFTC found that this claim was not true and that, in fact, Tether only had enough fiat currency in its bank accounts to back Tether tokens less than 30% of the time during a twenty-six-month time, from 2016 through 2018.[237]

The CFTC also found:

> that, instead of holding all USDT token reserves in U.S. dollars as represented, Tether relied upon unregulated entities and certain third-parties to hold funds comprising the reserves; commingled reserve funds with Bitfinex's operational and customer funds, and held reserves in non-fiat financial products. The order further finds that Tether and Bitfinex's combined assets included funds held by third-parties, including at least 29 arrangements that were not documented through any agreement or contract, and that Tether transferred Tether reserve funds to Bitfinex, including when Bitfinex needed help responding to a "liquidity crisis.[238]

The CFTC also found that Tether had not completed an audit of Tether's reserves.[239]

[5] Digital Asset Pump & Dump Case[240]

In July of 2022, the CFTC announced that a U.S. District Court had entered a consent order imposing sanctions on Jimmy Gale Watson of Dallas, TX.

The CFTC had previously filed an action against Watson and John McAfee alleging that they engaged in a manipulative and deceptive digital asset scheme. The defendant had engaged in what could be called "classic" pump-and-dump strategy. He

236. CFTC, "Tether to Pay $41 million Over Claims that Tether Stablecoin Was Fully Backed by U.S. Dollars," Release Number 8450-21, online at cftc.gov, October 15, 2021.
237. *Ibid.*
238. *Ibid.*
239. *Ibid.*
240. U.S. CFTC, Press Release Number 8558-22, "Federal Court Orders Texas Man to Pay Over $290,000 for Manipulative and Deceptive Digital Asset Pump-and Dump Scheme," online at: cftc.gov, July 18, 2022, accessed August 8, 2022. *See also*, U.S. CFTC, Press Release Number 8366-21, "CFTC Charges Two Individuals with Multi-Million Dollar Digital Asset Pump-and Dump Scheme," online at: cftc.gov, March 5, 2021, accessed August 9, 2022.

acquired a large position of digital assets and then arranged for misleading, positive endorsements to be published on social media. This increased the price of those assets, and the defendant then sold them at an inflated profit. The scheme involved a variety of digital products, including Verge (XVG), Dogecoin (DOGE) and Reddcoin (RDD).

The consent order issued by the U.S. District Court for the Southern District of New York included a permanent injunction, financial sanctions (payment of over US$ 290,000) and a requirement of disgorgement of ill-gotten gains against defendant Watson.

[6] South African Bitcoin Fraud Case[241]

At the end of June 2022, the CFTC brought charges against a South African pool operator and CEO relating to an alleged US$ 1.7 billion fraud involving Bitcoin. This is the largest fraud case involving Bitcoin brought by the CFTC at that time. The South African company involved is Mirror Trading International Proprietary Limited (MTI), and the CEO is Cornelius Johannes Steynberg. The scheme involved MTI in setting up an international foreign currency commodity pool that accepted only Bitcoin to participate in the pool. Participation in the pool was promoted on social media among other ways. The value of the money collected by MTI was over US$ 1.7 billion. It is alleged that the defendants misappropriated for themselves all of the Bitcoin received from participants in the pool.

The CFTC is seeking full restitution to investors, disgorgement of ill-gotten gains, permanent registration and trading bans, injunctions against future rule violations, and civil monetary penalties.

[7] The Gemini Trust Company Case[242]

At the beginning of June 2022, the CFTC filed a complaint in the U.S. District Court for the Southern District of New York against Gemini Trust Company LLC (Gemini), alleging false and misleading statements were made by the defendant in connection with Bitcoin futures products. The "false or misleading" statements allegedly related to, among other things, information relevant to whether Gemini-offered Bitcoin Futures Contracts were susceptible to manipulation.

[8] The EminiFX, Inc. Case[243]

In May of 2022, the CFTC filed an enforcement action in federal court in New York against Eddy Alexandre and his company EminiFX, Inc. They were charged with

241. *Ibid.*, 8549-22, "CFTC Charges South African Pool Operator and CEO with $1.7 Billion Fraud Involving Bitcoin," online at: cftc.gov, June 30, 2022, accessed August 9, 2022.
242. *Ibid.*, 8540-22, "CFTC Charges Gemini Trust Company for Making Material False or Misleading Statements and Omissions to the Commission," online at: cftc.gov, June 2, 2022, accessed August 9, 2022.
243. *Ibid.*, 8527-22, "CFTC Charges Long Island Resident and His Firm in Ongoing $59 Million Fraud Scheme," online at: cftc.gov, May 13, 2022, accessed August 10, 2022.

fraudulent solicitation and misappropriation for soliciting clients to trade foreign currencies, commodity futures contracts and cryptocurrencies.

It is alleged that the defendants promised customers returns of 5% per week. Defendants collected around US$ 59 million from customers for trading purposes. However, they only used about US$ 9 million to do trading that was allegedly dramatically unprofitable. It is alleged that the defendants lost about 70% of the amount used for trading. Much of the remaining money was appropriated by the defendants to run a type of "Ponzi scheme" and to pay for personal luxuries that defendant Alexandre acquired for himself.

In parallel with the CFTC civil case, the U.S. Attorney's Office for the Southern District of New York also filed a parallel criminal action against the defendants.

[9] *BitMEX* Case[244]

In early May of 2022, the CFTC brought a case against the three cofounders of the BitMEX cryptocurrency derivatives trading platform. As a result, the U.S. District Court for the Southern District of New York announced enforcement orders requiring the BitMEX cofounders to pay a total of US$ 30 million in civil penalties. They were also enjoined from future violations of law and CFTC regulations.

The CFTC's Acting Director of Enforcement Gretchen Lowe said:

> Individuals who control cryptocurrency derivatives trading platforms conducting business in the U.S. must ensure that their platform complies with the applicable federal commodities laws, including CFTC registration and regulatory requirements such as Know-Your-Customer and Anti-Money Laundering Regulations.[245]

In addition to allegations that the defendants were operating an illegal trading platform, it was also alleged that:

> BitMEX operated as a futures commission merchant (FCM) without CFTC registration, failed to implement a Customer Information Program (CIP) and Know-Your-Customer procedures and failed to implement an adequate Anti-Money-Laundering (AML) program.[246]

[10] *Kitkit & Mess Investments, LLC* Case[247]

In March of 2022, the CFTC obtained a consent order in the U.S. Federal Court for the Western District of Texas against Abner Alejandro Tinoco and his company Kitkit & Mess Investments, LLC, finding that they had misappropriated more than US$ 7.2

244. *Ibid.*, 8522-22, "Federal Court Orders BitMEX's Three Co-Founders to Pay a Total of $30 Million for Illegally Operating a Cryptocurrency Derivatives Trading Platform and Anti-Money Laundering Violations," online at: cftc.gov, May 5, 2022, accessed August 10, 2022.
245. *Ibid.*
246. *Ibid.*
247. U.S. CFTC, Press Release Number 8507-22, "Court Finds El Paso Man and His Firm Liable for Defrauding Forex and Cryptocurrency Clients of More Than $7.2 Million," online at: cftc.gov, March 29, 2022, accessed August 11, 2022.

million from customers who expected to trade forex and cryptocurrency in "managed accounts." The order imposed injunctions on the defendants and banned them from trading and future registration with the CFTC. The defendants were also found liable for fraud.

The defendants had obtained money from more than 300 clients and promised that the money would be used to trade foreign exchange and cryptocurrency on behalf of the clients. It is alleged the defendants did not trade as promised but used the money for their personal expenses and luxury purchases. Some of the money was used to pay false profits to clients in a kind of "Ponzi" scheme. The CFTC also indicated that it would pursue restitution, disgorgement and civil money penalties against the defendants.

[11] Golden, Patel, Egerton and Aggesen Case[248]

In early March of 2022, the CFTC filed a civil enforcement action in the U.S. court for the Eastern District of New York charging Dwayne Golden, Jatin Patel, Marquis Edgerton and Gregory Aggesen with operating Ponzi schemes involving Bitcoin where they fraudulently solicited more than US$ 40 million from clients and misappropriated much of it for themselves. Their "Ponzi scheme" paid millions of dollars in fake profits to clients, and appropriated millions of dollars for their personal use. Defendants Golden, Edgerton and Aggesen were also charged in a parallel criminal indictment with wire fraud, and money laundering.

[12] Crypto Dating Fraud[249]

In connection with digital asset trading and other financial trading, it is reported that a particularly loathsome type of scam has arisen in connection with interest in finding a romantic partner. In early February 2022, U.S. regulatory agencies joined in publishing an alert that romance scams on dating and social media websites have extracted millions of dollars from victims.

The CFTC and other federal agencies have launched an awareness effort entitled *Dating or Defrauding?*

The Federal Agencies warn:

> "While romance scams are not new, they can defraud people of any age including individuals who are more comfortable with online dating and buying digital assets.

248. U.S. CFTC, Press Release Number 8498-22, "CFTC Charges Four Operators for $44 Million Bitcoin Ponzi and Misappropriation Schemes," online at: cftc.gov, March 8, 2022, accessed August 11, 2022.
249. U.S. CFTC, Press Release Number 8492-22, "CFTC Customer Advisory Warns Online Daters and Social Media Users about Trading Scams," online at: cftc.gov, February 7, 2022, accessed August 11, 2022.

> Fraudsters may use comprehensive social media profiles and well-practiced scripts to convince their victims that they want to start a romantic relationship. Within a few weeks or even less, the fraudsters may coax their victims into believing they are in a caring relationship."
>
> "Eventually conversations turn to money, salaries, and the markets. The fraudsters then pose as successful traders or have a friend or relative that is supposedly a successful trader, and offered to help the victims trade forex, precious metals, or digital assets. However, the trading platforms the fraudsters recommend are fraudulent."

[13] Fingerhut **Case**[250]

In November of 2021, the CFTC obtained an order from the U.S. District Court for the Southern District of Florida granting injunctions against Florida resident, Daniel Fingerhut and other defendants, residents of Israel, requiring them to pay a total of US$ 7 million in penalties for violations of the CEA and CFTC regulations.

The CFTC complained that defendants had fraudulently solicited tens of millions of customers and prospective customers into opening off-exchange options and digital asset trading accounts. These were operated by unregistered brokers.

It is alleged that these solicitations were made using hypothetical and fictitious trading results and fabricated customer testimonials.

Fingerhut was also charged with making false statements to the CFTC in connection with the investigations.

[14] The Primefx **Case**[251]

In September of 2021, the CFTC filed an enforcement action in the U.S. District Court of Massachusetts against Alexander Uti Bassey of Lagos, Nigeria and several other defendants who lived in U.S. states, alleging that defendants, operating as Primefx.org, fraudulently solicited and misappropriated over US$ 1.2 million from US and international customers for a purported foreign currency and Bitcoin trading scheme. The CFTC sought financial penalties against the defendants.

The CFTC alleged that as part of the solicitation, defendants directed the customers to send their funds to personal bank accounts of the defendants, who misappropriated virtually all the customer funds for the defendants' personal use.

---

250. *Ibid.*, Press Release Number 8460-21, "Federal Court Orders Florida Man and Foreign Defendants to Pay $7 Million for Roll in Fraudulent Binary Options and Digital Assets Scheme," online at: cftc.gov, November 17, 2021, accessed August 12, 2022.

251. *Ibid.*, Press Release Number 8441-21, "CFTC Charges Nigerian and American Citizens Operating as PrimeFX with Forex and Bitcoin Fraud and Misappropriation," online at: cftc.gov, September 30, 2021, accessed August 12, 2022.

[15] Kraken Case[252]

At the end of September 2021, the CFTC charged Payward Ventures, Inc. d/b/a Kraken (Kraken) for illegally offering margined retail commodity transactions in digital assets such as Bitcoin and failing to register as a Futures Commission Agent FCM.

Kraken was ordered to pay US$ 1.25 million in financial penalties and cease and desist from further violations.

§3.10 US DEPARTMENT OF JUSTICE (DOJ) CRYPTOCURRENCY TASK FORCE

In October of 2021, The U.S. DOJ announced the creation of a National Cybercurrency Enforcement Team (NCET). It was established to conduct investigations and prosecutions of over-the-counter cybercurrency crimes including "crimes committed by virtual currency exchanges, "mixing and tumbling services," and money laundering infrastructure actors."[253]

According to Assistant Attorney General Kenneth Polite, Jr., the DOJ's concern was:

> With the rapid innovation of digital assets and distributed ledger technologies, we have seen a rise in their illicit use by criminals who exploit them to fuel cyberattacks and ransomware and extortion schemes; traffic in narcotics, hacking tools and illicit contraband online; commit thefts and scams; and launder the proceeds of their crimes.[254]

On February 17, 2022, the DOJ announced the appointment of Eun Young Choi to serve as the first Director of the National Cybercurrency Enforcement Team (NCET). Miss Choi had served with the DOJ in several capacities, including as Cybercrime Coordinator when she was an Assistant U.S. Attorney for the Southern District of New York.[255]

[A] DOJ Enforcement

[1] BitConnect Cybercurrency Indictment

In February 2022, the founder of BitConnect, Satish Kumbhani, was indicted by a grand jury in San Diego for establishing BitConnect as a "fraudulent cyber currency investment platform." It is alleged that he misled investors about a BitConnect "lending

---

252. *Ibid.*, Press Release Number 8433-21, "CFTC Imposes a $1.25 Million Penalty Against Kraken for Offering Illegal Off-Exchange Digital Asset Trading and Failing to Register as Required," online at: cftc.gov, September 28, 2021, accessed August 12, 2022.
253. U.S. DOJ, "Deputy Attorney General Lisa O. Monaco Announces National Cryptocurrency Enforcement Team," online at justice.gov, October 6, 2021.
254. *Ibid.*
255. U.S. DOJ, "Justice Department Announces First Director of National Cryptocurrency Enforcement Team," online at justice.gov, February 17, 2022.

program." BitConnect's program was purported to generate "substantial profits and guaranteed returns" by trading on cybercurrency exchanges. BitConnect was alleged to have claimed that its proprietary software was able to produce such profits and returns. However, it is alleged that this so-called lending program was actually a Ponzi scheme. It is alleged that the scheme took approximately US$ 2.4 billion from investors.[256]

§3.11 FEDERAL RESERVE

The Federal Reserve (Fed) is the "central bank" of the United States. In this capacity, it is tasked with performing several significant monetary functions.[257] These include the following:

- It is responsible for U.S. monetary policy.
- It is supposed to promote financial stability and counter systemic risks.
- It monitors the impact of financial institutions on the U.S. financial system.
- It establishes safe and efficient payment and settlement systems.
- It promotes consumer protection.
- It issues U.S. currency and strives to protect and maintain confidence in that currency.

Given the importance of the Fed's responsibility for U.S. currency, there are strict laws forbidding others from issuing competing currency or copying Fed-issued U.S. currency, or the fiat currency of other nations.

The US needs to be particularly cautious because the U.S. dollar is so widely used in world trade as a payment or pricing currency that a significant shift of payments away from U.S. currency or carefully regulated U.S. payment systems could destabilize the world economy. There are also other countries that authorize U.S. dollars as a legal medium of exchange in their country. These include the British Virgin islands, British Turks and Caicos, El Salvador, Panama, the Marshall Islands, Micronesia, Palau, East Timor and Zimbabwe. Also, more than sixty-five countries peg their currency to the U.S. dollar.[258]

U.S. Federal law says:

> "[w]however, with the intent to defraud, falsely makes, forges, counterfeits, or alters any obligation or other security of the United States, shall be fined ... or imprisoned not more than 20 years, or both." (18 U.S.C.A. Section 471).

In addition, 18 U.S.C.A. section 486 makes it a criminal offense to make or pass any metal coins "intended for use as current money, whether in resemblance of coins of the United States or of foreign countries or of original design."

---

256. U.S. DOJ, "BitConnect Founder Indicted in Global $2.4 Billion Cryptocurrency Scheme," online at justice.gov, February 25, 2022.
257. Board of Governors of the Federal Reserve System, "About the Fed"; "Currency," online at federal reserve.gov, accessed November 15, 2022.
258. Official Use of the U.S. Dollar, Investopedia, online, accessed February 23, 2022.

The law also forbids possessing any of the tools required to create counterfeit currency, and this extends to computers and digital equipment.[259]

Nevertheless, the temptation to grow rich by issuing instruments competing with genuine official currency has been irresistible to some.

Perhaps the best-known example of giving in to that temptation is attempts by certain people to issue "private" currencies. The U.S. government takes a very dim view of the issuance of private currencies. In 2011, it was reported that a gentleman named Bernhard von NotHaus was prosecuted by the U.S. Justice Department and convicted or issuing currency in coin form called "Liberty Dollars."[260]

Mr. von NotHaus reportedly founded the Royal Hawaiian Mint to produce gold and silver medallions. He was convicted of counterfeiting and additionally was accused of terrorism. The Liberty Dollar was made of nearly pure silver and began manufacture sometime around 1998. By 2006, Mr. NotHaus had managed to get millions of his coins in circulation in eighty U.S. cities.

However, in that year, the U.S. Mint sent NotHaus a letter telling him that using his Liberty Dollars "as circulating money" was criminal offense. Mr. NotHaus ignored the letter. In 2007, the U.S. government agents seized Liberty Dollars which featured the image of a Texas Congressman named Ron Paul. NotHaus was prosecuted and convicted of counterfeiting in 2011.[261] NotHaus was sentenced to six months of house arrest.[262]

[A] US Adoption of a National Cryptocurrency?

With the appearance of cryptocurrency, and the rapid expansion and the support it has gained in a number of sectors, the U.S. government has had a number of serious discussions about how the US may be able to use cryptocurrency to its benefit.

In late 2021 and early 2022, the U.S. Federal Reserve (Fed) along with other prominent institutions engaged in discussions about whether it would make sense for the US to adopt a digital currency or as it is referred to by the Fed as CBDC.[263]

In its discussion of this issue, the Fed pointed out that people have used digital currency for years in the form of online transactions, online bank accounts and online payment apps. However, the important difference between existing kinds of digital currency is that CBDC would be an obligation of the central bank rather than just an obligation of a private commercial enterprise. Consequently, the value of that digital currency would be supported by the full faith and credit of a national central bank.

In the United States, there would be two kinds of national legal tender: traditional currency issued by the national government and the digital currency balances held on

259. 18 U.S.C, Chapter 25, sections 471-504.
260. Alan Feuer, "Prison May Be the Next Stop on a Gold Currency Journey," The New York Times, online, October 24, 2012.
261. *Ibid.*
262. George Leef, "Protecting Us From A 'Terrorist' Who Made Pure Silver Coins: The Bernard von NotHaus Case," Forbes, online, December 8, 2014.
263. Board of Governors of the Federal Reserve System, "What is a Central Bank Digital Currency?," online, federalreserve.gov.

the system of the central bank. In both cases, the value of this currency would be supported by the full faith and credit of the national central bank. This would make it more generally acceptable and probably less volatile than the many private digital currencies being issued today by a variety of organizations with considerably different levels of credibility.

In January of 2022, the Federal Reserve issued a paper to discuss the issues relating to the development of digital currency and whether adoption of a digital currency could make any significant improvements to the money and payment systems of the United States. The Fed considers this an important part of its remit because it is tasked with conducting the monetary policy of the US to encourage maximum employment while maintaining stable prices, in a safe and efficient manner.[264]

According to the Fed, the key element that supports a nation's economy is confidence in the nation's money and its payment services. As the "central bank" of the United States, it is the duty of the Fed to support this confidence.[265] The purpose of the Fed's discussion paper is to examine whether the issuance of a U.S. CBDC could maintain and possibly enhance that confidence.

For the purpose of its discussion, the Fed defines a CBDC as "a digital liability of a central bank that is widely available to the general public. In this respect, it is analogous to a digital form of paper money."

The Fed points out that payment transfer systems have evolved from the use of the telegraph to a system that the Fed commenced building in 2019 called the "FedNow Service," "which will provide real time around the clock interbank payments every day of the year."[266]

The Fed's basic conclusions about a U.S. CBDC are that it should, among other things, do the following:

- provide benefits to ordinary citizens, businesses and the economy that outweigh its costs and risks;
- provide those benefits better than any alternatives;
- complement, rather than replace, existing money and financial services;
- protect consumer privacy;
- defend against criminal activity; and
- provide extensive support to key stakeholders.[267]

The Fed indicates that it has not reached a final conclusion on the usefulness of CBDC yet but will continue to examine the issue and solicit the views of those it affects while continuing to play an active role in developing international standards for the creation and regulation of Central Bank Digital Currencies.

264. Board of Governors of the Federal Reserve System, "Money and Payments: The U.S. Dollar in the Age of Digital Transformation," online, federalreserve.gov, p. ii.
265. *Supra* at p. 1.
266. *Ibid.*
267. *Supra*. pp. 1-2.

The Fed believes that if a CBDC were created in the US, it might potentially offer advantages of being "privacy protected, intermediated, widely transferable, and identity-verified."

But the Fed does emphasize that it has not yet adopted a specific policy on CBDC and takes no position on the ultimate decision of whether issuing a CBDC would be good for the US.

In its discussion paper, "Money and Payments: the US Dollar in the Age of Digital Transformation," the governors of the Federal Reserve consider the pros and cons of a potential U.S. CBDC, and make the following observations.

In its introduction, the paper points out that because of recent technological innovation, several "digital assets with money like characteristics" have appeared. They are described as having a combination of cryptographic and distributed ledger (or blockchain) technologies. These enable the creation of a decentralized peer-to-peer payment system.

The Fed defines money as being the following types:[268]

- Central bank money: This is a liability of a national central bank. In the US, the Fed has that role. Central bank money in the US constitutes physical currency issued by the Federal Reserve and the digital balances held by commercial banks at the Fed.
- Commercial bank money: This is money held in accounts at commercial banks.
- Nonbank money: This is digital money balances with nonbank financial providers. Transfers of this money are often made technologically, using a range of tools, including apps.

The different kinds of money have different relationships to credit and risk. The Fed says that central bank money is the safest form of money because it does not have either credit or liquidity risk. That is the view of the Fed, but that may not entirely be true. It is true that nationally supported central bank currency may be more liquid and less risky than the kinds of money issued or held on the accounts of noncentral bank entities. But there are many historical examples of central bank currencies declining dramatically in value (in relation to the central bank currencies of other nations) because of loss of confidence that results in runaway inflation. However, it is true that the U.S. dollar is relatively well respected around the world.

Other kinds of money derive much of their value from the ease with which they can be converted to or substituted for central bank currencies. As shown above from the federal and state laws regulating Money Services Businesses and Money Transmission, use of central bank fiat currency in these systems diminishes potential risk and liquidity problems. The entities that operate such services are usually subject to strict government supervision and regulations.

268. *Supra* p. 5.

However, some new cryptocurrency systems are operated by entities that are not government supervised or as strictly regulated.[269] Consequently, the growth of these payment systems could result in a significant shift of money from systems that offer a number of government-mandated protections. This would mean the lesser regulated payment systems would be subject to greater potential risks to value, liquidity and reliability. This could undermine confidence in and the stability of the overall national financial system.

§3.12 STATE BANKING REGULATIONS AND CRYPTO

Each U.S. state has its own banking laws. The extent to which they have any regulatory impact on cryptocurrency varies from state to state. In some cases, cryptocurrency may be affected by general regulations relating to money transfer. In any particular state, there may be laws and regulations that affect digital assets, including cryptocurrency more directly.

[A] Getting Accurate U.S. State Legal Advice

Below is a summary of some of the state regulations that may affect dealings in cryptocurrency.[270] However, this is not a complete legal review of the state laws that may affect digital assets, nor is it legal advice. To obtain legal advice about the laws and regulations that can relate to digital assets in any U.S. state, it will be necessary to obtain advice from qualified legal advisors in that state.

To get a general idea, although not necessarily a complete legal explanation, of the money transmission licensing requirements and other regulations relating to digital assets such as cyber currency, tokens and NFTs in different U.S. states, there are some websites which have been set up to summarize certain relevant regulations in the different states. These include a site provided online by Bloomberg Law, and another online site called Money Service Business Licensing—Nationwide Licensing Support. As indicated, some of the references below are to these and other sites.

It is important to remember that with respect to state law in the US, each U.S. state (and the District of Columbia) licenses the practice of law under their own strict laws and regulations. An attorney qualified in one jurisdiction is usually not permitted to practice law or give legal advice in another jurisdiction without express permission. Therefore, when seeking legal advice about the laws of a particular state or other U.S. legal jurisdiction, it is important to obtain legal advice from a lawyer expressly qualified to give legal advice in the relevant U.S. state or legal jurisdiction in question.

269. There is little clarity about how many cryptocurrencies exist. It has been reported that there were more than twenty thousand in 2022. Chris Jones, "Are there too many cryptocurrencies" COINTELEGRAPH, September 21, 2022; There are also about five-hundred cryptocurrency exchanges. Farran Powell, "10 Best Crypto Exchanges of 2022," Forbes Avisor, online at forbes.com, November 2, 2022.

270. "Cryptocurrency Laws and Regulations by State," online at pro.bloomberglaw.com, March 30, 2022.

[B] North American Securities Administrators Association

One website that gives an idea of what the overall attitude of North American securities regulators is respecting cryptocurrencies and crypto-related investments is the website of the North American Securities Administrators Association (NASAA). This is an organization of the state and provincial securities regulators in the United States, Canada and Mexico. Their stated goal is to protect investors from fraud and abuse by providing communication and some coordination with respect to the licensing and registration of key investment workers, investigating investor complaints, reviewing certain kinds of investments, including digital investments, and "Advocating passage of strong, sensible and consistent state securities laws and regulations."

[C] National Multistate Licensing System and Registry

With respect to regulating digital assets including cryptocurrency, NFTs and tokens, all of the U.S. states have adopted policies about how they are to be treated when they involve residents of that state. These rules are often imposed in conjunction with state banking, investing, money services, and money transmission regulations. Consequently, individuals and companies that are involved in dealing with digital assets are frequently required to be licensed to perform certain financial services activities within a state.

This often includes a complex application procedure, paying required fees, and may require obtaining a bond to cover the activities in question. The qualifications that are required to engage in those activities are determined by the states or other relevant jurisdictions themselves, but the application procedure in a number of states and other regulatory jurisdictions under U.S. law is frequently subcontracted to an organization called the Nationwide Multistate Licensing System (NMLS).

The Nationwide Multistate Licensing System is the system of record for nondepository financial services licensing or registration in participating state agencies, including the District of Columbia and U.S. territories of Puerto Rico, the U.S. Virgin Islands and Guam. In these jurisdictions, the NMSL is the official system for companies and individuals seeking to apply for, amend, renew, and surrender licenses. As of this writing, those processes are managed through NMLS for sixty-six state or territorial governmental agencies.

The NMLS itself does not grant or deny license authority. The qualifications for obtaining and holding money services business licenses are determined by the relevant state regulatory agencies themselves.

Fifty-nine U.S. jurisdictions use the NMLS for mortgage licensing. Fifty-five use the system to manage licensing for other nonbank entities (e.g., money services businesses, consumer finance and debt).

NMLS was created by the Conference of State Bank Supervisors (CSBS) and the American Association of Residential Mortgage Regulators and began operations in

January 2008. It is owned and operated by the State Regulatory Registry LLC, a wholly owned subsidiary of CSBS.[271]

Under the heading "State Licensing Requirements," the NMLS provides a helpful online guide to the various licensing requirements of the states that use the NMLS.[272]

[D] The Individual U.S. States and Jurisdictions

As is true throughout this book, the following comments are not legal advice. Any policies, legislation or regulations referred to herein are likely to be subject to change. Advice about the laws of any particular jurisdiction will need to be obtained from advisors legally qualified in that jurisdiction.

[1] Alabama

Alabama has been cautious in its approach to digital asset regulation, including cybercurrency. In May of 2018, the Alabama Securities Commission (ASC) posted the following advisory online: "Are You An Informed Investor? Be Cautious of the Crypto Investment Craze."

The posting said that to sell or issue any money-type instruments, including those used for payment, storing, transmitting, or receiving any money or monetary value, one needs a license. Any "medium of exchange," whether an official fiat or a virtual currency (redeemable in money or not), comes within the definition of "monetary value."[273]

In January of 2022, the ASC issued a press release identifying what it considered to be the "top investor threats for 2022." With respect to cryptocurrency, the press release said:

> "[T]he Alabama Securities Commission (ASC) today released an annual list of top investor threats and urged caution before purchasing popular and volatile unregulated investments—especially those involving cryptocurrency and digital assets. ... ."
>
> "The ASC revealed that investments related to cryptocurrencies and digital assets is our top investor threat. ... Stories of 'crypto millionaires' attracted some investors to try their hand at investing in cryptocurrencies or crypto-related investments this year, and with them, many stories of those who bet big and lost big began appearing, and they will continue to appear in 2022."
>
> "The top 2022 threats were determined by a survey of securities regulators conducted by the North American Securities Administrators Association (NASAA). The annual survey is designed to identify the most problematic products, practices or schemes facing investors. The following were cited most often by state

271. NMLS Resource Center, "About NMLS," online at: censingsystem.org, accessed May 24, 2022.
272. NMLS Resource Center, "State Licensing Requirements," online at: censingsystem.org, accessed May 24, 2022.
273. Alabama Code, sections 8-7A-2 and 8-7A-5.

and provincial securities regulators: 1. Investments tied to cryptocurrencies and digital assets, … ."[274]

[2] Alaska

In Alaska, "money services" are within the jurisdiction of the Alaska Division of Banking and Securities. The Division website says:[275]

> "Companies dealing with fiat and virtual currencies (cryptocurrencies) must apply for a money transmitter license, then enter into a Limited Licensing Agreement (LLA) with the State of Alaska."
>
> "All licensing activity is done through the NMLS system."[276]

The conditions for applying for such a license are set up in the Alaska Uniform Money Services Act.[277]

"Money Services" include "selling or issuing payment instruments or stored value or receiving money or monetary value for transmission."[278]

[3] Arizona

In 2021, the Arizona House of Representatives passed House Bill 2544 to establish the Blockchain and Cryptocurrency Study Committee. The purposes of the Committee are stated to be:

> (1) review data on the scope of blockchain and cryptocurrency throughout the country; (2) determine the current status of blockchain and crypto currency in relation to previously enacted Arizona legislation on the subjects; (3) compile an overview of potential legislation; and (4) solicit ideas and opinions of industry experts on additional legislation on or before December 31st 2021, to submit an initial report, on or before December 31st 2022, and submit a final report regarding the committee's findings and recommendations of legislative priorities that will foster a positive blockchain and cryptocurrency economic environment in this state to the Speaker of the House of Representatives and the President of the Senate and provide a copy of this report to the Secretary of State.

There are no blockchain or cryptocurrency reports shown on the Secretary of State's website at the time of this writing.[279]

---

274. ASC, "Alabama Securities Commission Announces Top Investor Threats for 2022," online at: www.asc.alabama.gov., January 10, 2022.
275. "Alaska Department of Commerce, Community and Economic Development, Division of Banking and Securities," online at: commerce.alaska.gov, accessed July 11, 2022.
276. NMLS, online at: mortgage.nationwidelicensingsystem.org.
277. Alaska Statutes, Chapter 55, Alaska Uniform Money Services Act, section AS.06.55.101, et.seq., online at: legis.state.ak.us, accessed July 11, 2022.
278. Alaska Statutes, section 06.55.990(15), online at: legis.state.ak.us, accessed July 11, 2022.
279. Arizona Secretary of State, online, at: azsos.gov, accessed July 11, 2022.

Money transmitters in Arizona need to be licensed. It is reported that both Binance and Coinbase have obtained money transmitter licenses in Arizona.[280]

[4] Arkansas

Cryptocurrency is included in the money transmission laws of Arkansas. Money transmitters are allowed to buy and sell cryptocurrency. Licenses are usually required.[281]

However, in at least a couple of cases, it is reported that Arkansas did expressly permit exemptions from licensing (for the in-game currency of a video game and where a person was selling their own Bitcoin holdings).[282]

In Arkansas:

> The term "engaged in the business of money services" unless otherwise provided, includes any person who holds himself out as being a currency dealer or exchange or; an issuer of traveler's checks, money orders, prepaid access, or stored value; a seller or redeemer of traveler's checks, money orders, prepaid access or stored value; or who receives money or monetary value for the purpose of transmitting said money or monetary value using a system outside that of a conventional financial institution.[283]

Under Arkansas regulations, the term "money transmission" means "selling or issuing payment instruments, stored value, prepaid access, or receiving money or monetary value for transmission."[284]

[5] California

California does have a Money Transition Act administered by the Department of Financial Protection and Innovation.

California Financial Code, section 2030 prohibits a person from engaging in the business of money transmission in California unless the person is licensed or exempt from licensure or is an agent of a person licensed or exempt from license shore.

Financial Code section 2003, Subdivision Q defines "money transmission" as receiving money for transmission, selling, or issuing stored value, or selling or issuing payment instruments. Financial Code section 2003, Subdivision U defines "receiving money for transmission" as receiving money or monetary value in the United States for transmission within or outside the United States by electronic or other means.

280. "Cryptocurrency Laws and Regulations by State," online at pro.bloomberglaw.com, March 30, 2022.
281. A.C.A. Sections 23-55-102 (12(A) and 23-55-701(b).
282. Bloomberg Law, *supra*, "Arkansas," *In re Mythical, Inc.* and *in re River Financial, Inc*, respectively.
283. Arkansas Securities Department, "Money Services Rules Effective February 2, 2020," PDF download, online at: securities.arkansas.gov., accessed July 11, 2022.
284. *Ibid.* Rule 102, Definitions, (10).

Financial Code section 2003, Subdivision X defines "stored value" as monetary value representing a claim against the issuer that is stored on an electronic or digital medium, and that is intended and accepted for use as a means of redemption for money or monetary value or payment for goods or services. The term does not include any stored value that is only redeemable by the issuer for goods or services provided by the issuer or its affiliates (closed loop).

In March of 2022, the State of California Department of Financial Protection and Innovation issued an Interpretive Opinion that analyzed the relationship between California money transmission law and cryptocurrency trading. That Opinion said the following:

> "The sale and purchase of cryptocurrency directly between [the trading platform in question (Platform)] and the customer where [the Platform] does not facilitate the exchange of the fiat currency or cryptocurrency with a third party, does not meet the definition of money transmission because it does not involve the sale or issuance of a payment instrument, the sale or issuance of stored value, or receiving money for transmission."
>
> "Likewise, the exchange of one cryptocurrency for another directly between two parties does not meet the definition of money transmission because it does not involve the sale or issuance of a payment instrument, the sale or issuance of stored value, or receiving money for transmission."
>
> "Likewise, the exchange of one cryptocurrency for another directly between two parties, such as the customer and [the Platform], does not meet the definition of money transmission. The customer can only redeem monetary values stored in an account [or 'wallet'] provided by [the Platform] for the benefit of the customer for digital currencies sold by [the Platform] or instruct [the Platform] to return it to the customer's bank account. Therefore, this stored value is a closed loop transaction and does not constitute regulated money transmission under the MTA [Money Transmission Act]."
>
> "The Department is not currently requiring [the Platform] to obtain an MTA license to operate its Platform that provides its customers with fiat and digital wallets to store and exchange cryptocurrency directly with [the Platform]. Please be aware, however, that this is subject to change. And at any time, the Department may decide this activity is subject to regulatory supervision. If [the Platform] chooses to operate in California, it would do so subject to these risks."[285]

Essentially, this describes a situation where a customer opens an account on a cryptocurrency trading platform. The Platform provides the customer with an account (wallet) to which the customer can transfer either fiat or cryptocurrency. When the customer makes a purchase on the Platform, the relevant amount of crypto or fiat currency is transferred from the customer's account to a special account (wallet) provided by the Platform for trading. When the trade is completed, any resulting currency is transferred back to the customer's account. The customer can obtain currency from the Platform only by withdrawing it from its own account (wallet) as

285. State of California, Department of Financial Protection and Innovation, Response to Request for Interpretive Opinion, March 23, 2022, online at: dfpi.ca.gov, downloadable as PDF file, accessed July 12, 2022.

they are labeled. Therefore, no sale or transfer is taking place outside the trading Platform to or from third parties, and consequently the DFPI does not currently consider that such transactions require a money transmission license. However, as noted, this can change.

[6] Colorado

In the spring of 2022, it was reported that "[Governor] Jared Polis is touting Colorado as a future cryptocurrency hub ..."[286]

In February of 2022, it was reported that "Colorado will become the first state to accept cryptocurrency as payment for state taxes and fees, Governor Jared Polis announced Wednesday":[287]

> "Polis said the state, which was also the earliest to use blockchain technology for government infrastructure, will take the digital coin payments and deposit the equivalent value in dollars into the state's treasury.
>
> "In Colorado, we've been laying the groundwork to be a center of crypto and blockchain innovation for a number of years." "Polis said in a statement. " "We see it as a critical part of Colorado's overall innovation ecosystem."[288]

However, Colorado's interest in digital assets does not exclude cybercurrency from laws and regulations relating to money transmission.

Under Colorado legislation:

> "Money transmission" means the sale or issuance of exchange or engaging in the business of receiving money for transmission or transmitting money within The United States or to locations abroad by any and all means including but not limited to payment instrument, wire, facsimile or electronic transfer.[289]

Colorado has issued "interim guidance" stating that cryptocurrency payment systems may require money transmission licenses.[290] It says:

> "Such licensure would be required when:
>
> - A person is engaged in the business of selling and buying cryptocurrencies for fiat currencies; and
> - A Colorado customer can transfer cryptocurrency to another customer within the exchange; and
> - The exchange has the ability to transfer fiat currency through the medium of cryptocurrency."

286. Mark Jaffe, Nancy Loftholm, "A Crypto Mine No One Is Quite Sure Exists," The Colorado Sun, online at: coloradosun.com, March 6, 2022.
287. Eric Faveulle, "Colorado to Become the First State to Accept Cryptocurrency as Payment for Taxes," *ABC News*, online at: abcnews.go.com, February 24, 2022.
288. *Ibid.*
289. Colorado Statutes, Chapter 11, Article 110, Money Transmitters, section 103 Definitions (11).
290. *See* Colorado Department of Regulatory Agencies, Division of Banking, Interim Regulatory Guidance, Cryptocurrency and the Colorado MTA, Issued September 20, 2018, online for PDF download at: banking.colorado.gov., accessed July 13, 2022.

> "If the person's business model has the ability to transfer fiat currency through the medium of cryptocurrency, the Division of Banking should be contacted at (303) 894-7575. The Division will individually analyze the entire course of a transmission to determine if licensure is required under the Money Transmitters Act, which is required before money transmission is conducted."[291]

In September of 2022, Colorado became the first state to allow state taxes to be paid in cryptocurrency.[292]

[7] Connecticut

According to the State of Connecticut Department of Banking (CDP), "virtual currency" which, in Connecticut, covers "cryptocurrency, digital currency and bitcoin" is regulated similarly to the way that cash or "fiat currency" is regulated under that state's money transmission laws.[293]

Transmitting digital currency in Connecticut requires a Money Transmitter License.

In providing licenses for Money Services Businesses including Money Transmission Licenses, the CDP does participate in the Multistate Money Services Business Licensing Agreement Program (MMLA).

The types of Money Services Business licenses that can be acquired through the MMLA include the following:[294]

- Check Cashing License.
- Consumer Collection Agency License.
- Debt Adjuster For-Profit License.
- Debt Adjuster Nonprofit License.
- Debt Negotiation License.
- Exempt Company Registration.
- Federal Student Loan Servicer Registrant.
- Lead Generator License.
- Money Transmission License.
- Mortgage Broker License.
- Mortgage Correspondent Lender License.
- Money Lender License.
- Mortgage Service License.
- Sales Finance Company License.
- Small Loan Company License.
- Student Loan Servicer License.

291. *Ibid.*
292. Namcios, "Colorado Becomes First US State As Payment For Taxes," BITCOIN Magazine, reported by NASDAQ, online at nasdaq.com, September 20, 2022.
293. State of Connecticut, Ct. gov (Official State Website), Department of Banking, "Virtual Currency Money Transmission FAQs," online at: ct.gov/DOB, accessed July 15, 2022.
294. NMLS Resource Center, State Licensing Requirements, Connecticut, online at: mortgage.nationwidesystem.org, accessed July 15, 2022.

Licenses are also provided for "branches" of the above-licensed businesses. Individuals can also obtain the following types of licenses:

- Loan Processor Underwriter License.
- Mortgage Loan Originator License.

There are also reserve requirements which require those holding such a license to keep reserves of the same kind and amount of digital currency as all of their outstanding transactions.

With respect to virtual currency Automated Teller Machines (ATMs), the operating of some in Connecticut may require a license, but that will depend on the types of transactions that the ATM can do.[295] The CDP has taken the position that in ATM will not need a license if it meets the following conditions:[296]

- The ATM is not connected to any financial institution.
- Transactions through the ATM are limited to buying and/or selling virtual currency in a simultaneous transaction in exchange for fiat currency.

> If any other transactions are available, the ATM may be required to be licensed as a money transmitter and a company seeking to engage in such activities is advised to contact the department for a determination of whether licensure is required prior to commencing activities. Please review the opinions linked here for more information.[297]

The CDP provides, on its website, PDF downloads of a number of opinions it has given about the licensure requirements of various types of ATMs. These often refer to cases where licensure is not required. For example, in December of 2019, the CDP issued and provided an opinion summarized as follows:[298]

> Company that operates virtual currency kiosks, which are stationary, unattended devices within the definition of "automated teller machine", but that do not involve a bank or financial institution, and essentially act as vending machines, limited to depositing cash into the kiosks and immediately receiving virtual currency from the kiosks inventory in return, not utilizing an exchange or other payment system, does not require licensure under the Money Transmission Act.

The CDP is also responsible for regulating what it defines as "virtual currency exchanges," which the CDP defines as businesses that allow customers to trade virtual currency for other assets such as conventional fiat money or other virtual currency. Regarding virtual currency exchanges, the CDP says:

> Depending on the activities in which the exchanges engaged, the exchange may be required to maintain a money transmission license. For example, an exchange that simply matches a buyer and seller of virtual currency through its software platform

295. *Ibid.*
296. *Ibid. See also*: Connecticut General Statutes (C.G.S.), section 36a-155(18).
297. *Ibid.*
298. *Ibid.*

> would not need to be licensed. However, if said exchange holds either party's currency (virtual or fiat), transmits virtual or fiat currency on behalf of other persons or advertises money transmission services, licensure would be required. Please review the opinions linked here for more information.[299]

Similarly to the information it has given on ATMs, the CDP provides downloadable PDF copies of opinions, such as an opinion the Department gave in January 2019 which is summarized as follows:

> Digital currency exchanges which hold or transmit fiat or virtual currency on behalf of Connecticut residents are engaging in money transmission in this state and require licensure under the Money Transmission Act.[300]

[8] Delaware

Under the Delaware banking law:

> No person, except those specified in section 2304 or agents of a licensee as provided in section 2311,[301] shall engage in the business of selling checks, or issuing checks, or engage in the business of receiving money for transmission or transmitting the same without first having obtained a license hereunder.

To obtain a license for transmitting money, application needs to be made to the Delaware Banking Commissioner.[302] The application requirements, conditions, qualifications, fees, etc., to obtain a money transmission license are set out in the Delaware Code.[303] The regulation does not expressly include cryptocurrency or other digital assets, but Coinbase and Binance, and other financial companies, are reported to have obtained money transmitter licenses in Delaware.[304]

[9] District of Columbia

Under the Code of the District of Columbia section 26-1002:[305]

> [N]o person shall engage in the business of money transmission without obtaining the license issued by the Superintendent [commissioner] under section 26-1009 except as provided in subsection (D) of this section and in section 26-1003.

---

299. *Ibid.*
300. *Ibid.*
301. The Delaware Code Online, Title 5, Banking, Other Businesses Under Jurisdiction of State Banking Department, Chapter 23. Sale of Checks and Transmission of Money, online at: delcode.delaware.gov., section 2304, Exemption from licensing, provided for banks, trust companies, credit unions, etc., already licensed under U.S. Federal or state laws.
302. *Ibid.* at Code sections under Chapter 23.
303. *Ibid.*
304. Bloomberg Law, *Supra*, "Delaware." *See*: Title 5 Delaware Code, section 2303.
305. Code of the District of Columbia, Title 26, Banks and Other Financial Institutions, Chapter 10, Money Transmissions, section 26-1002 License Required, online at: code.dccouncil.us.

In DC, money transmission, including dealing in cryptocurrency, requires a license.[306]

Under the District of Columbia Code, "money transmission":

> means the sale or issuance of payment instruments or engaging in the business of receiving money for transmission or transmitting money within the United States, or to locations abroad, by any and all means, including but not limited to payment instrument, wire, facsimile, or electronic transfer.[307]

The term "payment instrument" is defined as:

> any written or electronic check, draft, money order, travelers check, or other electronic or written instrument or order for the transmission or payment of money which is sold or issued to one or more persons, whether or not such instrument is negotiable. The term "payment instrument" does not include any credit card voucher, any letter of credit, or any instrument which is redeemable by the issuer in goods or services.[308]

[10] Florida

In May of 2022, Florida governor Ron DeSantis signed a new law redefining and easing the regulation on cryptocurrency in Florida. This law was to become effective on January 1, 2023.

The Money Services Businesses in Florida are governed under Chapter 560 of the Florida Statutes.[309]

A downloadable PDF of the text of the bill is available online.[310]

Under the Definitions section of those Statutes, the term "money services" business[311] is defined as:

> any person located in or doing business in this state, from the state, or into this state from locations outside this state or country who acts as a payment instrument seller, foreign currency exchanger, check casher, or money transmitter.[312]

Prior to the effective date of this new law, the term "money transmitter" was defined as:

> a corporation, limited liability company, limited liability partnership, or foreign entity qualified to do business in this state which receives currency, monetary value, or payment instruments for the purpose of transmitting the same by any

306. Bloomberg Law, *Supra*, "District of Columbia." *See*: *United States v. Harmon*, 474 F. Supp. 3d 76, 89 (D.D.C. 2020).
307. Code of the District of Columbia, Title 26, Banks and Other Financial Institutions, Chapter 10, Money Transmissions, section 26-1001, Definitions, (10), online at: code.dccouncil.us.
308. *Ibid*. Definitions, (12).
309. Florida Statutes, Chapter 560, online at: lawserver.com.
310. CS/HB 273: Money Services Businesses, Effective Date 1/1/2023, online at: flsenate.gov. The bill provides amendments to Florida Statutes, Chapter 506. Sections 103, 123, 125, 204, 208, 208.5, 210, 211, 212, and others. For more detailed information, obtain qualified professional advice about impact of full text of bill.
311. Florida Statutes, Chapter 560.103, Definitions, online at: lawserver.com.
312. *Ibid*., "Money services business," online at: lawserver.com.

> means, including transmission by wire, facsimile, electronic transfer, courier, the Internet, or through bill payment services or other businesses that facilitate such transfer within this country, or to or from this country.[313]

Under Florida Statutes:

> no person shall engage for consideration, nor in any manner advertise that they engage, in the selling or issuing of payment instruments or in the activity of a funds transmitter, without first obtaining registration under the provisions of this part.[314]

The Statutes provide detailed instructions on how to proceed as an applicant for registration.[315]

Florida also provides a lengthy set of rules for Money Transmitters.[316]

A Florida State appellate court case ruled that money transmission includes transactions in cryptocurrency.[317] Prior to this case, Florida considered digital tokens tied to ownership of physical gold to be covered by the money transmission regulations. It has not yet been ruled whether tokens tied to less tangible assets are also covered.

Florida regulation also provides an element of flexibility in financial services innovation that affects some cryptocurrency transactions.

At the end of 2020, the Florida Office of Financial Regulation (FOFR) said it would create something called a "Financial Technology Sandbox" (FTS)[318] that would allow financial technology startups to test new products and services to a limited extent under the watchful scrutiny of the FOFR but without breaking existing financial regulations. This idea was borrowed from a similar experiment which was launched in the UK in 2015. Being allowed to participate in this project required applying for an FTS license and paying filing fees. Certain background checks were also required.[319] The difference that this made to cryptocurrency innovators is that qualifying entities with an FTS license could benefit from limited exclusion from money transmitter regulations.[320]

[a] Local Interest in Florida

The growth of interest in cryptocurrency seems to have stimulated the imaginations of numerous politicians in Florida on both the state-wide and more local levels.

---

313. *Ibid.*, "Money transmitter," online at: lawserver.com.
314. *Ibid.*, Chapter 560.204, online at: lawserver.com.
315. *Ibid.*, Chapter 560.205 and 560.206, online at: lawserver.com.
316. Florida Administrative Code and Florida Administrative Register, Chapter 69V-560, 1000, et seq., online at flrules.org./gateway.
317. *Ibid. See, State v. Espinoza*, 264 So. 3d 1055 (Fla. Dist. Ct. App. 2019).
318. Florida Statutes, Chapter 559, section 952, online at: lawserver.com. Note that there have been some amendments that will take effect on January 1, 2023, under CS/HB 273, *see* text above relating to that new law.
319. Omni Public, "What you need to know about Florida's fintech sandbox," online at bizjournals.com, December 1, 2021.
320. Bloomberg Law, *Supra*, "Florida." *See*: Fla. Stat. Sections 559.952(4)(a)(3) through (14).

It has been reported that the Mayor of Miami, Francis Suarez, has decided that he wants to raise money for the city through cryptocurrency. His plan is that Miami will issue its own cryptocurrency to be called "MiamiCoin." Suarez is reported to believe that MiamiCoin could raise so much revenue for the city that Miami residents will no longer have to pay municipal taxes.

Mr. Suarez is apparently a great believer in the future of cryptocurrency. He has even asked that he be paid his salary in Bitcoin.[321]

However, Mr. Suarez is not the only U.S. mayor to try to profit from cryptocurrency. In this, he is competing with the mayor of New York City.[322]

Mr. Suarez has followed up his enthusiasm by making Miami a center of cryptocurrency conferences. He held one in 2021 that attracted 12,000 participants from every sector of the financial industry, including banks, computer executives and crypto industry entrepreneurs. He was so pleased with the results that he is planning more.

[11] Georgia

Under Georgia law, "virtual currency," defined as "digital representation of monetary value," does come within the money transmission laws that require a license for receiving or transmitting "monetary value." Georgia regulators are also authorized to enact regulations that are specific to cryptocurrency.[323]

In Georgia, "money transmitter" is defined as follows:

> A money transmitter is an individual or business that engages in the transmission of money or monetary value. Money transmission means engaging in the business of receiving money for transmission or transmitting money within the United States or to locations abroad.[324]

With some exemptions for state or federally chartered banks, etc., those that fall within the definition of transmitting money are required to comply with the licensing requirements of the Georgia Department of Banking. Like many other states, application for such licenses needs to be made through the Nationwide Multistate Licensing System which manages money transmitter licenses for the State of Georgia, and other states.[325]

321. Romaine Bostick, Taylor Riggs, and Caroline Hyde, "Miami Mayor Seeks Wider Crypto Use After Taking Pay in Bitcoin," Bloomberg, online at bloomberg.com, December 3, 2021.
322. Lucy Hooker, "Miami is Banking on Cryptocurrency and New York Wants in," *BBC News*, online, December 14, 2021.
323. Bloomberg Law, *supra*, "Georgia." *See*: Georgia laws: O.C.G.A. Sections 7-1-680(13) and (26); O.C.G.A sections 7-1-681 and 7-1-690. For additional information also *see* the following from the Georgia Department of Banking and Finance. "Money Transmission and the Sale of Payment Instruments" and; Department of Banking and Finance Orders CampBX, Bitcoin Trading Platform, to Cease and Desist (July 26, 2018).
324. Georgia Department of Banking and Finance, "Money Services Businesses," "Money Transmitters," online at: dbf.georgia.gov., accessed July 19, 2022.
325. Georgia Department of Banking and Finance, "Information for New Money Transmitter Applicants," online at: dbf.georgia.gov., accessed July 19, 2022.

The Secretary of State of Georgia has published at least three investor alerts about the dangers of cryptocurrencies and digital assets. Their purpose is to warn investors about investment frauds concerning cryptocurrency-related investment and business opportunities. Their warnings refer not only to cryptocurrencies generally but also to coins and tokens because "while both terms are similar, there are differences in how coins and tokens operate."[326] The Secretary warns:

> [F]raudsters often used the novelty of cryptocurrencies to lure investors into scams. We have become aware of a number of Internet promotions, including on social media, claiming to raise capital for products and services or that cryptocurrency is a safe asset in times of financial markets turmoil. We urge investors to be wary of these promotions, and to be aware of the substantial potential for fraud at this time.[327]

Among the "fraudulent cryptocurrency investments" that the Investor Alert lists are:

- Pump and Dumps.
- Multi-level Marketing Platforms.
- "Guaranteed" High Investment Returns.
- Unsolicited Offers.
- High Pressure to Buy.
- Volatility.
- Uninsured.
- Unregulated.
- Hackable.
- Vulnerable.

"Like any investment product, investors in cryptocurrencies should be prepared to lose the entire amount of their investment."[328]

[12] Hawaii

Under the Hawaii Money Transmitters Act (MTA),[329] "monetary value" is defined as "a medium of exchange whether or not redeemable in money."[330]

326. Georgia Secretary of State, "Investor Alert—Cryptocurrencies and Digital Assets," online at: sos.ga.gov, accessed July 19, 2022.
327. *Supra*, Georgia Secretary of State, "Investor Alert—Cryptocurrencies and Digital Assets," online at: sos.ga.gov, accessed July 19, 2022.
328. *Ibid.*
329. 2021 Hawaii Revised Statutes, Title 26. Trade Regulation and Practice, 489D. MTA, online at: law.justia.com, accessed July 20, 2022.
330. 2021 Hawaii Revised Statutes, *supra*, 489 D-4, Definitions, "Monetary value."

"Money transmission" means to engage in the business of:

- selling or issuing payment instruments; or
- receiving money or monetary value for transmission to a location within or outside the United States by any and all means, including wire, facsimile or electronic transfer.

"Money transmission does not apply to career services."[331]

"Payment instrument" is defined as:

> any electronic or written check, draft, money order, traveler's check, or other electronic instrument or written instrument or order for the transmission or payment of money, sold or issued to one or more persons, whether or not the instrument is negotiable. The term "payment instrument" does not include any credit card voucher, any letter of credit, or any instrument that is redeemable by issuer in goods or services.[332]

In 2020, the Hawaii Division of Financial Institutions (DFI), Department of Commerce and Consumer Affairs, and the Hawaii Technology and Development Corporation (HTDC) created a partnership to look at the potential of digital currencies and explore a potential regulatory scheme. This project was named the Digital Currency Innovation Lab (DCIL). Any entity that achieved successful admission to the DCIL was permitted to conduct business in Hawaii without having to obtain a state money transmitter license. This project was originally intended to expire on June 30, 2022, but in June of 2022, the program was given a two-year extension until June 30, 2024. This seems to allow cryptocurrency businesses to stand outside of the usual money transmission requirements of Hawaiian law.[333]

[13] Idaho

The Idaho MTA is administered and enforced by the Securities Bureau of the Department of Finance.[334]

The Department says on its website:

> "Any person, unless exempt, that sells or issues payment instruments or who engages in the business of receiving money for transmission or engaging in the business of money transmission, by any and all means including but not limited to payment instruments, wire, facsimile or electronic transfer" is required to have an Idaho Money Transmitter license.

331. *Ibid.*, "Money transmission."
332. *Ibid.*, "Payment instrument."
333. State of Hawaii, Department of Commerce and Consumer Affairs, News Release: "Digital Currency Innovation Lab Extended Two Years," online at: cca.hawaii.gov, accessed July 20, 2022.
334. Idaho Department of Finance, Idaho Money Transmitters Section, online at; finance.idaho.gov., accessed July 20, 2022.

The money transmitters license requirement also covers "Virtual Currency Exchangers":

> If you act as a virtual/digital currency exchanger and accept legal tender (e.g., government-backed and issued "fiat" currencies) for later delivery to a third party in association with the purchase of a virtual currency, then you must be licensed as a money transmitter with the Department of Finance.

However, there are some businesses that are exempted by the Department of Finance under the heading, "Who does not need this license?" This refers to government agencies, licensed banks, etc.

The Department of Finance has issued several "no action letters" with respect to a number of businesses involved in digital currency. For example, crypto ATMs are exempt from licensing requirements. Other no-action and opinion letters can be found on the website of the Idaho Department of Finance.[335]

[14] Illinois

In January of 2020, the Illinois legislature passed new legislation known as the "Blockchain Technology Act."[336]

Section 10 of the Act described "permitted use of blockchain," including, among other things, that:

> (a) a smart contract, record, or signature may not be denied legal effect or enforceability solely because blockchain was used to create, store, or verify the smart contract, record or signature.[337]

Section 15 of the Act describes "limitations to the use of blockchain," including, among other things:

> (a) if the parties have agreed to conduct a transaction by use of a blockchain and a law requires that a contract or other record relating to the transaction be in writing, the legal effect, validity, or enforceability of the contract or other record may be denied if the blockchain containing an electronic record of the transaction is not in a form that is capable of being retained and accurately reproduced for later reference by all parties or other persons who are entitled to retain the contract or other record.

According to an article in the *Chicago Tribune* in June of 2021, the state of Illinois was keen to become a center of the "booming cryptocurrency industry."[338] At that time, the Illinois State legislature was considering a new piece of legislation that would allow Illinois to become, after Wyoming, the second state "to allow special trusts to

---

335. Idaho Department of Finance. No Action and Opinion Letters, Money Transmitters, Digital Currency, online at: finance.idaho.gov., accessed July 20, 2022.
336. Illinois Public Act 101-0514, online at ilga.gov., accessed July 21, 2022.
337. *Ibid.*
338. Robert Channick, "From Bitcoin mining to ATMs, Illinois is positioning itself as a center for the booming cryptocurrency industry," Chicago Tribune, online, June 18, 2021.

hold cryptocurrency." Kraken, a cryptocurrency exchange, became a chartered bank in the state of Wyoming in 2020.[339]

In furtherance of allowing establishment of these "special purpose depository trusts" in Illinois, a bill was introduced in the Illinois General Assembly in February of 2021 for the purpose of amending the Blockchain Business Development Act to provide the Department of Financial and Professional Regulation with the authority to adopt rules, opinions, or interpretive letters regarding the custody of digital assets, including digital consumer assets, digital securities, and virtual currency.[340]

In Illinois, the money transmission laws do not specifically mention cryptocurrency.

Under the Illinois Transmitters of Money Act,[341] "money" is defined as:

> a medium of exchange that is authorized or adopted by a domestic or foreign government as a part of its currency and that is customarily used and accepted as a medium of exchange in the country of issuance.[342]

With respect to cryptocurrency, this definition is somewhat ambiguous because there are countries, such as El Salvador which have adopted cryptocurrencies (in that case Bitcoin) as "as part of its currency."

Under the Transmitters of Money Act, the term "transmitting money" is defined as:

> the transmission of money by any means, including transmissions to or from locations within the United States or to and from locations outside the United States by payment instrument, facsimile or electronic transfer.[343]

Under section 10 of the Transmitters of Money Act, a License is required under the following circumstances:

> no person may engage in the state in the business of selling or issuing payment instruments, transmitting money, or exchanging, for compensation, payment instruments or money of the United States government or a foreign government to or from money of another government without first obtaining a license under this act. Separate licenses shall not be required, however for persons acting as authorized sellers of licensees under this Act.[344]

Under the Act, "payment instrument" is defined as:

> a check, draft, money order, travelers check, stored value card, or other instrument or memorandum, written order or written receipt for the transmission or payment of money sold or issued to one or more persons whether or not that instrument or order is negotiable. Payment instrument does not include an

339. *Ibid.*
340. Illinois General Assembly, HB3968, November 28, 2021, Bill Status, online at: ilga.gov/legislation. Not yet law, as of July 22, 2022.
341. Illinois General Assembly, Illinois Compiled Statutes, Financial Regulation, 205 ILCS 657, Transmitters of Money Act, online at: ilga.gov/legislation/ilcs.
342. *Supra*, at 205 ILCS 657, section 5 "Money."
343. *Ibid.*, section 5 "Money transmitter."
344. *Ibid.*, section 10 "License required."

> instrument that is redeemable by the issuer in merchandise or service, a credit card voucher, or a letter of credit, a written order for the transmission or payment of money that results in the issuance of a check, draft, money order, travelers check, or other instrument or memorandum that is not a payment instrument.[345]

Although the definitions quoted above do not expressly mention cryptocurrency or digital assets, they do seem broad enough to require some cryptocurrency businesses to require a license under the Act.

Guidance on when this is required has been published by the Department of Financial and Professional Regulation on their website.

In June of 2017, the Illinois Department of Financial and Professional Regulation issued a document entitled "Digital Currency Regulatory Guidance."[346] That document gives a number of examples of digital currency transactions which do qualify as money transmission and require a license and also lists activities not qualifying as money transmission.

For example, the following were listed as "activities generally qualifying as money transmission" (although it is stated that "this is a non-exhaustive list"):

- Exchange involving both digital currency and money through a third-party exchanger is generally considered to be money transmission.
- Exchange of digital currency for money through an automated machine is generally considered to be money transmission. This includes many transactions on cryptocurrency ATMs, although some ATMs can be configured to avoid the licensing requirement.

Illinois General Assembly had a bill introduced in March of 2022 to allow payment of state taxes to be paid in cryptocurrency. However, as of this writing, that bill has not passed.[347]

In addition, the Illinois Department of Financial Institutions frequently publishes "non-binding statements" giving their opinion on which crypto businesses need to be licensed. These statements are published on the website of the Department of Finance.[348]

A number of crypto exchanges are reported to be operating in Illinois.

[15] Indiana

The state government of Indiana has set up a website called the Indiana Cybersecurity Hub, "Taking Cyber in Indiana to the Next Level."[349] On that website, the government

345. *Ibid.*, section 5 "Payment instrument."
346. Illinois Department of Financial and Professional Regulation, "Digital Currency Regulatory Guidance," Last updated: June 13, 2017, online at: idfpr.illinois.gov., accessed July 22, 2022.
347. Illinois General Assembly, HB5287, March 3, 2022, Bill Status, online at: ilga.gov/legislation. Not yet law, as of July 22, 2022. In September of 2022, Colorado became the first state to allow state taxes to be paid in cryptocurrency.
348. Bloomberg Law, *supra*, "Illinois." *See*: 205 ILCS 657/5.
349. Online at: in.gov/cybersecurity.

also includes access to downloads to two documents approved by the Indiana Executive Council on Cybersecurity (IECC) in 2021: the 2021 *Indiana Cybersecurity Strategic Plan* and *The State of Cyber Report, 2017-2021*. The website also invites readers to "visit our Indiana cyber blog and download our free *Cybersecurity for Education Toolkit*."[350]

Free subscriptions are offered to the Indiana Cyber Blog which is purported to offer:

> the latest news, resources and perspectives from cyber security experts including Indiana's Cybersecurity Program Director and guest bloggers from state and local government in a wide range of businesses/industries/markets.[351]

Also offered is a podcast series entitled "Days of Our Cyber Lives" which is touted as "no soap opera."[352]

The website says, "Here in Indiana, cybersecurity is a top priority."[353]

In the *Indiana Cybersecurity Strategic Plan*, one of the objectives of the IECC Finance Committee is to "develop a Finance Sector Disruption Plan for the State of Indiana by Qtr. three of 2023."[354]

Indiana is another state where crypto assets are not specifically mentioned in their legal definition of "money transmission."

The 2022 Indiana Code defines "money transmission" as follows:[355]

> (a) As used in this chapter, "money transmission" means an activity that:
> (1) involves:
> (A) the sale or issuance of payment instruments primarily for personal, family, or household purposes; or
> (B) engaging in the business of:
> (i) receiving money for transmission from; Or
> (ii) transmitting money to:
> any location and by any means, including a payment instrument, wire, facsimile, or electronic transfer, primarily for personal, family, or household purposes; and
> (2) is performed:
> (A) from an office or place of business, wherever located; or
> (B) over the Internet or by any other means of transmission.
> (b) The term includes any activity described in subsection (a) that is performed by an authorized delegate, wherever located.

350. *Ibid.*
351. *Ibid.*
352. *Ibid.*
353. *Ibid.*
354. IECC, Indiana Cybersecurity Strategic Plan, September 2018, p. 20, "Finance Committee," "Deliverable: Disruption Plan and Communication Evaluation, Objective 1."
355. Indiana Code 2022, IC 28-8-4, Chapter 4, Money Transmitters, section 28-8-4-13 "Money transmission."

Under the Indiana Code, a "payment instrument" is defined as follows:[356]

(a) As used in this chapter, "payment instrument" means:
  (1) a check;
  (2) a draft;
  (3) a money order;
  (4) a traveler's check;
  (5) a stored value card, other than a closed system stored value card; or
  (6) an instrument or written order for the transmission or payment of money; sold or issued to one (1) or more persons, whether such instrument is negotiable.
(b) as used in this chapter, "payment instrument" does not include:
  (1) a credit card voucher;
  (2) a letter of credit;
  (3) an instrument that is redeemable by the issuer in goods or services; or
  (4) a closed system stored value card.

The dividing line in that state seems to be whether or not a crypto asset is used for making current payments. If it is, such as many cryptocurrencies are, it may require licensing as a money transmitter. However, if it is an asset not used for making payments, such as certain tokens or NFTS, it may not require such a license. For example, it is reported that cryptocurrency exchanges do not usually require a money transmitter license.

In order to check whether a particular digital asset does fall within those categories that require licensing, it will be necessary to consult qualified Indiana attorneys.[357]

[16] Iowa

Under the Iowa Uniform Money Services Act:[358]

"Money" means a medium of exchange authorized or adopted by a domestic or foreign government as part of its currency and that is customarily used and accepted as a medium of exchange in the country of issuance. The term includes a monetary unit of account established by an intergovernmental organization or by agreement between two or more governments.[359]

"Money services" means "money transmission or currency exchange."[360]

"Money transmission" means any of the following:[361]

a. Selling payment instruments to one or more persons or issuing payment instruments which are sold to one or more persons.
b. Conducting the business of receiving money or monetary value for transmission.

356. *Ibid.*, section 28-8-4-15 "Money transmission."
357. Bloomberg Law, *supra*, "Indiana." *See*: Ind. Code section 28-8-4-13.
358. Iowa Statutes, 2003 Acts, Chapter 96, section 1, 42, Chapter 533C, accessed August 1, 2022.
359. *Ibid.*, section 1, 42, Chapter 533C.102, Definitions, 13, "Money," accessed August 1, 2022.
360. *Ibid.*, Definitions, 14, "Money services," accessed August 1, 2022.
361. *Ibid.*, Definitions, 15, "Money transmission," accessed August 1, 2022.

c. Conducting the business of receiving money for obligors for the purpose of paying obligors' bills, invoices, or accounts.

Under the Iowa Uniform Money Services Act, some cryptocurrency businesses, such as the New Jersey crypto lending platform, BlockFi, have obtained money services licenses:

> We're excited to announce that we've received our Money Services License in Iowa.[362]

These licenses are issued and supervised by the Iowa Division of Banking.[363] However, it is also important to note that many regulations relating to the sale of securities, which can relate to some cryptocurrency businesses (such as that of BlockFi LLC), are regulated by the Iowa Insurance Division.

It should be noted that on June 29, 2022, the Iowa Insurance Division issued the following press release on its website:[364]

> Iowa Insurance Commissioner Doug Ommen recently issued a consent order against BlockFi Lending LLC (BlockFi) after BlockFi offered and sold securities in Iowa that were not registered or permitted for sale in Iowa as well as offering and selling securities in Iowa without being registered as a broker-dealer or agent. BlockFi was ordered to pay at administrative fine in the amount of $943,000 and cease and desist from making any untrue statement of material facts regarding securities.
>
> ***
>
> The consent order is part of the conclusion of a broader multi-state investigation, where The US Securities and Exchange Commissioner (SEC) and state securities regulators from 53 jurisdictions came together as members of the North American Securities Administrators Association (NASAA) to investigate. BlockFi will pay settlements of up to $50 million in total to the 53 jurisdictions following the investigation as well as another $50 million to the SEC. The consent order found that in addition to offering and selling unregistered securities, BlockFi made misrepresentations and omissions about the level of risk in its loan portfolio which did not allow investors to have complete and accurate information to evaluate the risk of the investment. Specifically, BlockFi stated in multiple website posts that its institutional loans were "typically" over-collateralized when in fact most of the loans were not over-collateralized.

[17] Kansas

Under the Kansas Money Transmitter Act, "monetary value" is defined as "a medium of exchange, whether or not redeemable in money."[365]

---

362. BlockFi, online at blockfi.com, June 28, 2022.
363. Bloomberg Law, *supra*, "Iowa." *See*, Iowa Code section 533C.103.
364. Iowa Insurance Division, Press Release, "BlockFi Ordered to Pay More Than $943,000 in Iowa for Failing to Register Securities," online at: iid.iowa.gov, June 29, 2022.
365. Kansas Statutes, K.S.A. 9-508, Kansas Money Transmitter Act, Definitions, (g), 2021 Kansas Consumer & Mortgage Lending Law Book, online at: osbckansas.org, accessed August 2, 2022.

"Money transmission" is defined as:[366]

> to engage in the business of the sale or issuance of payment instruments or of receiving money or monetary value for transmission to a location within or outside the United States by wire, facsimile, electronic means or any other means, except that money transmission does not include currency exchange where no transmission of money occurs.

"Payment instrument" is defined as:[367]

> any electronic or written check, draft, money order, travelers check or other electronic or written instrument or order for the transmission or payment of money, sold or issued to one or more persons, whether or not such instrument is negotiable. The term "payment instrument" does not include any credit card voucher, any letter of credit or any instrument which is redeemable by the issuer in goods or services.

Digital currency is thought to come within the definition of money transmission that requires a license under Kansas law. However, guidance issued by the Office of the State Banking Commissioner indicates that a license would not be required if the transmission of the cryptocurrency is of a "decentralized digital currency." However, if the currency of a sovereign government is involved, a license might be required.[368]

The licensing requirements for money transmission are set out in the Kansas Statutes at K.S.A 9-509.[369] Subsection (a) says:

> no person shall engage in the business of selling, issuing or delivering its payment instrument, check, draft, money order, personal money order, bill of exchange, evidence of indebtedness or other instrument for the transmission or payment of money or otherwise engage in the business of money transmission with a resident of this state, or, except as provided in K.S.A. section 9-510, and amendments thereto, act as agent for another in the transmission of money as a service or for a fee or other consideration, unless a person files a complete application and obtains a license from the commissioner.[370]

Other details regarding money transmission licensing are set out in the other subsections of K.S.A. 9-509.[371]

366. *Ibid.*, Definitions, (h), 2021 Kansas Consumer & Mortgage Lending Law Book, online at: osbckansas.org, accessed August 2, 2022.
367. *Ibid.*, Definitions, (j), 2021 Kansas Consumer & Mortgage Lending Law Book, online at: osbckansas.org, accessed August 2, 2022.
368. Bloomberg Law, *supra*, "Kansas." *See*, Office of the State Bank Commissioner, "Regulatory Treatment of Virtual Currencies Under the Kansas Money Transmitter Act." Also *see*: K.S.A. section 9-508(h).
369. Kansas Statutes, K.S.A. 9-509, Kansas Money Transmitter Act, 2021 Kansas Consumer & Mortgage Lending Law Book, online at: osbckansas.org, accessed August 2, 2022.
370. *Ibid.*, (a), 2021 Kansas Consumer & Mortgage Lending Law Book, online at: osbckansas.org, accessed August 2, 2022.
371. *Ibid.*, (b)-(j), 2021 Kansas Consumer & Mortgage Lending Law Book, online at: osbckansas.org, accessed August 2, 2022.

[18] Kentucky

The Kentucky Department of Financial Institutions is responsible for the supervision and regulation of various industries that perform services for the citizens of Kentucky.[372]

Kentucky money transmission law does not expressly refer to cryptocurrency. The Kentucky Money Transmitter Act[373] defines "Money transmission" as:

> engaging in the business of receiving money or monetary value to transmit, deliver, or instruct to be transmitted or delivered, money or monetary value to another location inside or outside the United States by any and all means, including but not limited to wire, facsimile, electronic transfer, or issuing stored value.

"Money transmitter"[374] is defined as:

> a person engaged in money transmission.

"Monetary value"[375] is defined as:

> a medium of exchange whether or not redeemable in money.

"Money"[376] is defined as:

> a medium of exchange that is authorized or adopted by the United States or a foreign government or other recognized medium of exchange, including a monetary unit of account established by an intergovernmental organization or by agreement between two (2) governments.

However, cryptocurrency dealers, such as Coinbase and others, have obtained Kentucky money services licenses from the Department of Financial Institutions.[377]

Recently, Kentucky has been offering incentives to attract the cybercurrency industry to bring business there. It is thought that this might help revive some of the business that has been lost by the decline of the coal mining industry in the state. It is reported that the Governor signed two laws in 2021 to favor the crypto mining industry. The first extended clean energy incentives to crypto companies if they invested a minimum of US$ 1,000,000 in capital in Kentucky. Another bill gave cryptocurrency miners a number of tax breaks.[378]

---

372. Kentucky Department of Financial Institutions, online at: kentucky.gov.
373. Kentucky Revised Statutes, Kentucky MTA, KRS 286 11-003, Definitions for subtitle, (17) "Money transmission," online at: apps.legislature.ky.gov.
374. *Ibid.*, (18) "Money transmitter," online at: apps.legislature.ky.gov.
375. *Ibid.*, (15) "Monetary value," online at: apps.legislature.ky.gov.
376. *Ibid.*, (16) "Money," online at: apps.legislature.ky.gov.
377. Bloomberg Law, *supra*, "Kentucky." *See*: KRS 286.11-003.
378. Jacquelyn Melinek, "Bitcoin Miners Are Dusting off Kentucky Coal Towns, Spurred by State Crypto Tax Incentives," TechCrunch, online at: techcrunch.com, March 30, 2022.

[19] Louisiana

In general, engaging in virtual currency business in Louisiana is expressly regulated and may require a license. To govern this business, Louisiana has enacted the Virtual Currency Businesses Act[379] (Act). Regulation under the Act is under the authority of the Louisiana Office of Financial Institutions.[380] The Act defines virtual currency as follows:[381]

> "(a) Virtual currency" means a digital representation of value that is used as a medium of exchange, unit of account, or store of value, and that is not legal tender, whether or not denominated in legal tender.
> "(b) Virtual currency" shall not include any of the following:
> "(i) a transaction in which a merchant grants, as part of an affinity or rewards program, value that cannot be taken from or exchanged with the merchant for legal tender, bank credit, or virtual currency."
> "(ii) a digital representation of value issued by or on behalf of a publisher and used solely within an online game, game platform, or family of games sold by the same publisher or offered on the same game platform."

The Act says:[382]

> A person shall not engage in virtual currency business activity, or hold itself out as being able to engage in virtual currency business activity with or on behalf of a resident unless the person is one of the following:
> (1) Licensed in this state by the department pursuant to R.S. 6:1385
> (2) Registered with the department and operating pursuant to R.S. 6:1390.
> (3) Exempt from licensure or registration pursuant to R.S. 6:1383. Acts 2020 No. 341, Section 1.

The Act defines virtual currency business activity as follows:[383]

> "Virtual currency business activity" means any of the following:
>
> (a) Exchanging, transferring, or storing virtual currency or engaging in virtual currency administration, whether directly or through an agreement with a virtual currency control services vendor.
> (b) Holding electronic precious metals or electronic certificates representing interests in precious metals on behalf of another person or issuing shares or electronic certificates representing interests in precious metals.

Definitions of "virtual currency administration" and "virtual currency control services vendor" are also provided by the Act.[384]

---

379. Louisiana Revised Statutes, Chapter 21, Virtual Currency Businesses, RS 6:1381, et. seq., online at: legis.la.gov., accessed August 4, 2022
380. Louisiana Revised Statutes, RS 6:1382, Definitions, (3) "Department," online at: legis.la.gov., August 4, 2022
381. *Ibid.*, (20) "Virtual currency," online at: legis.la.gov., August 4, 2022
382. Louisiana Revised Statutes, RS 6:1384, "Licensure, general," online at: legis.la.gov., accessed August 4, 2022
383. Louisiana Revised Statutes, RS 6:1382, "Definitions" (22), online at: legis.la.gov., accessed August 4, 2022
384. *Ibid.*, (21) and (23), online at: legis.la.gov., accessed August 4, 2022

(c) Exchanging one or more digital representations of value within one or more online games, game platforms, or family of games for either of the following:
  (i) virtual currency offered by or on behalf of the same publisher from which the original digital representation of value was received.
  (ii) "Legal tender or bank credit outside the online game, game platform, or family of games offered by or on behalf of the same publisher from which the original digital representation of value was received."

In June of 2022, the Governor of Louisiana signed a Legislative bill:[385]

> To allow financial institutions and trust companies to serve as custodians of digital assets ... .

The provisions of the bill permit banks and trust companies to provide safekeeping facilities for cryptocurrency and other digital assets. In connection with that, those that provide those services are required to have effective risk management systems and adequate insurance coverage.

Cryptocurrency business does require a license in Louisiana. Some exceptions are provided for situations such as cryptocurrency that is already regulated under the securities laws of Louisiana or for academic use or for personal purchases using virtual currency. State guidance says that cryptocurrency users (who are not "exchanging" the crypto for fiat currency, funds or other virtual currency) do require a money transmission license.[386]

[20] Maine

Section 6103 of the Maine Revised Statutes[387] says:

> 1. *License required.* On or after January 1st 1998, a person, except one exempt pursuant to section 6104, may not engage in the business of money transmission without a license as provided in this subchapter.

Money transmitters are required to get a license under the Maine Money Transmitter Act from the Maine Office of Consumer Credit Regulation.[388] Money transmission in Maine is governed by the Department of Professional and Financial Regulation. Under the heading "Consumer Credit Protection," the Department publishes the following about the requirements for a Money Transmitter License:

385. Louisiana House Bill No. 802, to be enacted as Chapter 22 of Title 6 of Louisiana Revised Statutes, Banks and Banking, sections 6:1401 and 1402, online at: legis.la.gov., accessed August 4, 2022
386. Bloomberg Law, *supra*, "Louisiana." *See*: La. Rev. Stat. Sections 6:1381 to 6:1394; 61383(B) and (C); 61032(13) and State of Louisiana Office of Financial Institutions, "Consumer and Investor Advisory on Virtual Currency" (August 2014), accessed May 5, 2022.
387. Maine Legislature, Maine Revised Statutes, Title 32: Professions and Occupations, Chapter 80: Money Transmitters and Check Cashers, section 6103, online at: legislature.maine.gov, accessed August 5, 2022.
388. Department of Professional and Financial Regulation, Consumer Credit Protection, online at maine.gov. *See* Statute 32 M.R.S. Section 6103. Forms and Applications are provided at this same website, accessed August 5, 2022.

> A person who does business of selling or issuing payment instruments or the business of receiving money for transmission or transmitting money within the United States or to a location abroad by any means, including, but not limited to, payment instrument, wire, facsimile or electronic transfer must be licensed with the Maine Office of Consumer Credit Regulation.
>
> All applicants must submit an application and application fee of $500 plus $50.00 for each delegate up to $2500, show a net worth of not less than $100,000, then an additional worth of $50,000 for each authorized delegate up to $500,000, a surety bond, irrevocable letter of credit or other similar security device in the amount of $100,000 running to the administrator (in lieu of bond, with the approval of the administrator, applicants may deposit cash, interest bearing stocks and bonds, notes, debentures, etc.).

Maine's money transmission definition does expressly include "virtual currencies."[389] It says:

> 10. Money transmission. "Money transmission" means the business of selling or issuing payment instruments or the business of receiving money, including virtual currencies, for transmission or transmitting money, including virtual currencies, within the United States or to locations abroad by any means, including, but not limited to, payment instrument, wire, facsimile or electronic transfer.[390]

"Virtual currency" is defined as follows:[391]

> 15. "Virtual currency":
> A. Means a digital representation of value that:
> (1) Is used as a medium of exchange, unit of account or store of value; and
> (2) Is not legal tender, whether or not denominated in legal tender; and
> B. Does not include:
> (1) A transaction in which a merchant grants, as part of an affinity or rewards program, value that cannot be taken from or exchanged with the merchant for legal tender, bank credit or virtual currency; or
> (2) A digital representation of value issued by or on behalf of a publisher and used solely within an online game, game platform or family of games sold by the same publisher or offered on the same platform.

[21] Maryland

In Maryland, regulation of money transmission does include "transmission of virtual currency."

In Maryland, financial services are regulated by the Maryland Department of Labor's Office of the Commissioner of Financial Regulation.[392] among the businesses

389. *Ibid.*, accessed August 5, 2022.
390. Maine Legislature, Maine Revised Statutes, Title 32: Professions and Occupations, Chapter 80: Money Transmitters and Check Cashers, section 6102, Definitions, 10, online at: legislature-.maine.gov, accessed August 5, 2022.
391. *Ibid.*, 15, online at: legislature.maine.gov, accessed August 5, 2022.
392. Maryland Department of Labor, Office of the Commissioner of Financial Regulation, online at: dllr.state.md.us.

that the commissioner expressly states that it regulates are "Money transmission, including transmission of virtual currency."[393]

On its website, the Maryland Department of Labor sets out the Financial Regulation for "money transmitters." Their description says:

> "A *Money Transmitter* is a business that sells or issues payment instruments or prepaid access, or receives currency, funds, or other value that substitutes for currency and transfers currency, funds or other value that substitutes for currency to another person or a location within or outside the United States by any means, including electronically, through the Internet, through a mobile application, through a network of persons, or through an informal transfer system. A Money Transmitter also includes providing bill payer services or accelerated mortgage payment services."
>
> "This license is required for the principal executive office of any person (defined in Md. Code Ann., Fin. Inst., Section 1-101) engaging in the business of money transmission, unless the person is an authorized delegate who is authorized by a license to engage in the business of money transmission under the name of a licensee at any location other than the place of business specified in the license. Refer to Md. Code Ann. Fin. Inst. Section 12-401 et seq. for legal requirements. For more detailed information on this license type please proceed to the NMLS Resource Center."[394]

Binance and Coinbase are reported to have Maryland money transmitter licenses.[395] To conduct money transmission services in Maryland requires a money transmitter license. Maryland uses the Nationwide Mortgage Licensing System and Registry (NMLS) for its money transmitter applications and licenses.[396]

[22] Massachusetts

With respect to money services, a Foreign Transmittal Agency requires a license in Massachusetts. This applies to:

> all persons who engage or are financially interested in the business of receiving deposits of money for the purpose of transmitting the same or equivalents thereof to foreign countries.

"Foreign Transmittal Agency" is defined as:[397]

> a person who engages or is financially interested in the business of receiving deposits of money for the purposes of transmitting the same or equivalents thereof to foreign countries; however, that the following activities shall not constitute activities requiring licensure by the division as a foreign transmittal agency:

393. *Ibid.*, "Regulated Financial Services Industries and Activities—Financial Regulation," online at: dllr.state.md.us.
394. Maryland Department of Labor, Money Transmitters—Financial Regulation," online at: dllr.state.md.us., accessed August 5, 2022.
395. Bloomberg Law, *supra*, "Maryland." *See*: Md. Code. Fin. Inst. Section 12-401(n)(1).
396. Maryland Office of the Commissioner of Financial Regulation, online at dllr.state.md.us.
397. Mass.gov, 209 CMR 45.00: The licensing and regulation of money services businesses, online at: mass.gov/regulations, accessed August 8, 2022.

(1) The transmission of money or its equivalents that is not primarily for personal, family, or household purposes; or
(2) A transaction in which the recipient of the money or other monetary value is an agent of the payee pursuant to a written contract and delivery of the money or other monetary value to the agent satisfies the payers obligation to the payee.

Under Massachusetts law:

> Anyone who takes part in receiving deposits from Massachusetts consumers and transmitting the money to foreign countries needs a license from the Division of Banks (DOB). Anyone who sells or issues checks must be registered.[398]

The Massachusetts DOB has published a number of opinions on virtual currency transactions.[399]

Licenses are to be applied for through the NMLS.[400]

Massachusetts restricts its regulation of money transmission to transmission of money to foreign countries.[401]

Determining whether these licensing requirements have expanded or developed beyond what is described above will require consultation with competent Massachusetts legal counsel.

[23] Michigan

Under the Michigan Money Transmission Services Act, "Money transmission services" is defined as:[402]

> Selling or issuing payment instruments for closed loop prepaid access or prepaid access devices or vehicles or receiving money or monetary value for transmission. The term does not include the provision solely of delivery, online, or telecommunications services or network access.

Michigan regulators have stated that maintaining funds in an "e-wallet" requires a money transmission license.

The cryptocurrency exchanges Binance and Coinbase are reported to have Michigan money transmission licenses. This is not surprising because Michigan State guidance has stated that an "administrator or exchanger" of cryptocurrency does require a transmission license if that entity would require a money transmission license

398. Division of Banks, Apply for a money transmitter license, online at: www.mass.gov., accessed August 8, 2022.
399. Commonwealth of Massachusetts, General Laws, Chapter 169, Receipts of Deposits for Transmittal to Foreign Countries, section 6, Licenses: multi-state licensing system, online at: malegislature.govl, acc computer accessed August 8, 2022.
400. *Ibid.*, section 1, Application of chapter, online at: malegislature.govl, accessed August 8, 2022.
401. Bloomberg Law, *supra*, "Massachusetts." *See*: 209 CMR 45.02
402. Michigan Transmission Services Act, section 3, MCL 487.1003, accessed August 8, 2022.

under federal law. The federal regulation referred to is registration with the federal Financial Crimes Enforcement Network (FinCEN).[403]

[24] Minnesota

Money transmission in Minnesota is licensed and regulated by the Minnesota Department of Commerce (MDC). They regulate individuals and businesses that cash checks, transmit money, own and operate ATMs, and provide electronic funds transfers.[404]

Under Minnesota law, money transmission is defined as "selling or issuing payment instruments or engaging in the business of receiving money for transmission or transmitting money." Guidance from the MDC says that licenses are required by: "businesses that cash checks, transmit money, own and operate ATMs, and provide electronic funds transfers." It is reported that cryptocurrency exchanges including Binance and Coinbase have Minnesota money transmission licenses.[405]

The MDC website states:

> Persons engaged in the business of money transmission must obtain a license from the Department of Commerce. A licensee may conduct business in Minnesota at one or more locations, or through one or more authorized delegates, or both under a single license.[406]

Minnesota law also provides a list of exemptions from the licensing requirements including:[407]

(a) Authorized delegates of a licensee who have a contract with a licensee.
(b) The U.S. government.
(c) The U.S. Postal Service.
(d) The state or any political subdivision.
(e) Banks.
(f) Credit unions.
(g) Savings associations.
(h) Bank holding companies.

With respect to cryptocurrencies and other digital assets, the Minnesota government urges people to "Be Cautious of the Crypto Investment Craze."[408]

---

403. *See*, "Virtual Currency: What Consumers Need to Know," online at michigan.gov. Accessed May 5, 2022. Bloomberg Law, *supra*, "Michigan."
404. MDC, Money Transmission, online at: mn.gov, accessed August 16, 2022.
405. Bloomberg Law, *supra*, "Minnesota."
406. *See* Minnesota Commerce Department, "Money Transmission," online at mn.gov., accessed May 6, 2022.
407. *Ibid*.
408. *See* Minnesota Commerce Department, "Be Cautious of the Crypto Investment Craze," online at mn.gov, accessed August 16, 2022.

The MDC has published a guidance document on the application of Minnesota money transmission law to "virtual currencies" in August of 2021.[409] The MDC guidance says:

> "Selling or exchanging virtual currency for other types of virtual currency generally does not constitute 'selling or issuing payment instruments' because virtual currency is not a 'payment instrument'. ... Recently, only fiat currency-not virtual currency—is considered 'money' for purposes of the MMTA [Minnesota Money Transmitters Act]. ..."
>
> "Therefore, whether the Department of Commerce will require a license for transmitters of virtual currency depends on whether and how fiat currency is involved in the transactions. ...Certain virtual currency transactions involving fiat currency may subject operators to the licensing requirements of the MMTA. Persons operating businesses which receive a customer's fiat currency to facilitate an exchange for virtual currency by making the money available to a third-party seller of virtual currency are likely engaged in money transmission."[410]

[25] Mississippi

In Mississippi, the provisions of the MTA are supervised and regulated by the Mississippi Department of Banking and Consumer Finance.[411]

Mississippi law contains a definition of "monetary value" that appears broad enough to include digital assets such as cryptocurrency. It says that monetary value is "a medium of exchange whether or not redeemable in money."[412]

"Money transmission" is defined as meaning:

> to engage in the business of the sale or issuance of checks or receiving money or monetary value for transmission to a location within or outside the United States by any and all means, included but not limited to wire, facsimile or electronic transfer.[413]

The Mississippi MTA requires that, with some exceptions,[414] any person in the business of money transmission needs to first obtain a money transmission license.[415]

[26] Missouri

The relevant law in Missouri relates to an activity called "Sale of Checks-Money Orders." Under Missouri Sale of Checks Law, a "check" is defined as:

---

409. *See* Minnesota Commerce Department, Financial Institutions Division, "Re: Guidance on Minnesota Money Transmitters Act and Virtual Currency," online at mn.gov., accessed August 16, 2022.
410. *Ibid.*
411. Mississippi Department of Banking and Consumer Finance, online at: dbcf.ms.gov.
412. Mississippi MTA, MS Code, section 75-15-3(f).
413. *See* MS Code, section 75-15-3(g).
414. *See* MS Code, section 75-15-7.
415. MS Code, section 75-15-5.

> any instrument for the transmission or payment of money and shall also include any electronic means of transmitting or paying money."[416]

This appears to be broad enough to cover transactions in cryptocurrency and other digital assets. Some cryptocurrency exchanges such as Binance are reported to have a Sale of Checks License for Missouri.[417]

Inquiries can be made to the Missouri Division of Finance.[418]

[27] Montana

As of this writing, Montana has not yet enacted a money transmission statute.

A money transmitter's license is not yet required in Montana:

> There is currently no legislation from the Montana Division of Banking regulating money service businesses (MSBs). MSBs do not have to be licensed with the Division. However, they do need to be registered as a business with the Montana Secretary of State.[419]

[28] Nebraska

Nebraska Money Transmitters Act (NMTA) is set out in the 2021 Nebraska Revised Statutes, Chapter 8—Money and Banking.[420]

Under the NMTA, "money transmission" is defined as:

> the business of the sale or issuance of payment instruments or stored value or of receiving money or monetary value for transmission to a location within or outside the United States by any and all means, including wire, facsimile or electronic transfer. Notwithstanding any other provision of law, money transmission also includes bill payment services not limited to the right to receive payment of any claim for another but does not include bill payment services in which an agent of a payee receives money or monetary value on behalf of such payee.[421]

"Monetary value" is defined as:

> "Monetary value" means "a medium of exchange, whether or not redeemable in money."
>
> Nebraska law requires money transmitters operating in that state to obtain a license. Licensees under the MTA need to obtain license and registration through

416. Missouri Sale of Checks Law, section 361.700 (1), "Laws & Regulations," online for download at: finance.mo.gov.
417. Bloomberg Law, *supra.*, "Missouri."
418. Missouri Division of Finance, Email: finance@dof.mo.gov.
419. "Money Service Businesses," Montana Division of Banking, online at: banking.mt.gov /moneytransmitters, accessed May 10, 2022.
420. NMTA, Chapter 8, Article 28, sections 8-2701-8-2748, available for download online at: ndbf.nebraska.gov.
421. NMTA, section 8-2716, Money transmission, defined.

> the Nationwide Mortgage Licensing System and Registry.[422] The licensing laws are also drafted to "ensure that money transmitters engage in ethical business practices."[423]
>
> In May of 2021, Nebraska signed into law the Nebraska Financial Innovation Act. This is intended to create "digital asset depositories or banks that trade cryptocurrency in the state."

In addition, other banks have an opportunity to hold and trade in cryptocurrency. This innovative financial area is to be under the supervision of the Nebraska Department of Banking and Finance. Nebraska became the second state, after Wyoming, to permit banks to hold cryptocurrency.[424]

It was reported that a cryptocurrency trading company, Telcoin announced that it would establish a crypto bank in the state of Nebraska. At the time, Telcoin was based in Tokyo, but the CEO of the company said he would consider moving his residency to Nebraska.[425]

Despite the new law, it is reported that there was still some confusion as to how Nebraska would classify cryptocurrency. A professor at the University of Nebraska who is said to be an expert in blockchain technology said:

> We do not pay our taxes in crypto currencies. They work as financial instruments. We deal with cryptocurrencies and then once we decide to pay our taxes, we have to convert that into real currency, such as dollars and then pay our taxes. It is a currency, it's a special type of currency that operates as a financial instrument, as a stock.[426]

[29] Nevada

The Nevada legislative definition of "check." says:

"'Check' means any check, draft, money order or other instrument used for the transmission or payment of money."[427] This appears broad enough to include virtual currency:

> A person shall not engage in the business of selling or issuing checks or of receiving for transmission or transmitting money or credits unless the person is licensed pursuant to this chapter.[428]

Licensees are also required to post bonds or deposits for the conduct of business in the state in amounts of between US$ 10,000 and US$ 250,000.[429]

---

422. NMTA, section 8-2730, Licensee; license and registration through Nationwide Mortgage Licensing System and Registry; department; powers; director; reports; duties.
423. NMTA, section 8-2724, Licensure requirement; applicability.
424. Aaron Bonderson, "State Legislature's Cryptocurrency Bill Designed to Regulate the New Financial Sector," Nebraska Public Media, online at: nebraskapublicmedia.org.
425. *Ibid.*
426. *Ibid.*, quoting Dr. Jaques Bou Abdu, Professor at the University of Nebraska at Kearney.
427. Nevada statute: NRS 671.010.1., online at leg.state.nv.us, accessed May 10, 2022.
428. Nevada statute: NRS 671.040.
429. Nevada Statutes, NRS 671.100 and NRS 671.110.

The Nevada Financial Institutions Division (NFID) has indicated that the above statutory requirements have undergone some modification since they were put in place. They issued a "Statement on the Regulation of Cryptocurrency in Nevada," which says in part:

> It is important to note the NFID issues a licensure determination based upon a review of an entity's specific business model in order to determine the relevant Chapter of the Nevada States (NRS) the entity is regulated under, if any. Generally, an entity engaging in the business of selling or issuing checks or of receiving for transmission or transmitting money or credits is required to have a license under NRS 671. However, if an entity proposes to serve as a digital custodian for any form of digital currency, then the business may be regulated as a trust company under NRS Chapter 669.[430]

[30] New Hampshire

Under New Hampshire law any person who does not qualify for an exemption and who transmits money from New Hampshire to persons within New Hampshire needs to obtain a money transmitter license from the state banking department.[431]

The legal definition of "money transmission" in New Hampshire means:

"(a) engaging in the business of selling or issuing payment instruments or stored value; or
"(b) receiving currency or monetary value for transmission to another location."[432]

The New Hampshire legal definition of "monetary value" is "a medium of exchange, whether or not redeemable in currency."[433] This definition appears broad enough to include cryptocurrency, although it is not clear whether all forms of digital assets such as "tokens" or NFTs would also be included.

However, they may be included in the NH definition of "convertible virtual currency" which is: "a digital representation of value" that:

"(a) Can be a medium of exchange, a unit of account, and/or a store of value;
"(b) Has an equivalent value in real currency or acts as a substitute for real currency;
"(c) May be centralized or decentralized; and
"(d) Can be exchanged for currency or other convertible virtual currency."[434]

The licensing statute also includes a fairly long list of "exemptions,"[435] some of which are:

430. NFID, online at: fid.nv.gov, accessed May 10, 2022.
431. New Hampshire Statute, RSA 399-G3, NH Rev. Stat. Section 399-G3 (2015), online at: law.justia.com, accessed May 12, 2022.
432. New Hampshire Statute, RSA 399-G1, Definitions, online at: gencourt.state.nh.us, accessed May 12, 2022.
433. *Ibid.*
434. *Ibid.*
435. New Hampshire Statute, RSA 399-G3, Exemptions, online at: gencourt.state.nh.us, accessed May 12, 2022.

- properly qualified banks, trust companies, credit unions, insurance companies, etc.;
- federal and state government departments;
- retailers "issuing stored value credits or gift cards";
- licensed "debt adjusters" Performing limited function limited money transmission functions; and
- "Other persons not within the intent of this chapter as the commissioner may designate by rule or order."

The status of cryptocurrencies and digital assets in New Hampshire has endured a considerable degree of uncertainty for some time, but the state governor undertook a serious effort to clarify things early in 2022.

Prior to that, a law was passed in 2016 requiring traders in digital currency to be licensed and bonded as "money transmitters."

In February of 2022, the Governor of New Hampshire signed an Executive Order establishing a Governor's Commission on cryptocurrencies and digital assets.[436] The purpose of establishing a governor's Commission was stated by the governor to be:

> "New Hampshire is a hub of financial innovation and this Executive Order will further our commitment to attracting high quality banking and financial businesses in a safe and responsible manner."
>
> "Federal and state governments must work to bring legal and regulatory certainty to the digital asset industry because clear rules of the road foster technology and innovation."

The Commission will reportedly focus on:

> reviewing and investigating the current status of United States federal and state laws and regulatory rules, and laws of other non-United States jurisdictions applicable ... to banks and other businesses that provide services with respect to cryptocurrencies and digital assets.

New Hampshire has been the site of some hard times for certain cryptocurrency businesses. In March of 2021, it was reported that the FBI arrested six people in New Hampshire for operating an unlicensed cryptocurrency exchange business in the town of Keene. Some were also alleged to be engaging in wire fraud, money laundering and other financial crimes.[437]

---

436. Kevin Helms, "NH Governor Signs Executive Order to Bring 'Regulatory Certainty' to Cryptocurrency Industry" online at: news.bitcoin.com, February 13, 2022. *See also*, Press Release, February 9, 2022, "Governor Chris Sununu Establishes Governor's Commission on Cryptocurrencies and Digital Assets," online at: governor.nh.gov/, accessed May 11, 2022.
437. Asher Klein, "FBI Arrests 6 Over NH Cryptocurrency Business," online at: nbcboston.com, March 16, 2022.

[31] New Jersey

New Jersey laws define "payment instrument" broadly enough so that cryptocurrencies are covered by the state's money transmission regulations. It is reported that both Binance and Coinbase have obtained money transmitter licenses in New Jersey.

The State of New Jersey Department of Banking and Insurance requires that a money transmitter license must be obtained by any person engaging in the following activities in that state:[438]

"(1) the sale or issuance of payment instruments for a fee, commission, or other benefit (payment instruments include checks, drafts, money orders, travelers checks or any other instrument or written order for the transmission or payment of money)

"(2) the receipt of money for transmission or the transmitting of money within the United States or to locations abroad by any and all means, including but not limited to payment instrument, wire, facsimile, electronic transfer, or otherwise, for a fee, commission or other benefit

"(3) the receipt of money for obligors for the purpose of paying obligor's bills, invoices or accounts for a fee, commission or other benefit paid by the obliger."[439]

[32] New Mexico

In New Mexico, no one may "engage in the business of money transmission or advertise, solicit or hold itself out as providing money transmission unless such person":

- is licensed; or
- or is an "authorized delegate" of a licensee.[440]

Under New Mexico law,[441] "money transmission" is defined as:

selling or issuing payment instruments, stored value or receiving money or monetary value for transmission.

"Payment instrument" is defined as:

a check, draft, money order, travelers check or other instrument for the transmission or payment of money or monetary value, whether or not negotiable. "Payment instrument" does not include a credit card voucher, letter of credit or instrument that is redeemable by the issuer in goods or services.

438. State of New Jersey Department of Banking & Insurance, "Foreign Money Transmitter/Money Transmitter, online at: state.nj.us, accessed May 12, 2022.
439. *Ibid.*
440. New Mexico Statutes, NM Stat. Section 58-32-201 (2018) Definitions, online at: nmonesource.com, accessed 13 May 2022.
441. *Ibid.* Section 58-32-102 (2018) Definitions, online at: nmonesource.com, accessed 13 May 2022.

New Mexico interprets "payment instrument" as including cryptocurrency. The definition also appears wide enough to include other digital assets which can be interpreted as representing "stored value."

The amount of the bond varies according to the business of the applicant, but it will be the larger of:[442]

- US$ 300,000.
- 1% of the total annual dollar volume of business in New Mexico.
- The projected total volume of business in New Mexico for the first year in which the applicant is licensed.

The maximum bond will not exceed US$ 2 million except where the state determines that the applicant's financial position is not satisfactory, which may require a bond as high as US$ 5 million.[443]

[33] New York

In New York, both the state Attorney General and the New York State Department of Financial Services (NYDFS) have taken strong roles in the regulation of cryptocurrency. Nevertheless, there is still some uncertainty as to exactly what the limits of the regulations are. Part of the problem is that some of the regulation overlaps in ways that cause confusion.[444]

Part of the problem is that day-to-day regulation is to a large extent left to the states because, although a number of federal regulatory agencies regulate digital assets in different ways (SEC, CFTC, Controller of the Currency, etc.), there is no single federal regulator providing comprehensive and consistent overall regulation.[445]

New York, in an effort to become a leading location for digital business has adopted a number of regulations to accomplish that goal.

In June of 2015, New York adopted a regulation called the "BitLicense."[446] In that month, the NYDFS started granting BitLicenses to virtual currency firms that had completed the required application procedure. These BitLicense regulations were applicable to activities relating to either the State of New York or New York State residents. Instead of attempting to make distinctions between types of digital assets based on traditional financial regulation categories such as "security" or "commodity," the BitLicense regulation applied to:

> any type of digital unit that is used as a medium of exchange or a form of digitally stored value. Virtual currency shall be broadly construed to include digital units of

442. *Ibid.* Section 58-32-203 (2018) Definitions, online at: nmonesource.com, accessed 13 May 2022.
443. *Ibid.*
444. Brian K. Mahanna, Zachery Goldman, Ariel E. Dobkin and Aric Jain, "Cryptocurrency at a Regulatory Crossroads in New York," New York Law Journal, online, December 2, 2021, accessed May 16, 2022.
445. *Ibid.*
446. 23 NYCRR Part 200.

exchange that: have a centralized repository or administrator; Are decentralized and have no centralized repository or administrator; Or may be created or obtained by computing or manufacturing effort. Virtual currency shall not be construed to include any of the following:

(1) digital units that:
   i. are used solely within online gaming platforms;
   ii. have no market or application outside of those gaming platforms;
   iii. cannot be converted into, or redeemed for, fiat currency or virtual currency; and
   iv. may or may not be redeemable for real-world goods, services, discounts, or purchases;
(2) digital units that can be redeemed for goods, services, discounts, or purchases as part of a customer affinity or rewards program with the issuer and or other designated merchants or can be redeemed for digital units with another customer affinity or rewards program, but cannot be converted into, or redeemed for, Fiat currency or virtual currency;
(3) Digital units as part of prepaid cards.

"Virtual currency business activity" is defined as:

the conduct of any one of the following types of activities involving New York or a New York resident:

(1) receiving a virtual currency for transmission or transmitting virtual currency, except where the transaction is undertaken for non-financial purposes and does not involve the transfer of more than a nominal amount of virtual currency;
(2) Storing, holding, or maintaining custody or control of virtual currency on behalf of others;
(3) Buying and selling virtual currency as a customer business;
(4) Performing exchange services as a customer business; or
(5) controlling, administering, or issuing virtual currency.

"Lead development and dissemination of software in and of itself does not constitute virtual currency business activity."[447]

Applying for a BitLicense in New York is an intensive process. A lot of documentation must be provided, and the DFS undertakes detailed background checks on the business, its history and the history of the people behind business. Details about the application process are set out in New York Statute 23 CRR-NY 200.4.

However, trading in cryptocurrency was not always smooth sailing in New York. Despite the stated desire to encourage the growth of innovative financial activity in New York and the establishment of a regulatory system that encourages digital asset business, the DFS does strictly enforce anti-fraud regulations against digital businesses that it believes to be betraying the public trust.

In 2018, the DFS brought cases against Bitfinex and Tether alleging that they were making false statements about large losses suffered by Bitfinex and Bitfinex's problems in accommodating customer withdrawals. In that case, the court ultimately ruled that Tether can be regulated as a "commodity" under New York law. The case was settled

447. WESTLAW, New York Codes, Rules and Regulations, 23 CRR-NY 200.2, online, accessed May 16, 2022.

by payment of an US$ 18.5 million penalty and imposition of injunctions including a bar to Bifinex and Tether doing any trading with New Yorkers.[448]

In September of 2021, the New York Attorney General:

> secured a judgement against the virtual currency trading platform Coinseed, ... that permanently halts their illegal and fraudulent operations and puts in place a permanent receiver to protect investors funds.[449]

In the first half of 2022, three founders of a cryptocurrency exchange operating in New York called the "Bitcoin Mercantile Exchange" (BitMEX) pled guilty in Manhattan federal court to various violations of federal law relating to currency trading including anti-money laundering regulations under the BSA. The investigation in this case was reportedly carried out by the FBI's New York Money Laundering Investigation Squad in cooperation with the CFTC. The prosecution was conducted by U.S. Attorney for the Southern District of New York's Money Laundering and Transnational Criminal Enterprises Unit.[450]

[a] New York City

Following the example of Miami[451] the Mayor of New York City, Eric Adams, who took office in January of 2022, said he wishes to make New York City the center of the cryptocurrency market. He has even suggested that city employees should be paid in cryptocurrency and that lessons about cryptocurrency should be taught in New York schools. Mr. Adams is promoting a cryptocurrency for the city to be called "NYC Coin." Learning that the mayor of Miami was doing so, Mr. Adams also asked to be paid in Bitcoin for his first three months' salary. Mr. Adams tweeted:

> In New York we always go big, so I am going to take my first THREE paychecks in Bitcoin when I become Mayor. NYC is going to be the center of the cryptocurrency industry and other fast growing, innovative industries! Just wait![452]

[34] North Carolina

In North Carolina, money transmission is regulated by the North Carolina Commissioner of Banks. A "money transmitter" is defined as:

> A business that helps a person to send and receive money within the United States or abroad, typically by means of wire transfer, money order, or stored value card.

---

448. Brian K. Mahanna, Zachery Goldman, Ariel E. Dobkin and Aric Jain, *supra*.
449. New York Attorney General, "Attorney General James Shuts Down Virtual Currency Trading Platform and Stops Cryptocurrency CEO From Continuing Fraudulent Conduct," online at: ag.ny.gov, September 13, 2021.
450. DOJ, U.S. Attorney's Office, Southern District of New York. "Third Founder Of Cryptocurrency Exchange Pleads Guilty to Bank Secrecy Act Violations," press release, online, March 9, 2022, accessed March 16, 2022.
451. *See* discussion of Florida, *supra*.
452. Eric Adams, Twitter, 5.25 PM, November 4, 2021.

> Money transmitters must have a license to operate and are regulated by the Office of the Commissioner of Banks.[453]

The Office of the Commissioner of Banks has also posted online a "Consumer Alert: Virtual Currencies" which is intended to caution those using virtual currencies to educate themselves about virtual currencies before buying or investing in cryptocurrencies.[454]

In the alert, "virtual currency" is defined as:

> Virtual currency is an electronic form of monetary value that does not have all the attributes of a real currency. There are many examples of virtual currency, such as Bitcoin and Litecoin, and other forms of virtual currency continue to appear in the market.

"Most virtual currencies are based on computer cryptography and derive their values solely from the market's perception of their value. These currencies are:

- not backed by any physical commodity, such as gold or silver;
- not backed by the United States or any other national government;
- not legal tender for debts; and
- not insured by the FDIC [Federal Deposit Insurance Company] or any other government agency."[455]

The Office of the Commissioner Banks (NCCOB) also states that it is "working diligently to license companies who promise to exchange real world currency for virtual currencies." It states that it is only these licensed companies that are in a position to provide some of the consumer protections available "for traditional money transmission."[456]

The NCCOB urges potential consumers of virtual currency to consider the following before buying or investing:

- Consumer Protections: Not all are available for virtual currencies. Consumers need to understand that they could lose the funds invested in virtual currencies.
- Price volatility.
- Possibility of theft.
- Limited access.
- Investor protection.
- Tax issues.

453. North Carolina Commissioner of Banks, "Money Transmitters Overview," online at: nccob.org., accessed May 23, 2022.
454. *Ibid.*
455. *Ibid.*
456. *Ibid.*

With respect to all of the above issues, the NCCOB is at pains to point out that virtual currencies can present different and sometimes more difficult problems than fiat currencies and, as a result, the risks of virtual currencies are significantly greater.[457]

On the web, the NCCOB provides a list of authorized money transmitters licensed in North Carolina.[458]

The term "money transmission" under North Carolina law does expressly include "virtual currency." The definition of money transmission is stated as follows:

> Money Transmission—to engage in the business of any of the following:
>
> a. sale or issuance of payment instruments or stored value primarily for personal, family, or household purposes; or
> b. Receiving money or monetary value for transmission or holding funds incidental to transmission within the United States or to locations abroad by any and all means, including payment instrument, stored value, wire, facsimile, or electronic transfer, primarily for personal, family, or household purposes. This includes maintaining control of virtual currency on behalf of others.

[35] North Dakota

The Official Portal for North Dakota State Government states:

> The purchase, sale, or exchange of virtual currency does not in and of itself require a money transmitter license. However, other activities related to these business lines may trigger this requirement, such as the transmission of fiat currency denominated assets to third parties.[459]

That website also answers a number of questions relating to the relationship of money transmission and cryptocurrency in North Dakota. The general attitude of the ND government seems to be that for many types of transactions involving cryptocurrency a license will not be needed.

However, anyone wishing to understand the position of North Dakota law on cryptocurrency will need to consult qualified local counsel on this issue.

The State Government has expressed considerable interest in attracting crypto-related business, such as crypto mining, to the state. It may surprise some to learn that North Dakota offers a big attraction for data centers and cryptocurrency miners—the weather.[460] On the US's border with Canada and being a place that experiences very cold winters, the cost of running cooling equipment for large arrays of computers is considerably less than other places in the United States such as Arizona (one of the

457. *Ibid.*
458. *Ibid.*
459. Official Portal for North Dakota State Government, Financial Institutions, "Frequently Asked Questions—Non-Depository," online at: nd.gov/dfi, accessed 28 June 2022.
460. Amy R. Sisk, "Cold North Dakota Ideal for Hot Cryptocurrency Data Centers," The Bismark Tribune, reported by the Associated Press, online at: usnews.com, January 22, 2022, accessed June 27, 2022.

hottest places on Earth),[461] or California (home to Furnace Creek—officially the hottest place on Earth).[462]

However, there is a concern in North Dakota communities:

> "The topic came up at the Bismarck City Commission meeting earlier this month [January 2022]. City officials have fielded inquiries from companies looking for spots for data centers in recent months, but Bismarck's ordinances do not allow for the standalone facilities. ... .
>
> "Data centers already exist in the city, but they are attached to businesses such as hospitals and telecom companies. ... .
>
> "The fans associated with a large standalone data center could generate a lot of noise, and city officials say that the facilities inquiring about coming to Bismarck may or may not place employees on site. Officials have expressed concerns about the potential for data centers to catch fire, as has happened in other North Dakota communities such as at a Grand Forks computer server farm in 2019."[463]

The state government of North Dakota has expressed a keen desire to attract cryptocurrency businesses including cryptocurrency miners to the state. Officials from the North Dakota Commerce Department (NDCD) attended the Miami Bitcoin conference in 2022 with the hope of attracting more Bitcoin mining business. The state has already attracted US$ 3 billion in crypto investment and hopes to attract about US$ 3 billion more.

It is not only the weather that attracts crypto miners. In recent years North Dakota has been home to an oil and gas production boom generated by the growing use of fracking to obtain hydrocarbons from previously unproductive shale oils and sands. One of the downsides to producing these hydrocarbons is that a large amount of unsalable natural gas is produced which is simply "flared" or burned off to dispose of it. The burning of all this gas is not only wasteful but also damaging to the environment because of the amount of carbon released into the atmosphere.

However, crypto miners who have set up data centers in or near these western North Dakota oil and gas fields have found that the waste gas can be used to generate relatively inexpensive energy to power their data centers. This provides North Dakota with a difficult-to-beat combination of attractions for data centers in that they can find both relatively inexpensive energy to power their datacenters, a cool climate to reduce the costs of cooling their equipment, and kudos from helping to reduce a serious climate change problem. This last also helps them ameliorate the criticism crypto miners receive because of the possible climate-damaging impact caused by their use of very large amounts of electricity, the generation of which can cause the release of increased amounts of carbon.

---

461. The city of Yuma, Arizona, has been identified as the hottest and sunniest city on Earth by the Automobile Association of America, Your AAA today, online at: magazine.northeast.aaa.com.
462. U.S. National Park Service, Death Valley, Weather, 134 degrees Fahrenheit, 57 degrees Celsius, recorded at Furnace Creek in Death Valley, California, online, at nps.gov.
463. *Ibid.*

This nonstandard way to generate power may not match Norway's ability to offer crypto miners 100% green, renewable energy from hydropower, but it is a step in the right direction.[464]

With respect to activities involving the use of digital currency, the NDCD urges caution. In June of 2022, it published online a memorandum entitled "Guidance for Digital Assets/Virtual Currency." It does not cover all transactions in virtual currency but is directed at North Dakota State-chartered credit unions. It states:

> The Department does not encourage or discourage a credit union's involvement in the virtual currency market, rather we are issuing this guidance to help ensure risks are considered and mitigated. This document contains the Department's current understanding of these risks. Any credit union intending to engage in, or currently engaged in, activities involving or related to digital assets should consult its legal counsel and Federal regulators as with any activity, credit unions must have procedures in place to appropriately measure, monitor, control, and mitigate potential risks.[465]

[36] Ohio

Under Ohio law, the term "transmit money" means:

> To receive, directly or indirectly and by any means, money, or its equivalent from a person and to deliver, pay or make accessible, by any means, method, manner, or device, whether or not a payment instrument is used, the money received or its equivalent to the same or another person, at the same or another time, and at the same or another place, ... [466]
>
> "Transmit money" also includes the sale of checks or other payment instruments.[467]

To operate as a money transmitter in Ohio, one needs to obtain a license required by the Ohio Division of Financial Institutions. The licensing procedure itself is supervised by the NMLS.

The NMLS states that a money transmitter license is required in Ohio under the following conditions:

> Any person, regardless of the location of that person, its facilities, or its agents, who receives directly or indirectly and by any means, money or its equivalent for transmission from a person located in this state is required to have this license.

464. Nicole Buckler, "North Dakota Hopes to Double the $3B of Clean Crypto Mining in the State," CoinTeleraph: The Future of Money, online at: cointelegraph.com, April 14, 2022.
465. Official Portal for North Dakota State Government, Financial Institutions, "Guidance for Digital Assets/Virtual Currency—Credit Unions," Wednesday, June 8, 2022—12:40 pm, online at: nd.gov/dfi, accessed June 28, 2022.
466. 2016 Ohio Revised Code, Title [13] XIII Commercial Transactions—Ohio Uniform Commercial Code Chapter 1315—Transmitters of Money: Check-Cashing Businesses section 1315.01 —Transmitters of money definitions, online at: Justia U.S. Law, www.justia.com, accessed May 24, 2022.
467. *Ibid.*

Ohio Revised Code Section 1315.02. Unless, that person receiving the money or its equivalent for transmission is a licensee, or otherwise exempt from licensure.[468]

[37] Oklahoma

Several cryptocurrency exchanges have acquired "money transmitter" licenses in Oklahoma. This indicates that they believe that their products and services are probably covered by that State's money transmitter laws.

In Oklahoma, any money transmitters that operate in the state need to have a money transmitter license under Oklahoma Code, Title: 85: Chapter 15, Subchapter 3-1.[469] Such licenses are obtained from the Oklahoma State Department of Banking (OSDB). Applicants must also obtain a bond.

Chapter 15 of the Oklahoma Code deals with Money Service Businesses. In the Definitions section,[470] "Money" is defined as:

> a medium of exchange that is authorized or adopted by the United States or a foreign government. The term includes a monetary unit of account established by an intergovernmental organization or by agreement between two or more governments.[471]

That definition, in itself, does not appear to cover privately issued digital assets such as cryptocurrencies tokens or NFTS. However, the Oklahoma Code definition of "Money transmission" stretches further.

"Money transmission" is defined as:

> receiving money for transmission of the money or value of the money by any means through a financial agency or institution, a Federal Reserve Bank or other facility of one or more Federal Reserve banks, the Board of Governors of the Federal Reserve System, or both or any other electronic network by which money or its value may be transmitted. Money transmission does not include the business of selling or issuing checks. That is required to be licensed under the Oklahoma Sale of Checks Act, Title 6, Section 2101 *et seq.*[472]

It appears to be the case that the words "money or the value of money" are intended to extend the definition of transmission of money beyond the simple transmission of what is described as "money" in the previous definition. Therefore, it is reasonable to assume that various digital assets including cybercurrency could also be covered. This may be the conclusion of the cybercurrency exchanges that have acquired Oklahoma money transmission licenses.

---

468. NMLS Resource Center, "State Licensing Requirements," "Ohio," online at: censingsystem.org, accessed May 24, 2022.
469. Oklahoma, "Administrative Rules Search," online at: rules.ok.gov/code, accessed May 26, 2022.
470. Oklahoma Code, Chapter 85: Chapter 15, Subchapter 1-2, "Definitions."
471. *Ibid.*, Subchapter 1-2 (12), "Money."
472. *Ibid.*, Subchapter 1-2 (13), "Money."

[38] Oregon

Financial services in Oregon are regulated by the Division of Financial Regulation (DFR).[473]

Oregon law does not require digital currency exchange companies, which turn cash into digital currency, to be licensed. However, companies that help transfer digital currency from one person to another are required to be licensed by the state as a money transmitter.[474]

Businesses that want to provide money transmission services in Oregon must have a license with the Division. Services include things such as electronic bill paying and wiring money within the US and abroad.[475]

Applications are submitted through the NMLS. An electronic surety bond is required, and a business must be registered with the Oregon Secretary of State.

The statutes governing money transmission are found under Chapter 717 of the Oregon Laws, "Money Transmission."[476]
Under that chapter, "Money transmission" is defined as:

> selling or issuing payment instruments or engaging in the business of receiving money for transmission, or transmitting money within the United States or to locations abroad by any and all means, including but not limited to payment instrument, wire, facsimile or electronic transfer.[477]

"Money" is defined as:

> a medium of exchange that:
>
> "(a) the United States or a foreign government authorizes or adopts; or
> "(b) represents a value that substitutes for currency but that does not benefit from government regulation requiring acceptance of the medium of exchange as legal tender.[478]

It seems likely that "a value that substitutes for currency" covers cryptocurrency and digital tokens that are exchangeable for benefits, including: goods, services or other currencies.

[39] Pennsylvania

The regulation of money transmission in Pennsylvania is under the Pennsylvania Money Transmitter Act (MTA), which states in Section 2:

---

473. Website online at: dfr.oregon.gov.
474. DFR, "Make Sure Digital Currency Exchange Is Licensed Within the State," online at: dfr.oregon.gov., January 22, 2018, accessed May 25, 2022.
475. Online at: dfr.oregon.gov, accessed May 25, 2022.
476. Online at: oregonlegislature.gov/bills_laws, accessed May 25, 2022.
477. *Ibid.* at: section 717.200 Definitions, subsection (11), accessed May 25, 2022.
478. *Ibid.*, subsection (10), accessed May 25, 2022.

> No person shall engage in the business of transmitting money by means of a transmittal instrument for a fee or other consideration without first having obtained a license from the Department of Banking nor shall any person engage in such business as an agent except as an agent of a person licensed or exempted under this act.[479]

The Pennsylvania Department of Banking and Securities (DoBS) has previously published a statement entitled "Money Transmitter Act Guidance for Virtual Currency Businesses," which said:

"Virtual currency, including Bitcoin, is not considered 'money' under the MTA." This view was issued in 2014,[480] but was confirmed in 2019. Local legal counsel should be consulted on whether this policy has changed since then.

[40] Rhode Island

In Rhode Island, "virtual currency" is expressly included under "currency transmission" requirements set out in Rhode Island laws. The relevant Rhode Island statute says:

> "Currency transmission" means engaging in the business of any of the following:
>
> (ii) "Receiving money or monetary value for transmission or holding funds by any and all means including payment instrument, stored value, wire, facsimile, or electronic transfer, primarily for personal, family, or household purposes. This includes maintaining control of virtual currency or transactions in virtual currency on behalf of others."[481]

A license for money transmission is required:[482]

> "(a) No person shall engage within this state in the business of: ... (3) providing currency transmission for a fee or other consideration ... without first obtaining a license or registration from the director or the director's designee. ... Special exemptions from licensing for each activity are contained in other chapters of this title."
>
> "(e) No person, except those exempt pursuant to [Section] 19-14.3-1, shall engage in the business of currency transmission in this state without a license as provided in this chapter."

Currency transmitter licenses for Rhode Island are obtained by application through the NMLS:[483]

479. Licensing Business of Transmitting Money or Credit, Act of 1965, P.L. 490, No. 249, section 2, Available as PDF download, online at: www.dobs.pa.gov., accessed May 26, 2022.
480. Documents, Newsletter 620, available as PDF for download.
481. JUSTIA, U.S. Law, online, 2021 Rhode Island General Laws, Title 19—Financial Institutions Chapter 19-14—Licensed Activities section 19-14-1—Definitions, accessed June 1, 2022.
482. *Ibid.*, section 19-14-2—Licenses required., accessed June 1, 2022.
483. State of Rhode Island, Department of Business Regulation, "All Other Licensees—Application, Forms & Other Information," online, dbr.ri.gov, accessed June 1, 2022.

"(f) A currency transmission licensee may conduct its business in this state at one or more locations, directly or indirectly owned, or through one or more authorized delegates, or both, pursuant to the license granted under this chapter."

"(g) A person is considered to be engaged in the business of currency transmission in this state if that person enters into a transaction with a person physically located in or resident in Rhode Island at the time the transaction is initiated."

The cryptocurrency exchange Binance was granted a Rhode Island currency transmitter license in May 2022.[484]

[41] South Carolina

South Carolina's view is that virtual currency is not really the same as "money" because it lacks the characteristics of a "medium of exchange." Therefore, virtual currency businesses do not need to be licensed in South Carolina.

However, certain financial products based on digital assets, such as cryptocurrency, can be considered securities in South Carolina and may not be sold in South Carolina, or in any U.S. jurisdiction, unless they are properly registered as securities.[485]

In 2022 a firm called BlockFi Lending LLC (BlockFi) agreed to a Consent Order requiring it to register its offerings as securities and to pay a US$ 50 million settlement. The Consent Order said:

> BlockFi is a New Jersey-based financial services company that offered and sold interest-bearing digital asset accounts called BlockFi Interest Accounts ("BIAs"), through which investors lend digital assets to BlockFi in exchange for BlockFi's promise to provide variable monthly interest payments ... BlockFi will cease and desist offering or selling BIA's or any security that is not registered, qualified or exempt to new clients in the United States, and BlockFi will cease accepting further investments or funds in the BIAs by current US clients, unless and until the BIAs or other securities are registered, qualified or otherwise exempt; and BlockFi shall pay up to a total of [$50 million] in settlement payments divided equally among the 50 states, the District of Columbia, Puerto Rico and the US Virgin Islands to each of the 53 jurisdictions that enter into a consent order pursuant to the terms of BlockFi's agreement with the Multistate Working Group; ... [486]

There have also been similar cases in South Carolina. For example, see the Voyager Digital group, Cease and Desist Order.[487]

Generally, it seems to be the case that although "money" regulations may not apply to cryptocurrency in South Carolina, securities regulations can apply to digital

484. Coincu, "Binance US Has Been Given a Rhode Island Currency Transmitter License," online at: news.concu.com, May 24, 2022.
485. *See*, Administrative Proceeding Before the Securities Commissioner of South Carolina, In the Matter of BlockFi Lending LLC, Respondent, Consent Order, Matter No. 20213960, March 4, 2022, accessed June 2, 2022.
486. *Ibid*.
487. *See*, Administrative Proceeding Before the Securities Commissioner of South Carolina, In the Matter of Voyager Digital Ltd, et al., Respondents, Order to Cease and Desist, Matter No. 20221067, April 6, 2022, accessed June 2, 2022.

asset-related financial products, including those related to cryptocurrencies. An investment guide published by the Office of the South Carolina Attorney General Securities Division says:

> Do not invest in cryptocurrency offerings unless you can determine some basic facts about the company. ... most important, deal with registered parties. State registration requirements should apply equally to traditional securities and emerging securities, including products tied to cryptocurrencies. Keep in mind that you will have little or no recourse if your money is stolen.[488]

The Guide goes on to warn potential investors:

> The Internet has been alive with the sound of cryptocurrency scams since late 2017. ... as a result, cryptocurrency-related cases have become a staple of the Securities Division's enforcement work.[489]

[42] South Dakota

Under South Dakota law, a license is required to engage in the business of "money transmission." This does include engaging in the transmission of virtual and cryptocurrencies.

The relevant South Dakota law says:

> No person, except a person who is exempt pursuant to the provisions of section 51A-17-3 [which can include government agencies, banks, etc.], may engage in the business of money transmission in this state without obtaining a license in accordance with this chapter and undergoing a criminal background investigation. A person is engaged in providing money transmission if the person provides those services to residents of this state, including any person who has no physical presence in this state. Each person subject to this section shall be licensed under and maintain a unique identifier through the Nationwide Mortgage Licensing System and Registry.[490]

"Money transmission" is defined as:

> engagement in the business of the sale or issuance of payment instruments or stored value or of receiving money or monetary value for transmission to a location within or outside the United States by any means including wire, facsimile, or electronic transfer.[491]

---

488. Office of the South Carolina Attorney General Securities Division, "South Carolina Investor Guide: Strategies for Investing Wisely and Avoiding Financial Fraud," 2022 Edition, online, p. 43.
489. *Ibid.*, p. 49.
490. South Dakota Statute: SDCL-17-4, online at: sdlegislature.gov/Statutes/Codified_Laws, accessed June 6, 2022.
491. South Dakota Statute: SDCL-17-1(13), online at: sdlegislature.gov/Statutes/Codified_Laws, accessed June 6, 2022.

"Monetary value" is defined as "any medium of exchange, whether or not redeemable in money."[492]

On May 25, 2019, the South Dakota Division of Banking issued a memo entitled "Virtual Currency Transmission in South Dakota" that said:

> It is the position of the South Dakota Division of Banking that, as it relates to SDSL Chapter 51-17, virtual currencies including crypto currencies like Bitcoin are "monetary value." Accordingly, entities that receive virtual currency, including cryptocurrencies like Bitcoin, for transmission within or outside the United States by any means, including wire, facsimile, or electronic transfer would likely be required to obtain and maintain licensure pursuant to SDCL chapter 51A-17 in order to operate in South Dakota.[493]

[43] Tennessee

Tennessee requires that a license is needed for "money transmission."[494]

Money transmission is defined as:

> the sale or issuance of payment instruments or engaging in the business of receiving money for transmission or transmitting money within the United States or to locations abroad by any and all means, including, but not limited to, payment instrument, wire, facsimile, or electronic transfer.[495]

This definition does not seem much different than other definitions of "money transmission" in other state laws which do include virtual currencies in their definition of the kinds of financial transactions that do require a money transmission license. However, Tennessee makes distinctions between virtual currencies and what Tennessee law considers to be "money" for the purposes of its Money Transmission Act. Because virtual currencies are said not to fit Tennessee's definition of "money," transactions in virtual currency do not require a license in Tennessee.

At present,[496] virtual currency does not qualify as "money" for the purposes of the Money Transition Act, and, therefore, a license is not required to engage in most virtual currency transactions in Tennessee.

The Tennessee Department of Financial Institutions has posted a section online entitled "Virtual Currency Guidance." Under that section, there is a memorandum available for download entitled "Regulatory Treatment of Virtual Currencies under the Tennessee Money Transmitter Act," dated December 16, 2015. The purpose of the

492. South Dakota Statute: SDCL-17-1(12), online at: sdlegislature.gov/Statutes/Codified_Laws, accessed June 6, 2022.
493. Division of Banking, Memorandum, "Virtual Currency Transmission in South Dakota" May 25, 2019, online, available for download, accessed June 6, 2022.
494. Tennessee Code Annotated, Title 45 Banks and Financial Institutions, Chapter 7 Money Transmission, section 45-7-102 License Required, online, advance.lexis.com, accessed June 7, 2022.
495. *Ibid.*, section 45-7-103 (10) "Money transmission," online, advance.lexis.com, accessed June 7, 2022.
496. As of June 2022.

Memo is stated to be "to establish the regulatory treatment of virtual currencies under existing statutory definitions."[497]

The memorandum defines "virtual currency" as:

> an electronic medium of exchange that does not have all the attributes of real currencies. Virtual currencies include crypto currencies, such as Bitcoin and Litecoin, which are not legal tender ... .

The memorandum goes on to say:

> Because crypto currency is not money under the Tennessee Money Transmitter Act, receiving it in exchange for a promise to make it available at a later time or different location is not money transmission. Consequently, absent the involvement of sovereign currency in a transaction, no money transmission can occur. However, when a cryptocurrency transaction does include sovereign currency, it may be money transmission depending on how the sovereign currency is handled. A licensing determination will be based on the handling of the sovereign currency.[498]

[44] Texas

Different kinds of currency transactions attract different kinds of regulation under Texas law. On April 1, 2019, the Banking Commissioner of Texas issued a Supervisory Memorandum explaining the distinctions under the Texas Money Services Act. The Memorandum sets out the policy of the Texas Department of Banking on the application of the Act to virtual currency transactions.[499]

The Memorandum asserts:

> One important characteristic of cryptocurrency is its lack of intrinsic value. A unit of crypto currency does not represent a claim on a commodity and is not convertible by law. ... Its value is only what a buyer is willing to pay for it.[500]

Virtual currencies are not considered "currencies" for the purposes of the Texas Financial Code:

> Code section 151.501 (b)(1) defines currency for purposes of currency exchange as "the coin and paper money of the United States or any country that is designated as legal tender and circulates and is customarily used and accepted as a medium of exchange in the country of issuance." ... Therefore, absent a legislative change to

497. Greg Gonzales, Commissioner, Tennessee Department of Financial Institutions, To: All Virtual Currency Companies Operating or Desiring to Operate in Tennessee, "Regulatory Treatment of Virtual Currencies under the Tennessee Money Transmitter Act," December 16, 2015, online at: tn.gov, accessed June 7, 2022.
498. As of this writing (June 2022), Tennessee policy does not appear to have change as a result of certain cryptocurrencies being recognized as "legal tender" by countries such as El Salvador.
499. Charles G. Cooper, Banking Commissioner, Texas Department of Banking, Supervisory Memorandum—1037, To: All Virtual Currency Companies Operating or Desiring to Operate in Texas, "Regulatory Treatment of Virtual Currencies Under the Texas Money Services Act," Texas Finance Code Chapter 151, online for download at: dob.texas.gov, accessed June 8, 2022.
500. *Ibid.* p. 2.

the statute, no currency exchange license is required in Texas to conduct any type of transaction exchanging virtual with sovereign currencies.[501]

However, not all transactions in cryptocurrency are exempt from licensing requirements under Texas law. There are circumstances under which they are subject to money transmission licensing requirements:

> Money transmission licensing determinations regarding transactions with cryptocurrency and sovereign-backed stablecoins turn on the single question of whether either should be considered "money" or "monetary value," under the Money Services Act. Under Finance Code Section 151.301, any transmission is the receipt of money or monetary value by any means in exchange for a promise to make the money or monetary value available at a later time or different location.[502]

Texas Finance Code section 151.301(b)(3) defines "money" or "monetary value" as:

> "Currency or a claim that can be converted into currency through a financial institution, electronic payments network, or other formal or informal payment system. ... Therefore, cryptocurrencies as currently implemented cannot be considered money or monetary value under the Money Services Act."[503]
>
> "However, when a cryptocurrency transaction does include sovereign currency, it may be money transmission depending on how the sovereign currency is handled. A licensing analysis will be based on the handling of the sovereign currency."[504]
>
> "Exchange of cryptocurrency for sovereign currency through a third-party exchanger is generally money transmission."[505]

It is important to note that the above guidance relates to "cryptocurrencies as currently implemented." This is an indication that if the nature of cryptocurrency transactions or Texas policy toward cryptocurrencies changes, there is no certainty that the legal status of cryptocurrencies in relation to financial regulation in Texas will remain the same. It will be important to refer to guidance from the Texas Department of Banking and qualified Texas legal counsel to be aware of any changes being proposed or implemented. Some relevant information will be found on the Texas Department of Banking website online.

[45] Utah

The Utah policy on digital assets, such as cryptocurrency, is not completely clear. However, there is an express exclusion of "blockchain tokens" from money transmission regulations in that state.

---

501. *Ibid.* p. 3.
502. *Ibid.*, p. 3.
503. *Ibid.* pp. 3-4.
504. *Ibid.*, p. 4.
505. *Ibid.*

The Utah Money Transmitter Act contains the following definitions:[506]

"(3) 'Blockchain' means an electronic method of storing data that is:

(a) maintained by consensus of multiple unaffiliated partners;
(b) distributed across multiple locations; and
(c) mathematically verified."[507]

"(4) 'Blockchain token' means an electronic record that is:

(a) recorded on a blockchain; and
(b) capable of being traded between persons without an intermediary."[508]

"(9) (a) 'Money transmission' means the sale or issuance of a payment instrument or engaging in the business of receiving money for transmission or transmitting money within the United States or to locations abroad by any and all means, including payment instrument, wire, facsimile, or electronic transfer.
(b) 'Money transmission' does not include a blockchain token."[509]

However, Utah maybe changing its attitude toward digital assets such as cryptocurrency, and digital tokens.

In April of 2022, new legislation was passed in Utah dealing with cryptocurrency. This took the form of three legislative bills that deal with the subject of digital assets. The first bill creates a "Blockchain and Digital Innovation Task Force." The stated purpose of the bill is to set up a task force to develop knowledge and expertise about blockchain and related technologies and make policy recommendations related to blockchain and related technologies. The task force is required to report annually to the Business and Labor Interim Committee and the Legislative Management Committee of Utah. The bill was signed by the Governor of Utah on March 24, 2022, and it went into effect on May 4, 2022.[510]

The second bill deals with payments in the form of "digital assets." the bill adds a number of definitions to Utah legislation relating to digital assets, the principle one being defining "digital asset" as follows:

"Digital asset means a representation of economic proprietary, or access rights that is stored in a computer readable format."

Further definitions refine what kinds of digital assets that are referred to in different situations. This bill was also signed by the Governor of Utah on March 24, 2022. It came into effect on July 1, 2022.[511]

The third bill purports to establish "a framework for the ownership of digital assets" and "provides a basis for understanding the ownership of digital assets." This

506. Utah Code, Title 7 Financial Institutions Act, Chapter 25 Money Transmitter Act, Part 1 General Provisions, section 102 Definitions (Effective 5/12/20), online at: le.utah.gov.
507. *Ibid.*, at 7-25-102(3).
508. *Ibid.*, at 7-25-102(4).
509. *Ibid.*, at 7-25-102(9).
510. Utah Bill H.B. 335, online at: le.utah.gov.
511. *Ibid.*, 406, online at: le.utah.gov.

bill was also signed by the Governor of Utah on March 24, 2022. It came into effect on May 4, 2022.[512]

There is no doubt that these new legislative provisions indicate a broader regulatory coverage of digital assets in Utah. It is not the place of this book to attempt to explain all of the details and implications of Utah legislation with respect to digital assets. That will require competent advice from a qualified advisor on the laws and regulations of Utah. However, these kinds of legislative changes are an indication of ongoing changes in how digital assets are being treated in U.S. States, and other U.S. jurisdictions.

[46] Vermont

Under Vermont law, "Money Services" is governed by a set of legislative provisions that includes provisions relating to "virtual currency."[513] There, "virtual currency" is defined as:[514]

> A digital representation of value that:
> (A) can be a medium of exchange, a unit of account, or a store of value;
> (B) has an equivalent value in money or acts as a substitute for money;
> (C) can be centralized or decentralized; and
> (D) can be exchanged for money or other convertible virtual currency.

"Money services" is defined as: "money transmission, check cashing, or currency exchange."[515]

"Money transmission" is defined as:

> To engage in the business of selling or issuing payment instruments, selling or issuing prepaid access, or receiving money or monetary value for transmission to a location within or outside the United States.[516]

Money transmission does require a license under Vermont law.[517]

[47] Virginia

The Virginia Bureau of Financial Institutions warns Virginia residents, "Virtual currencies are highly volatile with the potential for complete loss of value. ... The Bureau

512. Utah Bill S.B. 182, online at: le.utah.gov.
513. The Vermont Statutes Online, Title 8: Banking and Insurance, Chapter 79: Money Services. online at: legislature.vermont.gov/statutes.
514. *Ibid.*, Subchapter 1: General Provisions, section 2500 Definitions, (13) "Virtual currency," online at: legislature.vermont.gov/statutes.
515. The Vermont Statutes Online, Title 8: Banking and Insurance, Chapter 79: Money Services, Subchapter 1: General Provisions, section 2500 Definitions, (8) "Money services," online at: legislature.vermont.gov/statutes.
516. *Ibid.*, section 2500 Definitions, (9) "Money transmission," online at: legislature.vermont .gov/statutes.
517. *Ibid.*, Subchapter 2: Money Transmission Licenses, online at: legislature.vermont.gov/statutes.

strongly cautions residents to consider the risks associated with the purchase and use of virtual currencies."[518]

Nevertheless, the Bureau says that it does not:

> currently regulate virtual currencies; However, to the extent of virtual currency transactions also involved the transfer of fiat currency (such as U.S. Dollars, Euros, and Japanese Yen), they may be regulated under Chapter 19 of Title 6.2 of the Code of Virginia open (Money Order Sellers and Money Transmitters) ... .[519]

This regulation could come about because under that statute[520] "Monetary value" is defined as "a medium of exchange, whether or not redeemable in money," and "Money transmission" is defined as "receiving money or monetary value for transmission by wire, facsimile, electronic means or other means or selling or issuing stored value." "Stored value" is defined as "monetary value that is evidenced by an electronic record." "Money transmitter" is defined as "a person engaged in the business of money transmission."[521]

Given the breadth of these statutory definitions, it is not difficult to see how certain commercial transactions involving virtual currency could considered to be "the business of money transmission" which is apparently required to be conducted by "licencees" under this statute.

There is enough ambiguity in Virginia's treatment of virtual currency, so that a person dealing with virtual currency who wishes to know their legal position in that state should consult qualified legal advisors.

[48] Washington

In the State of Washington, cryptocurrency is included in the "money transmission" definition found in the Uniform Money Services Act[522] (Act). The definition of "Money transmission" is:

> "Money transmission" means receiving money or its equivalent value (equivalent value includes virtual currency) to transmit, deliver or instruct to be delivered to another location, inside or outside the United States, by any means including but not limited to by wire, facsimile or electronic transfer. "Money transmission" includes selling, issuing, or acting as an intermediary for open loop prepaid access and payment instruments, but not closed loop prepaid access. 'Money transmission' does not include: the provision solely of connection services to the Internet, telecommunication services, or network access; units of value that are issued in affinity or rewards programs that cannot be redeemed for either money or virtual

518. Virginia Bureau of Financial Institutions, "Notice to Virginia Residents Regarding Virtual Currency," revised August 25, 2021, online at: scc.virginia.gov, accessed June 10, 2022.
519. *Ibid.*
520. Code of Virginia, Title 6.2, Chapter 19 Money Order Sellers and Money Transmitters (6.2-1900 thru 6.2 1921), 6.2 1900 Definitions, online at: law.justia.com/codes/virginia, accessed June 10, 2022.
521. *Ibid.*
522. Washington State Legislature, "Uniform Money Services Act," RCWs, Title 19, Chapter 19.230, online, accessed June 13, 2022.

currencies; and units of value that are used solely within online gaming platforms that have no market or application outside of the gaming platforms.[523]

The Act defines "Virtual currency" as follows:

"Virtual currency" means a digital representation of value used as a medium of exchange, a unit of account, or a store of value, but does not have legal tender status as recognized by the United States government. "Virtual currency" does not include the software or protocols governing the transfer of the digital representation of value or other uses of virtual distributed ledger systems to verify ownership or authenticity in a digital capacity when the virtual currency is not used as a medium of exchange.

The government organization that determines whether a license is needed to engage in money transmission is the Washington State Department of Financial Institutions (DFI). Guidance published online by the DFI states:

Companies wishing to transmit money for Washington residents in a digital currency form can contact DFI for a determination whether licensure under UMSA is required. If it is, a license is required before the company can engage in the activity.[524]

The Uniform Money Services Act states in section 19.230.30:[525]

Money transmitter license required:

(1) A person may not engage in the business of money transmission, or advertise, solicit, or hold itself out as providing money transmission unless the person is:
    a) Licensed as a money transmitter under this chapter;
    b) And authorized delegate of a person licensed as a money transmitter under this chapter; Or
    c) Excluded under RCW 19 point 230.020.

(2) A money transmitter license is not transferable or assignable.

The Washington State statutes also set out additional regulations about becoming and acting as a money transmitter.[526]

[49] West Virginia

West Virginia regulates cryptocurrency as part of its currency transmission and/or money transmission regulations by defining those activities as including "other value that substitutes for money by any means." Under this definition, cryptocurrency may not escape regulation in West Virginia. It is also reported that the West Virginia

523. Washington State Legislature, RCW 19.230.010, "Definitions," (18) "Money transmission," online accessed June 13, 2022.
524. Washington State Department of Financial Institutions, Guidance, "Virtual Currency Regulation," online (PDF), accessed June 13, 2022.
525. Washington State Legislature, RCW 19.230.030, "Money transmitter license required," online, accessed June 13, 2022.
526. Washington State Legislature, RCW 19.230, Uniform Money Services Act, online, accessed June 13, 2022.

legislature is considering a number of proposed pieces of legislation that refer to cryptocurrency in the context of criminal law, property law in other legal contexts.[527]

West Virginia law defines "currency transmission" or "money transmission" as:

> (1) engaging in the business of selling or issuing checks or the business of receiving currency, the payment of money, or other value that substitutes for money by any means for the purpose of transmitting, either prior to or after receipt, that currency, or (2) payment of money or other value that substitutes for money by wire, facsimile, or other electronic means, or through the use of a financial institution, financial intermediary, the Federal Reserve System, or other funds transfer network. It includes the transmission of funds through the issuance and sale of stored value or similar prepaid products' cards which are intended for general acceptance and used in commercial or consumer transactions. It also includes payroll processing services. It does not include the provision of solely online or telecommunications services or network access.

Unless exempt under West Virginia Code section 32 A-2-3:

> A person may not engage in the business of currency exchange, transportation, or transmission in this state without a license issued under this article. For purposes of this article, a person is considered to be engaging in those businesses in this state if he or she makes available, from a location inside or outside this state, and internet website that West Virginia citizens may access in order to enter into those transactions by electronic means.[528]

[50] Wisconsin

The Wisconsin Department of Revenue defines virtual currency as:

> a form of currency or medium of exchange that is electronically created and stored. It is defined by the U.S. Department of Treasury as a 'medium of exchange that operates like a currency in some environments but does not have all the attributes of real currency.' While real paper money and coins are legal tender, virtual currency does not have the status as legal tender. Some other names for virtual currency are virtual money, digital money, and cryptocurrency.

However, as of the beginning of 2022, there were no particular virtual currency regulations in Wisconsin specifying that a license is needed for transactions involving such things as "money transmission." Wisconsin has apparently been reluctant to place regulatory restrictions on digital assets.

Whether that policy will continue remains to be seen. As one legal commentator has written:

> As cryptocurrency and blockchain technology continues to evolve in practice and popularity, it will be vital to keep up with current digital asset legislation in states.

527. For examples and references, *see* NCSL, "Cryptocurrency 2022 Legislation," online at ncsl.org, accessed June 14, 2022.
528. West Virginia Code, section 32A-2-2, License Required, online at: code.wvlegislature.gov., accessed June 14, 2022.

Licensure agreements are becoming more standard with virtual currency transactions.[529]

[51] Wyoming

Wyoming has gone out of its way to provide exemptions from its money transmission law for transactions in virtual currency. In June of 2019, Wyoming, following the example of Arizona, created a "financial technology sandbox" under the Wyoming FTS Act.[530] The stated purpose of the Sandbox Act is to permit approved firms to offer innovative financial products or services to consumers under the conditions set out in the Sandbox Act.[531]

A person wishing to qualify to take advantage of the benefits offered by the Sandbox Act must make an application and meet a number of conditions including, among other things, the following:

- have a physical presence in the state and not merely a "registered office or agent";[532]
- submit to a specified "criminal history background check";[533]
- deposit a fee of US$ 500 into the "financial technology innovation account";[534] and
- provide detailed information about the product, the business plan, the risks, etc., as specified under the Act.[535]

[52] Puerto Rico Attracts Crypto

A US, non-state, jurisdiction that is attracting digital asset-related business is the U.S. territory of Puerto Rico.

In early 2018, it was reported that several successful cryptocurrency and Blockchain entrepreneurs were moving to Puerto Rico to avoid U.S. state and federal taxes on their growing fortunes.

529. Mary McCarthy, "Wisconsin Slow to Regulate Cryptocurrency," online at: ostermcbride.com, December 6, 2021.
530. WY Stat section 40-29-104 (2021), Justia U.S. Law, online at: law.justia.com, accessed June 17, 2022.
531. WY Stat section 40-29-104(f)(i) (2021), Justia U.S. Law, online at: law.justia.com, accessed June 17, 2022.
532. WY Stat section 40-29-104(b) (2021), Justia U.S. Law, online at: law.justia.com, accessed June 17, 2022.
533. WY Stat section 40-29-104(d) (2021), Justia U.S. Law, online at: law.justia.com, accessed June 17, 2022.
534. WY Stat section 40-29-104(e) (2021), Justia U.S. Law, online at: law.justia.com, accessed June 17, 2022.
535. WY Stat section 40-29-104(f) (2021), Justia U.S. Law, online at: law.justia.com, accessed June 17, 2022.

It is even reported that they had hoped to build a "crypto utopia" by building a new city in Puerto Rico where all money would consist of cryptocurrency to show the rest of the world how a crypto economy could work.[536]

It is reported that by the spring of 2022, thousands of cryptocurrency and blockchain entrepreneurs and enthusiasts had moved to Puerto Rico because of the beaches, the climate and the low taxes. In its way, it has sort of become the "Silicon Valley of Crypto":[537]

> "'A lot of us really do think technology can save the world,'" says Evan Ortega, 38, who has lived in Puerto Rico for four years. "Ortega is a former cannabis entrepreneur who made a small fortune in crypto and is now helping to launch a tech-enhanced art community center in old San Juan."[538]

The entrepreneurs and crypto enthusiasts that have moved to Puerto Rico are reportedly making some rather dramatic claims about how what's going on there represents the future of both technology and the economy. Amanda Cassatt who reportedly founded a marketing firm centered on crypto business is quoted as expressing the following view:

> Decentralize everything. ... Currency is just the beginning. Decentralize the energy markets This is the embryo stage of a new economy.[539]

Whether this new world dawns and laws and regulations are created and/or adjusted to support it remains to be seen, but there is little doubt that the crypto community in Puerto Rico has lots of enthusiasm.

An important legal change that has attracted these young enthusiasts to Puerto Rico is the fact that from 2012 the Puerto Rico government passed a number of laws providing tax incentives to American investors who were willing to become residents in Puerto Rico. These incentives attracted approximately ten thousand members of the American financial community to move and do business there. It is reported that around three thousand of these new residents were wealthy from cryptocurrency profits.[540]

[53] Puerto Rico Tech Tax Breaks[541]

Puerto Rico is an unincorporated U.S. territory. This gives it the advantage, under the U.S. Internal Revenue Code, of being exempt from U.S. Federal tax.[542]

---

536. Nellie Bowles, "Making a Crypto Utopia in Puerto Rico," The New York Times," online, February 2, 2018.
537. Josh Glancy, "Why Are Cryptocurrency Evangelists Flocking to Puerto Rico?," The Sunday Times, online, April 24, 2022.
538. *Ibid.*
539. *Ibid.*
540. *Ibid.*
541. This book does not provide legal advice. It simply provides summaries to aid understanding of issues that may arise. Only qualified legal experts can provide legal advice on any particular issue described in this book.
542. U.S. Internal Revenue Code, section 933.

Because of the economic hardships suffered by Puerto Rico as a result of hurricane damage, Puerto Rico has made serious efforts to attract U.S. citizens and businesses by enacting laws that provide significant benefits to U.S. citizens moving to Puerto Rico.

In 2019, Puerto Rico enacted a law known as the Incentives Code of Puerto Rico. The purpose of these incentives was to boost the economy. There are a number of tax incentives offered falling into six different categories. However, some of these had been particularly attractive to tech entrepreneurs and particularly to cyber currency businesses.[543]

The two principal laws that Puerto Rico passed providing tax benefits to U.S. citizens moving to Puerto Rico are Act 20 and Act 22.

Act 20 focuses on providing tax benefits to businesses in Puerto Rico that are exporting services to those outside Puerto Rico. In order to be considered to be genuinely entitled to these tax benefits with respect to corporate or income tax, property tax or dividends, certain legal tests must be satisfied, including whether one's office is in Puerto Rico, whether the services are being provided to those outside Puerto Rico and whether the services provided are related to Puerto Rican trade or business. There is a long list of "services" that may qualify for these exemptions, including various digital businesses and related activities such as research and development.

Puerto Rico makes available three kinds of tax breaks that tech entrepreneurs may be able to benefit from. The first is a 4% fixed income tax or corporate tax rate, the second is a 100% exemption on export service dividends, and the third is a property tax exemption of 100%.

In order to benefit from these tax rates, one has to be a U.S. citizen and become a genuine resident of Puerto Rico.

Act 22 is called the individual investors act. For those who qualify, it provides a complete exemption from income taxes in Puerto Rico on any passive income received by a bona fide Puerto Rican resident.

However, careful consideration and caution should be exercised by those who moved to Puerto Rico to take advantage of tax incentives. It has been reported that the U.S. IRS has been taking a careful look at the tax returns of those who have relocated to Puerto Rico. The IRS is seeking to identify taxes that should have been reported on U.S. tax returns but were not.[544]

To benefit from these laws, and escape the more onerous U.S. Federal tax laws, a U.S. citizen needs to become a "bona fide resident" of Puerto Rico. To be considered a bona fide resident, a person needs to satisfy three basic tests. To summarize,[545] these tests are:

543. PWC, "Puerto Rico—Tax Credits and Incentives," online at taxsummeries.pwc.com. February 21, 2022

544. "IRS Targeting Those Who 'Relocated' To Puerto Rico in the Wake of Act 22," National Law Review, online, September 23, 2021.

545. Please be aware that this is simply a summary guide. It is not a complete examination of all the factors that tax authorities may consider in determining whether the conditions that determine whether one is legally a "bona fide resident" of Puerto Rico. To know the full picture, one will need to consult qualified legal and tax experts.

- For 183 or more days in a taxable year, one must be physically present in Puerto Rico.
- In any taxable year, one cannot be a tax resident of any jurisdiction outside Puerto Rico.
- One's connection to Puerto Rico must be closer than to any other foreign country or the United States.

To get a complete understanding of whether the services that one provides could qualify for the Puerto Rican tax benefits, it will be necessary to consult qualified tax experts about all of the related legal details.

There is no substitute for timely, competent tax advice.

[54] Proposed State Legislation

The above summaries of U.S. state/jurisdiction legislation and regulation of cryptocurrency and other digital assets are referenced to the time period that this book was written—2022-2023. However, anyone that wishes to improve their understanding of how cryptocurrencies and other digital assets are regulated under U.S. state/jurisdiction law needs to be aware that these laws and regulations are continually changing and being modified. State and other U.S. jurisdiction legislatures are always in a continuous process of considering proposed legislation on various topics including cryptocurrencies and other digital assets.

One website that provides information about proposed state legislation on various topics, including cryptocurrency legislation, is the website of the National Conference of State Legislatures (NCSL). There, one can find lists of examples and references to proposed legislation. However, the NCSL information may not always be up-to-date, so it is important to consult qualified advisors in the states or jurisdictions in question to learn the most recent information about digital asset law and regulation in any particular state or legal jurisdiction.[546]

[55] Legal Tender and Mediums of Exchange

One issue that U.S. jurisdictions will need to look at is the impact on their policies and legislation of their definitions of money. A number seem to include things that are recognized as "legal tender" or "mediums of exchange" by the US or foreign countries as falling within their definitions of "money" that is included in their regulation of "money transmission." These definitions are used to exclude from or include within crypto assets with respect to their money transmission regulations. These states will need to consider whether the designation of certain cryptocurrencies, such as Bitcoin, as legal tender or legitimate mediums of exchange by countries such as El Salvador changes the scope of their money transmission regulations.

546. For examples and references, *see* NCSL, online at ncsl.org.

§3.13 CRYPTO BANKRUPTCY ISSUES

Concern was raised that the crash of a widely traded cryptocurrency or a group of cryptocurrencies could have a dangerously negative impact on the wider digital asset market. Unfortunately, this has been tested by the financial problems of some major crypto businesses.

For example, Coinbase Inc. (COIN.O) is a widely known and used crypto exchange that operates in the US, and the name of that frequently comes up in the context of crypto asset regulation.

Coinbase Inc. is licensed to engage in "money transmission" in most U.S. jurisdictions. Most of its licenses cover transmissions relating to U.S. dollar wallets and transfers. In some states, the license also covers cryptocurrency transmissions. In some states, no money transmission license is required to operate a cryptocurrency business.

The U.S. Bank Secrecy Act (BSA) requires Coinbase to verify customer identities, maintain records of currency transactions for up to five years and report certain transactions. Under the U.S. Patriot Act, Coinbase must designate a compliance officer to ensure compliance with applicable laws and two produce procedures and controls to ensure compliance, adequate training and periodic review of the compliance program.

However, it was reported in May of 2022:

> "Brian Armstrong, co-founder and chief executive of Coinbase Global, attempted to reassure investors and users this week that the popular digital currency exchange has "no risk of bankruptcy" after a regulatory disclosure raised alarm.
>
> "In its latest quarterly filing Coinbase said that, in the event of bankruptcy, crypto assets held by the exchange could be considered property of the bankruptcy proceedings and customers could be treated as unsecured creditors."[547]

An "unsecured creditor" is someone who is owed a debt by a debtor but has no legal claim on any particular asset possessed or controlled by the debtor. In other words, if a debtor goes bankrupt, an unsecured creditor will be entitled only to a pro rata share of any liquidated assets of the creditor, but the amount of the unsecured creditor's share is not known until all unsecured creditors have registered their claims and the total of those claims is compared to the total realized value of the liquidated unsecured assets owned by the bankrupt.

This report caused something of a backlash among commentators such as shown by this comment:

> Not a penny of taxpayer's money should go into bailing out feckless get rich quick gamblers. There are close to 20,000 cryptos now and they are all intrinsically worthless ... .[548]

The most dramatic example of the impact that one crypto company can have on others in the market was the bankruptcy of the popular crypto exchange, FTX, in November of 2022. FTX was reported to owe billions of dollars to creditors. A month

547. Jones, *supra*.
548. Comment by "Zebedee," Martin, *supra*.

after FTX filed for bankruptcy, its founder, Sam Bankman-Fried, was arrested in the Bahamas and charged with fraud and other crimes by the U.S. regulatory and law enforcement authorities. He was extradited to the United States to face a number of regulatory and criminal charges.

Several crypto companies had exposure to FTX, and this affected their value as well as overall confidence in the crypto asset markets. Investigations and legal actions involving FTX and those connected with it will undoubtedly go on for some time. But the collapse of FTX and the accusations of irresponsibility and illegality that have arisen in connection with that collapse will undoubtedly negatively impact the crypto asset markets and may well have a negative impact on the wider investment business.[549]

§3.14 THOUGHTS ON U.S. CRYPTO REGULATION

The US attitude toward the existence and use of cryptocurrency, particularly within the United States, is not yet completely clear. The division of regulation of assets between so many different federal, state and industry organizations is likely to cause overlap, contradiction, confusion, and hesitation to act.

It seems reasonable to suggest that the US, as the world's largest financial marketplace, should organize a single, central regulator for virtual assets. Their jurisdiction and remit should include all immaterial assets, including crypto assets and derivatives. This could provide a central repository for registration, transaction reporting. A single rulebook administered by a single federal agency, in possession of complete information about the state of markets and their participants, would be a useful tool to avoid unexpected market manipulations and crashes. Perhaps a Federal Virtual Asset Commission?

549. There have been many reports on, and analyses of, the FTX problems. For example, *see*, Emily Nicolle, Olga Kharif and Stacy-Marie Ishmael, "All The Ways That Crypto Broke in 2022," Bloomberg online at: bloomberg.com, December 22, 2022.

CHAPTER 4

EU Law

§4.01 EBA WARNING ON VIRTUAL CURRENCIES

In December of 2013, the European Banking Authority (EBA) issued an online warning to consumers on virtual currencies.[550] The warning explained what virtual currencies are, how they work, and highlighted the following risks that consumers should be aware of:

- You may lose your money on the exchange platform.
- Your money may be stolen from your digital wallet.
- You are not protected when using virtual currencies as a means of payment.
- The value of your virtual currency can change quickly, and could even drop to zero.

As EU parliament member Stefan Berger is reported to have said:

> The recent fall in the value of digital currencies shows us how highly risky and speculative they are.[551]

The EBA is one of three financial supervisory authorities which form parts of the European System of Financial Supervision (ESFS). Two others are the European Securities and Markets Authority (ESMA) and the European Insurance and Occupational Pensions Authority. Other parts of the ESFS are the European Systemic Risk Board, the Joint Committee of European Supervisory Authorities and the national supervisory authorities of the Member States of the EU.[552]

550. EBA, News and Press, "EBA Warns Consumers on Virtual Currencies," online at: eba.europa.eu, December 13, 2013, accessed July 27, 2022.
551. *Ibid.*
552. Detailed information about the EBA is available online at: eba.europa.eu.

§4.02 MARKETS IN CRYPTO ASSETS REGULATION (MICA)

At the end of June of 2022, in the midst of a dramatic fall in cryptocurrency prices, the EU drafted new cryptocurrency rules and regulations to control what it considered and "Wild West" digital asset market.[553]

Before EU legislators now are a series of proposals for regulating cryptocurrencies and other digital assets.

The new legislation is called the MiCA.

In its newsletter of July 26, 2022, the EU gave more details as to what these regulations will cover. The publication notes that crypto asset markets were at the heart of disruptive financial change and policy attention. Prior to the issuance of this publication, there have been significant movements in the markets that have resulted in changes in value of Bitcoin, stablecoins and other crypto assets.

The intended purpose of the new rules being proposed for crypto assets by the EU is to allow these markets to develop on the bases of a reasonable regulatory framework, to prevent crypto transactions from being used for crimes such as money laundering and terrorist financing but to allow for innovation and growth in these increasingly important markets.

On June 30, 2022, EU legislators reached a provisional agreement on MiCA.[554]

According to the provisional agreement (PA), MiCA will have the following elements:[555]

- Issuers of crypto products and providers of crypto asset services (collectively, Crypto Businesses), to the extent that this is not already provided for, will need to be authorized by their national competent authority (Financial Regulator).
- Once they have obtained the authority of their Financial Regulator, they will be allowed to passport their services throughout the EU.
- Disclosure and transparency requirements for "unbacked" crypto assets will be imposed.
- Stricter requirements will be imposed for the issuance of "stablecoins." Different types of stablecoins are referred to. The first is "asset-referenced tokens" and the second is "e-money tokens." Both types will require EU Financial Regulator authorization. The business issuing these tokens must also be established within the EU. Also, both types of tokens will require a reserve whereby the issuer will be required to hold in reserve the same asset as their reference and for the same amount as the total amount of crypto assets issued.
- "Algorithmic coins"[556] cannot meet the above requirements set for stablecoins and consequently could only be marketed as "unbacked" crypto assets. These

553. Robert Milner, "EU Tackles 'Wild West' Bitcoin Market," The Times, online, July 3, 2022.
554. European Commission, Article, "Crypto-asset Markets," July 26, 2022, online at: ec.europa.eu.
555. Council of the EU, "Digital Finance: Agreement Reached on European Crypto-assets Regulation (MiCA)," Press Release, June 30, 2022, online at: consilium.europa.eu.
556. An "algorithm" is a set of digital instructions that determines a digital process. An algorithmic coin or token is called that because its backing rests solely on an imbedded algorithm that

crypto assets would not be permitted to claim that their value is "pegged" to any official national or fiat currency.

- "Asset-referenced tokens" are another category of stablecoins; they claim to be "stable" because they are referenced to other assets such as fiat currencies, commodities or other crypto assets. Under MiCA, holders of asset-referenced tokens will have a redemption right against the issuer. To ensure that redemption right, asset-referenced tokens are required to be fully backed by a reserve of assets which is subject to prior authorization and supervision by the relevant Financial Regulators.
- Certain "significant" asset-referenced and e-money tokens will be under stricter EU supervision that will be conducted by the EBA. It is hoped that this additional supervision will encourage greater confidence in those digital assets and reduce the likelihood of market turbulence.
- Strong consumer protection will be a feature of MiCA. Protection will be extended to consumers as they transact with crypto assets on authorized exchanges, use crypto asset wallets and use trading platforms to buy, trade and transfer crypto assets. MiCA will include provisions to increase the availability of information in crypto markets. For example, publication of crypto asset white papers will be required to inform potential holders of the characteristics of a particular crypto asset. There will also be a monthly publication of data on the number of tokens in circulation as well as the mandatory requirement of independent reserve asset audits.
- Issuers of crypto assets and crypto trading markets will have an obligation to disclose information about the environmental impact of the crypto assets they offer.
- Consumers will be granted a right of withdrawal within 14 days of the purchase of crypto assets (with exceptions for asset-referenced tokens and e-money tokens).
- Crypto asset service providers will be obligated to protect and preserve investor funds and will be liable for the loss of investor funds.
- Throughout the EU, MiCA will set common rules on crypto assets. This will make EU a leading major international jurisdiction to impose such common rules. The US and the UK have been somewhat slower in completing their regulatory frameworks for crypto assets. It is the hope of the EU that other international jurisdictions will cooperate in adopting similar common regulations for the buying, selling, holding and trading of crypto assets.

---

controls a relationship between the algorithmic token or coin and another cybercurrency that supposedly supports the algorithmic coin or token. Examples are: terraUSD, magic Internet money and neutrino usd. Ekin Genc, 'Algorithmic Stablecoins: What They Are and How They Can Go Terribly Wrong: The stunning crash of UST stablecoin and LUNA, its sister token, has many questioning if an algorithmic stablecoin can be trusted.," CoinDesk, May 18, 2022, online at: coindesk.com.

The provisional agreement is subject to approval by the Council and the European Parliament before going through the formal adoption procedure.[557]

The Committee on Economic and Monetary Affairs of the European Parliament issued a press release[558] that announced that key provisions of the new regulations would require:

- A uniform legal framework for crypto assets in the EU.
- Consumer protection and safeguards against manipulation and financial crime.
- Significant crypto assets providers would be required to disclose their energy consumption.
- Provisions on supervision, consumer protection, environmental safeguards for all crypto assets, including cryptocurrencies.

The new rules require cryptocurrency traders to have a license and to put customer protections in place if they wish to sell digital assets within the EU.

The new provisions will cover such things as the issuing and trading of crypto assets, including cryptocurrency and tokens, transparency, disclosure, authorization and supervision of crypto transactions. They will require that consumers should be better informed about the risks, costs and charges of cryptocurrency transactions. There will also be requirements relating to market integrity and financial stability that relate to public offers of digital assets. There will also be additional measures against market manipulation and to prevent money laundering, terrorist financing and other criminal activities.[559]

§4.03 MONEY LAUNDERING

Prior to the EU agreement to impose these new rules, digital assets were largely unregulated by the EU with the principal regulation imposed on cryptocurrency traders being the avoidance of money laundering.[560] Transactions in virtual currency may be misused for criminal activities, including money laundering.

As a way of preventing money laundering, the ESMA may set up a public register of noncompliant crypto market companies that are offering products and services in the EU without obtaining authorization.[561]

The EU recognizes that there are differences between NFTs and cryptocurrencies. However, it is the intention of the EU that the rules should reclassify NFTs as either regulated financial instruments or as crypto assets subject to other crypto asset and money laundering compliance regulations.[562]

557. *Ibid.*
558. European Parliament, "Cryptocurrencies in the EU: Deal Struck Between Parliament and Council," Press Release 22-22, June 30, 2022.
559. *Ibid.*
560. Milner, July 3, 2022.
561. *Ibid.*
562. *Ibid.*

§4.04 CLIMATE CHANGE

Because climate change is an important issue to the EU, there will be regulations intended to control the carbon footprint of cryptocurrency production and trading. Crypto companies of a certain size will be required to disclose their energy consumption. ESMA is urged to prepare technical standards on how these disclosure obligations are to be complied with.

EU Member of Parliament (MP) Stefan Berger said:

> We are the first continent to have crypto-asset regulation. ... reliable authorization and supervisory structures for new tokens are now being created for the first time.[563]

The MiCA bill was approved by the European Council in October of 2022.[564] A full vote of the European Parliament is expected in February of 2023.[565] MiCA is expected to take effect in 2024.

§4.05 THE DIGITAL EURO?

There is no question that the EU is taking digital currency seriously. In July of 2022, the ECB published an article on its website discussing what a "digital euro" would mean in the European euro currency system.[566]

They speculate that the digital euro would be similar to euro banknotes but would, of course, be in digital form. It would be issued by the euro system, which consists of the ECB and national central banks of the euro area. The digital euro would be accessible to all European citizens and businesses.

ECB says that the digital euro would not replace euro fiat currency in cash form but would be a compliment to it. It would give people another choice about how to pay and receive money and would make it easier to do so. They say this would improve the accessibility and inclusion of EU citizens into the EU financial system.[567]

Of course, a significant degree of care would have to be exercised in issuing official digital euros. The safety of EU citizens in conducting their financial affairs is a principal priority. Christine Lagarde, president of the ECB, said:

> Our work aims to ensure that in the digital age citizens and firms continue to have access to the safest form of money, central bank money.[568]

This statement not only is intended to reassure EU citizens and businesses but also subtly indicates a degree of concern about the competition presented by privately

563. *Ibid.*
564. Rahul Nambiapurath, "European Council Approves Crypto Regulation Bill," Investopedia, online at investopedia.com, October 6, 2022.
565. Kate Prescott, "Crypto's Alphabet Soup is Crying Out for Three More Letter: the FCA," The Times, online, November 16, 2022.
566. ECB, Eurosystem, "A Digital Euro," online at: ecb.europa.eu, accessed September 14, 2022.
567. *Ibid.*
568. *Ibid.*

issued eurocurrency to official central bank euro currency. The issuance of an official digital euro is obviously intended to prevent a significant number of financial transactions from moving from official EU-issued currency to private cryptocurrency markets.

The ECB's online publication goes on to explain further details about what the digital euro will be, how it will be used, and how it will affect the Eurosystem.

On July 13, 2022, the ECB published an article entitled "The Case for a Digital Euro: Key Objectives and Design Considerations."[569]

A reason given for issuing a digital euro is that it would provide EU citizens with digital form of money "in the fast-changing digital world."

However, it is recognized that introduction of a digital euro could have some undesirable effects. To avoid those, the ECB concedes that the digital euro should be carefully designed. One thing that the ECB wants to avoid is having the issuance of the digital euro cause sudden large shifts of bank deposits to the digital euro.[570]

The ECB says that the digital euro should be issued by "supervised intermediaries" in a way that minimizes any IT project risk associated with its issuance, or unforeseen delays or unexpected costs.

Regulatory standards by all members of the Eurosystem should be complied with.

Additional dangers may be posed by use of the digital euro outside the euro area. Consequently, those organizations providing services within the Eurosystem will need to be highly resistant to cyber threats that might be posed by introduction of the digital euro.[571]

There are also important legal issues associated with the issuance of a digital euro that will need to be resolved. Different design features may entail different legal implications, and there will be issues about the applicability of existing EU legislation on financial transactions to the new digital euro. These will need to be resolved and settled before the digital euro can be injected into the Eurosystem.

It is interesting to see the issues that the ECB believes are important when considering adopting a digital euro within the euro system. However, any jurisdiction, including the US and the UK, which is considering the adoption of a digital currency will need to confront the same types of issues. There are bound to be differences in the way they are resolved.

§4.06 INTERNATIONAL COOPERATION

However, it would be best for the international financial markets if there was discussion and cooperation among the major markets on resolving these issues so that unnecessary conflicts between different financial regulation systems can be avoided.

569. *Ibid.*
570. *Ibid.*
571. *Ibid.*

CHAPTER 5
United Kingdom Law

§5.01 CRYPTO IN THE UK

In March of 2022, it was reported that the UK was beginning to take serious steps toward regulating cryptocurrency. It was reported that:

> City regulators have taken the first step toward creating a British rule book for cryptocurrencies amid worries that the fast-growing $1.7 trillion market will eventually pose a threat to the wider financial system.[572]

It has taken a fairly long time for this reaction to develop but for the reasons stated above it is obvious that such action by financial regulators in the UK is absolutely necessary in order to protect the UK and international financial markets from the kind of disruptions that were experienced in 2008. For some time, there has been an understanding that the rapid growth of the cyber currency market will probably have a significant impact on the financial markets. Regulators in the UK and elsewhere now appear to be waking up to the fact that in order to prevent that impact from being damaging, well-thought-out regulations will need to be put in place before the damage occurs.[573]

There are three specific areas of financial services regulation which may be of concern to issuers and users of cyber currency. They are as follows:

- Banking law.
- Investment law.
- Currency law.

572. Ben Martin, "We Must Set Cryptocurrency Rules, Admits Bank of England," The Times, online, March 25, 2022.
573. For more detail on the UK approach to regulation of crypto, *see* Chapter 5.

The reason that they may be important with respect to cyber currency is because of the way the cyber currency is described by its issuers and other users of cyber currency.

It is therefore important to examine the role that the cyber currency business seems determined to establish for itself in the world of finance and the regulatory laws that governments expect to apply to the world of finance. Therefore, it is useful to examine each of the areas of finance law described above and compare them to how those in the cyber currency market appear to view their roles in the cyber currency business.

§5.02 BANKING LAW

Although there are international treaties and conventions that apply to the conduct of banking law, this area of law has significant differences in different countries and different legal jurisdictions.

A common legal definition of a "bank" is a government-regulated entity that is entitled to receive deposits of money, to make loans, and to issue promissory notes.

These are usually among the most strictly regulated financial institutions functioning within any legal jurisdiction. It is usually the case the prior to being authorized to operate as a bank, the entity in question needs to undergo a rigorous application process to satisfy and a number of conditions that need to be met before the entity is permitted to publicly operate as a bank. Following that authorization, a bank is expected to adhere to a number of strict operational and reporting regulations and to be willing to undergo periodic regulatory inspections and reviews of its operations. As a result of these conditions, the number of entities permitted to operate as banks is usually limited to a relatively few. Although there may be thousands or tens of thousands of regulated financial institutions permitted to operate within a particular legal jurisdiction, the number of banks is usually significantly smaller.

As a financial market center, the UK has maintained significant awareness of the growth of the crypto asset markets. It has been reported that there is significant public interest in the UK in owning crypto assets. In July of 2022, it was reported that:

> "As many as one in 10 adults in Britain have bought crypto-assets such as Bitcoin, far more than previously thought.
>
> "Research commissioned by HM Revenue and Customs found that about 6.7 million adults owned or have bought crypto-assets. This is almost three times higher than estimates from the Financial Conduct Authority, the City regulator.[574]
>
> In November of 2022, it was reported that "nearly one in five people in the UK own some cryptocurrency ... ."[575]

574. Lily Russell-Jones, "One in Ten Britons Have Bought Crypto Assets Despite Warnings," The Times, online, July 6, 2022.
575. Katie Prescott, "Crypto's Alphabet Soup Is Crying Out for Three More Letters: the FCA," The Times, online, November 16, 2022.

The FCA has said:

> Crypto-assets are considered very high risk, speculative investments. If you buy these types of crypto-assets you are unlikely to have access to the Financial Ombudsman Service or the Financial Services Compensation Scheme (FSCS) if something goes wrong. If you invest in crypto-assets, you should be prepared to lose all your money.[576]

Despite that official pronouncement on risk:

> Reportedly, fewer than 10% of crypto investors in the UK their investment as "a gamble." About 20% regarded it as a "core part of their investment portfolio." Less than half were reportedly aware that they might need to pay tax on their holdings. This is particularly disturbing since HMRC is reportedly conducting about 20 criminal investigations relating to tax evasion involving digital assets.[577]

[A] Bank of England

Toward the end of 2021, the Bank of England expressed the view that expanding use of cryptocurrencies in the financial system posed a significant risk to overall financial stability.[578] It said that before banks and other financial institutions began using cryptocurrencies extensively, they should wait until financial regulators around the world put in place adequate financial regulations to protect against the disruptive effects and potential volatility of cryptocurrency.[579]

The Bank stated that it would be dangerous if financial institutions accumulated large positions in cryptocurrency and then experienced dramatic falls in their value.[580]

This could become an issue because of the volatility cryptocurrencies have experienced in the past when changes in market confidence led to significant reductions of their value.

In response to the perceived risk of crypto assets, the Bank's Financial Policy Committee (FPC) published an outline in March of 2022 as to how you thought cryptocurrency should be regulated and supervised in the future.

The Bank recognized that cryptocurrencies have largely been unregulated, and this posed problems which could possibly develop into a disruption of the type experienced in 2008 and the years following.

The Bank's view was that crypto should be regulated in much the same way as other financial services under existing financial market rules. The FPC said:

> Where crypto technology is performing and equivalent economic function to one performed in the traditional financial sector, the FPC judges that this should take

576. FCA, "Cryptoassets," online at fca.org.uk, May 23, 2022.
577. FCA, August 12, 2022, cited above.
578. "Crypto's Rise Carries High Risk of Market Turbulence, Bank Warns," The Times, online, December 14, 2021.
579. *Ibid.*
580. *Ibid.*

> place within existing regulatory arrangements, and that the regulatory perimeter be adapted as necessary to ensure an equivalent regulatory outcome.[581]

The UK regulators have been motivated by their awareness that the volatility of the crypto markets has caused numerous people in the UK and elsewhere to lose money in the crypto markets. There is also significant concern that crypto is being used in a variety of financial crimes, including money laundering, hacking for ransom, and fraud.[582]

There had also been a worrying dramatic rise in the number of people advertising get-rich schemes on the Internet that involved cryptocurrency.[583]

[B] Investment

Members of the British Parliament are reported to have pressured financial regulators to stop permitting financial firms to promote cryptocurrencies by referring to them as "investments."

Members complained that referring to cryptocurrencies as investments gives them undeserved credibility. One MP said, "the words 'your investment' endorse the idea that this is an investment on par with a FTSE 100 company or a unit trust."[584]

The Chief Executive of the FCA responded with a slightly different view, saying that:

> Personally, I would suggest we simply say that anything crypto-related should not be entitled to compensation, so that consumers are clear about that when they are investing. We'll have a discussion about what the wording should be.[585]

The UK FCA is a regulator of the financial services industry in the UK. Their roles include consumer protection, protecting industry stability and promoting reasonable competition between financial service providers.[586]

These roles give the FCA important responsibility for oversight of the crypto asset business. The FCA defines its "work on crypto assets" as being:

> to ensure that consumers are protected, market integrity is upheld, and that competition works in the interest of consumers.[587]

However, reading regulatory policy statements on crypto assets, one can be forgiven for thinking there is a significant amount of confusion in the UK about

---

581. Ben Martin, cited above, March 25, 2022.
582. *Ibid.*
583. David Byers, "TSB Bans Cryptocurrency Amid Fraud Concerns With Binance and Kraken," The Times, online, June 19, 2021.
584. Scott Chipolina, "UK Politicians Tell Regulator Bitcoin 'Is Not an Investment'," The Times, online, December 9, 2021.
585. Scott Chipolina, December 9, 2021, cited above.
586. UK Government, "Financial Conduct Authority," online at: gov.uk, accessed September 2, 2022.
587. FCA, "Cryptoassets: Our Work," August 12, 2022, online at: fca.org.uk, accessed September 2, 2022.

whether, and to what extent, crypto assets are regulated in the UK. As examples of this ambiguity, there is a press release from the FCA dated September of 2022 in which the FCA refers to Advertising Standards that govern the marketing of cryptocurrency. It is stated that such advertising should include statements that "cryptocurrency is not regulated by the FCA and not covered by financial compensation schemes." The was a report in *The Times* on November 16, 2022, following the dramatic collapse of the FTX crypto exchange, that said:

> The Financial Conduct Authority can only warn people of potential risks with crypto. The sector has no capital requirements, as there are in banking, and no financial compensation scheme. ... When the Treasury Select Committee held a session on the sector on [14 November 2022], Ian Taylor, Executive Director at the industry body CryptoUK,[588] said pointedly that "founder members" had testified to it in 2018 that they wanted regulation, and that had there been some four years later perhaps these recent events might not have been allowed to happen.[589]

It seems a little unfair that the UK and particularly the FCA are criticized for not paying enough attention to regulating crypto assets. An examination of the record shows that the UK has been expanding its regulation of crypto assets for some years.

Part of the confusion is probably because UK regulators have long been aware that they are saddled with a double responsibility in the financial markets. One aspect of that is to protect the UK's position as a leading financial market and to foster its expansion and growth. The second rule is to protect the integrity and stability of the financial markets and to protect the consumers that participate in financial market transactions. There is some conflict within this dual role to both encourage and protect. It is not easy to craft a regulatory system that does both equally well without one goal undermining the other.

§5.03 THE SANDBOX

The attempt to balance these goals was reflected in the 2016 decision of the UK government to allow the creation of a financial market "sandbox."

However, the UK being aware that it is important to support London's position as an important financial market, has understood that it is necessary to adjust to some of the dramatic changes brought about in the financial markets by innovations such as digital assets. Consequently, the FCA has established a "Regulatory Sandbox" (initially in 2016, but with modifications since then) that "allows firms to test innovative propositions in the market with real customers."[590]

---

588. CryptoUK describes itself as an independent trade body that represents the UK Crypto and Digital Assets sector. It also provides a secretariat for the Crypto and Digital Assets All Party Parliamentary Group, which provides a forum for parliamentarians, regulators, governments and companies in the crypto sector. Website at: cryptouk.io.
589. Katie Prescott, November 16, 2022, cit. above.
590. FCA, "Regulatory Sandbox," online at: fca.org.uk, August 24, 2022, accessed September 22, 2022.

On their website the FCA describes the benefits of their Regulatory Sandbox to innovative financial companies as follows:

> "The Regulatory Sandbox provides innovators, both incumbents and new players, with access to regulatory expertise. It's open to applications from all sectors of the financial services market and gives firms:
>
> - The ability to test products and services in a controlled environment.
> - The opportunity to find out whether a business model is attractive to consumers, or how a particular technology works in the market.
> - A reduced time to market at potentially lower cost.
> - Support in identifying consumer protection safeguards that can be built into new products and services."
>
> Among the sandbox benefits offered by the FCA, those that qualify for the Sandbox will have "a dedicated case manager to provide support in the development and implementation of a test."

The FCA does not envision that those using the Sandbox opportunity will be allowed to market their innovation to the public generally. The Sandbox provides an opportunity to test a new product for a limited time with a limited number of consumers. Although participating in the Regulatory Sandbox does not impose the same requirements as a full application for authorization with the FCA, there are still formal requirements that need to be complied with before a firm is permitted to operate a test in the Regulatory Sandbox.

Obtaining access to Regulatory Sandbox status requires an application to the FCA which, if granted, permits "restricted authorization or registration" where a firm can test an innovative product or service with the limitations agreed with the FCA. The FCA will provide guidance, which, although not as detailed as would be provided to a fully authorized firm, will help point the Sandbox firm in the right direction. The FCA will give an "informal steer" To help the testing firm understand what regulatory rules may apply to their innovative business. However, because the steer is informal, a Sandbox company has to understand that the steer may not provide the full implications of what the regulatory position of the innovative business will be if it applies for formal authorization. The testing firm may not fully understand regulatory requirements that will apply to its innovative business. The FCA will help firms understand and interpret how the regulatory rules will apply to the Sandbox test and how they might apply if the innovative product becomes formally authorized. If the application of a particular regulatory rule is unclear or ambiguous, the FCA may be willing to temporarily waive an FCA rule. However, Sandbox firms need to understand that the FCA is not able to waive national or international law. In cases where the FCA is not able to fully understand what the impact of an innovative the business being tested in the regulatory Sandbox will be, the FCA may be able to issue a "no action letter" which will stay FCA disciplinary action for the duration of the Sandbox test.[591]

591. *Ibid.*

The FCA says:

> We accept applications from firms of all sizes, at all stages of development and from all sectors of financial services .... We're open to all types of propositions.[592]

[A] Evolving Crypto Regulation

In March of 2018, the UK government established a Cryptoassets Task Force as part of its Financial Technology (Fintech) Strategy. The Task Force was to include Her Majesty's Treasury, the Bank of England and the FCA to together assess the impact of crypto assets and to consider policy responses. That Task Force published a report on October 26, 2018. An important conclusion of the Task Force Report was:

> There is a lack of regulatory clarity in the UK.[593]

Consequently, the Task Force said the following should be done:

> The task force has concluded that strong action should be taken to address the risks associated with crypto assets that fall within existing regulatory frameworks. Further consultation and international coordination is required for those crypto assets that pose new challenges to traditional forms of financial regulation, and fall outside the existing regulatory framework. The authorities plan to engage with international bodies to ensure a comprehensive response.[594]

Given the comments above, made in 2022, it is apparent that there are doubts that the UK regulatory system had achieved the necessary clarity by that time.

However, between 2018 and 2022, the UK, step by step, began to increase its regulation of "crypto-assets."

[B] Archax Ltd.

In the UK, an important step forward toward participation in the digital asset economy is the founding in 2018 of the digital asset exchange Archax Ltd. (Archax).[595]

Archax describes itself as "an FCA-regulated digital asset exchange, broker and custodian targeted at professional and institutional clients globally. Archax operates in London, Hong Kong and the Philippines."[596]

In August of 2022, the UK investment manager, Abrdn, which has over £500 billion under management, said that it was taking a large "stake in the block chain-focused startup Archax."[597]

---

592. *Ibid.*
593. HM Treasury, FCA, Bank of England, "Cryptoassets Taskforce: final report," October 2018, p. 52. Available for review/download from: gov.uk/government/publications/cryptoassets-taskforce.
594. Cryptoassets Task Force, Final Report, cited above, Forward, p. 3.
595. Ben Martin, "Abrdn Takes Stake in Crypto Start-up Archax," The Times, online, August 12, 2022.
596. Archax, online at: archax.com.
597. *Ibid.*

Abrdn owns more shares of Archax than any other outside investor and will have a seat on the board. Steven Bird, the CEO of Abrdn said that this stake would give them a "meaningful footprint" in a rapidly developing market. Bird called Archax "one of the most promising UK players in an area expected to see high growth."[598]

However, according to the FCA, the FCA-authorized firm Archax Ltd. has been an unfortunate victim of a particular kind of financial crime. This crime is "cloning" an FCA-authorized firm, such as Archax Ltd. A clone firm has been reported to the FCA that operates under the name "Archax Trade" (archaxtrade.com).[599]

This is an example of unfortunate development that has been detailed by the FCA[600] as follows:

> Fraudsters are using the details of firms we authorize to try to convince people that they work for a genuine, authorized firm. ... .
>
> This is what we call a "clone firm"; and fraudsters usually use this tactic when contacting people out of the blue, so you should be especially wary if you have been cold-called. They may use the name of the genuine firm, the "firm reference number" (FRN) that we have given the authorized firm, or other details.

To avoid being scammed by such firms, the FCA urges people to check the Financial Services Register to ensure they are dealing with an actual FCA-authorized firm.[601]

The FCA issues regular announcements about crypto-related firms it believes may be providing financial services or products in the UK without FCA authorization. Some examples that FCA has included in such announcements are the following:

- 02/09/2022: bitftradez.
- 26/08/2022: Bitcoin Vault.
- 24/08/2022: Cryptojet/Cryptojet Ltd Trading Ltd.
- 19/08/2022: Hash Miner Ltd.
- 19/08/2022: Prime Coin.

These are just a few examples.[602] Indeed, FCA Enforcement Data Annual Report, 2020/21 showed that the most common enforcement actions brought by the FCA, by far, were cases dealing with unauthorized business.[603]

598. *Ibid.*
599. *Ibid.*
600. UK FCA, Warnings, "Archax Trade (Clone of an FCA Authorized Firm)," online at: fca.org.uk., August 19, 2021, accessed August 15, 2022.
601. *Ibid.*
602. FCA, Press Releases, By Year, online at: fca.org.uk., accessed September 6, 2022.
603. FCA, "Enforcement Data—Annual Report 2022/21," July 15, 2021, online at: fca.org.uk, accessed September 6, 2022.

[C] Registration with FCA

In January of 2020, the FCA acquired regulatory powers allowing the FCA to supervise how crypto asset businesses manage money laundering risks and counterterrorist financing.

These required crypto asset businesses in the UK to comply with the Money Laundering Regulations (MLRs) and to register with the FCA.

From January 10, 2020, the FCA became the anti-money laundering and counterterrorist financing supervisor for crypto asset firms, including firms that exchange money to and from crypto assets and those that held customers' crypto assets.

[D] Regulation of Cryptocurrency Companies

The British government has taken the regulation of cryptocurrency seriously and has established a path to bring it under the type of full regulation that covers traditional financial investments.

In December of 2020, the FCA set up a temporary register that allowed companies that were undergoing an FCA review process of their applications for full regulatory approval. In part, this was intended as an encouragement to companies who sought registration but were unable to obtain it within the time they hoped because their initial efforts did not meet the FCA's full approval.[604]

Prior to the establishment of this temporary register, the FCA did have some regulatory authority over the digital asset companies. As of January 2020, the FCA gained responsibility for supervising the anti-money laundering and anti-terrorist financing efforts of companies which included cryptocurrency businesses. This did require those businesses to register with the FCA and to take the required steps to meet the FCA requirements to prevent money laundering and terrorist financing from being done through them.[605]

Those cryptocurrency businesses that did not opt to be on the temporary register would be required to stop operating their businesses in the UK. However, this did not solve the problem completely because those that did not wish to be on the register could move their operations to an overseas location and still be in a position to seek customers in the UK from their foreign location over the Internet. At least one company was reported to be taking this route. Global Block a crypto broker that is listed on Canada Toronto Stock Exchange did operate in the UK through a subsidiary on the temporary register. However, in February of 2020, it learned that its application for permanent regulation in the UK was unlikely to meet with FCA approval. The firm subsequently announced that it was going to shift its business to Lithuania, which is an

604. Ben Martin, "Crypto Firms May Move Abroad As Deadline Looms," The Times, online March 30, 2022.
605. *Ibid.*

EU Member that Global Block apparently believed would give them opportunities to sell their services in the UK and throughout the EU.[606]

The FCA set up their temporary registration regime for crypto companies so that it would end on March 31, 2022.[607] From the government's point of view, it was hoped that establishing this temporary registration process would encourage a number of cryptocurrency companies to come forward and at least allow the FCA to be aware that they were doing business in the UK and to provide a certain level of regulatory insight into their activities. A number of cryptocurrency companies appear to have considered that it is in their public relations interest to be on this FCA temporary register.[608]

Since then, the UK's reputation as a major financial center has inspired more than thirty crypto businesses to go through the FCA's permanent registration processes and successfully complete them.

[E] FCA Definitions of Crypto Assets

Crypto asset firms were required to be registered with the FCA by January 10, 2021. As of January 10, 2020, new crypto asset firms were required to obtain full FCA registration before beginning business.[609]

The FCA defines "cryptoassets" as follows:

> Cryptoassets are cryptographically secured digital representations of value or contractual rights that use some type of Distributed Ledger Technology (DLT) and can be transferred, stored or traded electronically.[610]

The FCA emphasizes that there are different kinds of crypto assets that might fall within the regulatory perimeter in different ways. The FCA divides the crypto asset spectrum as follows. First, there are "regulated tokens" which include both "security tokens" and "e-money tokens." "Security tokens" can be regulated by the FCA because they constitute a "specified investment" within the UK's Regulated Activities Order (RAO).

Security tokens, which do not include e-money tokens, may provide ownership, repayment of a defined sum of money, or entitlement to shares in future profits. They might also be transferable securities or financial instruments under the EU's markets in Financial Instruments Directive. These tokens are considered to be probably within the perimeter of FCA regulation.

"E-money tokens" are tokens that fall within the definition of e-money under the E-Money Regulations (EMRs). These are regulated by the FCA.[611]

---

606. *Ibid.*
607. *Ibid.*
608. *Ibid.*
609. FCA, "FCA Establishes Temporary Registration Regime for Cryptoasset businesses," Press Release, December 16, 2020, online at fca.org.uk.
610. FCA, August 12, 2022, cited above.
611. *Ibid.*

[F] FCA Ban on Retail Sales

In October of 2020, it was reported that the FCA had announced a ban on the sale of crypto derivatives to retail clients. The FCA is reported as saying:

> Retail customers can't reliably assess the value and risks of derivatives like contracts for differences (CFDs), futures, options, and exchange traded notes (ETNs) that reference certain crypto-assets.

Forbes expressed the view that this ban would be detrimental to the UK's desire to remain a leading international financial center. They said it would also damage the UK's reputation as a promoter of financial technology.[612]

In its announcement on October 16, 2020, the FCA said:

> "The FCA considers these products to be ill-suited for retail customers due to the harm they pose. These products cannot be reliably valued by retail consumers because of the:
>
> - The inherent nature of the underlying assets, which means they have no reliable basis for valuation.
> - Prevalence of market abuse and financial crime in the secondary market (e.g. cyber theft).
> - Extreme volatility in crypto-asset price movements.
> - Inadequate understanding of crypto-assets by retail consumers.
> - Lack of legitimate investment need for retail consumers to invest in these products ... ."
>
> "To address these harms, the FCA has made rules banning the sale, marketing and distribution of all retail consumers of any derivatives (i.e. contracts for differences—CFDs, options and futures) and ETNs that reference unregulated transferable crypto-assets by firms acting in, or from, the UK."
>
> "The FCA estimates that retail consumers will save around 53 million pounds from the ban of these products."

"Sheldon Mills, Interim Executive Director of Strategy and Competition at the FCA, said:

> This ban reflects how seriously we view the potential harm to retail consumers in these products. Consumer protection is paramount here."

The ban came into effect on January 6, 2021.[613]

612. Lawrence Wintermeyer, "FCA Crypto Ban Is a Setback For The U.K. In the Race to Lead the Growing Global Digital Assets Market," Forbes, October 20, 2020, online at: forbes.com, accessed August 31, 2022.
613. FCA, Press Releases, "FCA Bans the Sale of Crypto-derivatives to Retail Consumers," October 6, 2020, online at: fca.org.uk, accessed August 31, 2022.

[G] Advertising Crypto Assets

In May of 2022, the FCA reminded the public that it had not been given regulatory oversight over *direct investments*[614] in crypto assets and NFTs. They said:

> There are no consumer protections for those who buy any crypto assets and NFTs, and they are not FSCS protected. As a result, if you buy crypto assets you should be prepared to lose all the money you invest.

They emphasize that those marketing crypto assets must follow the guidelines set out by the Advertising Standards Authority (ASA). These require that marketers state:

- these crypto assets are not regulated by the FCA; and
- these crypto assets are not protected by financial compensation schemes.

The FCA says that among the crypto adverts that have been investigated by the ASA, many did not make it clear that the products were not regulated or protected in the UK.[615]

In August of 2022, the ASA published detailed advice on crypto assets and their advertising.

They state that their advice is not "legal advice" and "does not bind CAP, CAP[616] advisory panels or the Advertising Standards Authority." However, their publication does provide information on the following both to consumers and crypto asset sellers.[617] The advice includes the following:

- What is a crypto asset?
- Regulation of crypto assets.
- Make clear that crypto assets are unregulated and not protected.
- Do not take advantage of consumers' inexperience or credulity.
- Include all material information.
- Make clear that value can go down as well as up.
- State the basis used to calculate any projections or forecasts.
- Make clear that past performance is not a guide for future performance.

§5.04 UK REGULATORY ENFORCEMENT

[A] FCA Binance Ban

In June of 2021, the FCA banned Binance from engaging in regulated activities in the UK after the FCA concluded that Binance did not comply with money laundering standards.

---

614. Purchases are not made from or through an FCA regulated entity.
615. Financial Conduct Authority, Press Releases, "FCA Reminds Consumers of the Risks of Investing in Cryptoassets," May 11, 2022, online at: fca.org.uk, accessed September 1, 2022.
616. Committee of Advertising Practice Ltd. CAP writes advertising codes applied by the ASA. *See*: ASA, "Who We Are and What We Do," online at: asa.org.uk.
617. Advertising Standards Agency (ASA), Advice and Resources, "Cryptoassets, Advice Online," August 17, 2022, online at: asa.org.uk, accessed September 1, 2022.

Binance is reported to have a Chinese/Canadian founder and to be one of the largest crypto marketplaces with more than 13 million customers.

One of the disadvantages that Binance suffered from the UK regulator's ruling was being denied access to the UK's Faster Payments Service, which speeds money transfers from one bank to another. However, in January 2022, Binance made an arrangement with Paysafe Financial Services, an institution that is authorized and regulated by the FCA to issue electronic money and to provide associated payment services. This reestablished Binance's access to the Faster Payments Service. However, the FCA has expressed continuing concern about Binance's—particularly regarding—money laundering issues.[618]

The FCA said:

> Our concerns about Binance remain. We received a notification of this business partnership but have limited powers to object two arrangements of this kind.

It was reported in September of 2022 that Lord Vaizey of Didcot had become an adviser to Binance. As reported in *The Times*:

> "Vaizey joining Binance is likely to raise eyebrows given the tough stance on the firm taken by the Financial Conduct Authority, the UK regulator."
>
> "Since June last year the FCA has warned the public about Binance and barred the firm's UK arm from carrying out regulated business here. It believes Binance 'is not capable of being effectively supervised' and that its products pose 'a significant risk to customers.'"
>
> "Vaizey, 54, was an MP and the culture minister in [Prime Minister] David Cameron's government."[619]

However, the company, although reportedly registered in the Cayman Islands, apparently has no headquarters, and has attracted investigations by several financial regulators.

[B] Negative Bank Rules on Crypto

[1] TSB Blocks Crypto Trading

In June of 2021, during a period of frenzied purchases and sales, and wildly fluctuating values, some powerful opposition to the use of cryptocurrency has been building. For example, in June of 2021, the Trustee Savings Bank (TSB), a large British bank, with more than 5 million customers, said that it was preparing to block its customers from sending money to cryptocurrency trading sites.

They had noticed that customers were losing money to scammers apparently using the Binance trading site, registered in the Cayman Islands. They reported that

618. "Financial Conduct Authority Still Worried Over Binance," The Times, online February 17, 2022.
619. Ben Martin, "Tory Peer Joins Banned Crypto Firm As Advisor" The Times, online September 23, 2022.

over eight hundred of their customers had said they lost money to scams connected to Binance accounts.

[2] Barclays Bank Ban

Following that, another large UK bank, Barclays, banned its UK clients from transferring funds to Binance (although customers could still make withdrawals from Binance).[620]

[3] Starling Bank

Starling Bank also suspended payments to crypto exchanges to protect customers from fraud.

In September 2021, it was announced that the FCA intended to take a closer look at the regulations of cryptocurrencies.

[4] The *Ben Delo* Case

In August of 2022, it was reported that a cryptocurrency billionaire who previously pled guilty to violating U.S. anti-money laundering regulations was bringing a novel legal case against the UK's data regulator, the Information Commissioner's Office.[621]

The billionaire in question is Ben Delo, a cofounder of BitMEX. Delo says he has permission for a judicial review of a decision by the Information Commissioner to refuse to hand over reports of suspicious activity allegedly made by a competitor, Wise Payments, to the National Crime Agency. It is speculated that these reports might be related to money laundering allegations.[622]

Delo's attorney is reported to have alleged:

> The Information Commission is meant to protect the data protection rights of individuals—and it hasn't done so in this case.[623]

§5.05 DIGITAL POUND?

[A] Britcoin: Digitalization of Central Bank Currency

Britain is considering creating its own cyber currency, tentatively referred to as: "Britcoin."

620. Ben Martin, "Barclays Blocks Customers Moving Cash to Binance After FCA Ban," The Times, online, July 6, 2021.
621. Jonathan Ames, "Cryptocurrency Tycoon Ben Delo in Legal Challenge Over Data Watchdog," The Times, online, August 12, 2022.
622. *Ibid.*
623. *Ibid.*

Britain, along with other countries, has understood that if the use of cybercurrency offers any national advantages, tying them to national currency issued by central banks may help reduce their volatility.

In June 2021, Andrew Bailey, Governor of the Bank of England, said that the Bank has been discussing the prospect of creating digital Pounds, and these have been given the name "Britcoins."

Bailly reportedly said that he supported the exploration of central bank use of what he considered to be a "critical innovation" in finance. He said he considered this innovation to have created a new era in finance which central banks such as the Bank of England should be considering using.[624]

Britcoin would be tied to the value of Pounds Sterling.

624. Callum Jones, "A Central Bank Digital Currency Would be Historic Innovation, says Andrew Bailey," The Times, online, June 12, 2021.

CHAPTER 6
Chinese Law

§6.01 CHINA

Historically, China has often been at the forefront of monetary policy and reportedly is heading that way again. There is evidence that China, during the Yuan Dynasty, introduced the first national paper currency.[625]

In the Five-Year Plan introduced by the Chinese in 2016, it was made clear that a key pillar of government policy was to increase the importance of Chinese currency in the international markets. This included becoming less sensitive to U.S. monetary policy, protecting the Chinese economy against the power of the U.S. dollar, and lowering borrowing costs.

However, it seems that China's policy of strict regulation will also extend to cryptocurrencies.

§6.02 CRYPTOCURRENCY

China clearly resents the fact that Chinese currency is far less important in the International Monetary markets then the U.S. dollar. For example, it is reported that around 60% of international foreign reserves are in dollars and only about 2% in Chinese currency.[626] Of course, there are many reasons for this, not all of which are results of monetary policy. As one commentator has pointed out:[627]

> Crucially, China's rule of law, trustworthiness and tightly controlled economy make investors skittish of relying on Chinese currency.

---

625. Sam Davidson, "Digital Dynasties: How China's Cryptocurrency Could Unseat the Dollar," Harvard International Review, August 29, 2022, online at: hir.harvard.edu.
626. *Ibid.*
627. *Ibid.*

However, the Chinese government's behavior over the last eight years has indicated that China believes that one thing that may help them in achieving more power in the monetary markets is introduction of a digital national currency ("digital yuan").

In 2014, the People's Bank of China (PBC) began exploring government-issued cryptocurrency. Prior to that time, the mining of cryptocurrency in China had become a huge activity, using so much electricity that the government noticed the unusual increases in power usage. In fact, the mining was so intensive that at that time over 90% of new cryptocurrency was being mined in China. The Chinese government reacted with horror. The introduction and use of private cryptocurrency were seen as a serious challenge to China's rigid social and financial regulations.[628]

Two things began to happen in China. First, China began a crackdown on private cryptocurrency business, and began to transition its national currency from paper to digital.

[A] Chinese Crackdown on Mining

When the government of China began its crackdown on Bitcoin creation (mining) in May of 2021, this caused the market price of Bitcoin to drop about thirty percent, and the overall value of the cryptocurrency to lose about a trillion U.S. dollars.[629] About two weeks previously, some of the China's largest banks were told that they were not allowed to hold or use cryptocurrency. This was a shock to the market because before that China was judged to be the location of the largest production of cryptocurrency. A state newspaper, *The Global Times*, reported that many bitcoin mines had been shut down. About 90% of China's mining capacity had been shut down.[630]

The Chinese government had decided that it was too big a problem that cryptocurrency mining diverted huge amounts of electric power from other uses:

> China's National Development and Reform Commission said it will work to cut off financial support and electricity supply for mining, which it said, spawns risks and hampers carbon neutrality goals.[631]

[B] China's Crypto Ban

In mid-June 2021, it was reported that the Chinese police arrested 1,100 people on suspicion of using cryptocurrency trades to launder money.[632]

628. *Ibid.*
629. Charlie Campbell, "Why China Is Cracking Down on Bitcoin Mining and What It Could Mean for Other Countries," Time, online, June 2, 2021.
630. Callum Jones, "Bitcoin Falls As China Clamps Down," The Times, online, June 22, 2021.
631. Alun John and Samuel Shen, Tom Wilson, September 24, 2021.
632. Patrick Hosking, "World's Banks Must Cover Risk of Bitcoin, says Regulator," The Times, online June 11, 2021.

However, it was only in September of 2021 that the main Chinese financial regulators cooperated together to impose such a comprehensive ban on cryptocurrency:

> "[The September 2021 ban] ... is the most detailed and expansive yet from the country's main regulators, underscoring Beijing's commitment to suffocating the Chinese crypto market.
>
> 'In the history of crypto market regulation in China, this is the most direct, most comprehensive regulatory framework involving the largest number of ministries,' said Winston Ma, NYU Law School, Adjunct Professor."[633]

While other countries have been trying to find some sort of balanced way to deal with the growing popularity of cryptocurrencies that responds to both their usefulness and the risk that they entail, China decided to ban all cryptocurrency transactions.[634] On September 23, 2021, China's regulators imposed a total ban on all cryptocurrency transactions and mining. Of course, this negatively affected the prices of cryptocurrencies such as Bitcoin as well as crypto and blockchain-related shares.

China's negative attitude toward cryptocurrency is not new. Chinese regulators have been placing restrictions on the use of cryptocurrencies since at least 2013. They have placed several bans on providing services relating to cryptocurrency business in that year, another in 2017 and then those of 2021.

China like other countries shares the worries that digital currencies were displacing nationally issued mediums of exchange thus reducing government control of financial markets and financial systems and their regulation of tax revenues.

[C] Negative Impacts of Crypto

In addition, digital currencies entailed significant financial risk, aided financial crime, and took investment away from traditional investment vehicles such as stocks and bonds.

China is also planning to introduce its own "digital yuan" and did not want privately created digital currencies to compete with that.

China's hardline regulatory attitude toward cryptocurrencies has provoked negative comment in other countries. In the US, a prominent Republican Senator tweeted:

> Beijing is so hostile to economic freedom they cannot even tolerate their people participating in what is arguably the most exciting innovation in finance in decades.[635]

633. Alun John and Samuel Shen, Tom Wilson, September 24, 2021.
634. Alun John and Samuel Shen, Tom Wilson, "China's Top Regulators Ban Crypto Trading and Mining, Sending Bitcoin Tumbling," Reuters, online, September 24, 2021.
635. Alun John and Samuel Shen, Tom Wilson, September 24, 2021.

On the other hand, China's view is that must prevent speculation in cryptocurrency to safeguard the property of its people and preserve economic, financial, and social stability.[636]

[D] Digital Yuan

Despite China's negative attitude toward privately issued cryptocurrencies, the country apparently sees some advantages to the issuance of government-sponsored digital currency. In response to that, it is reported that China has been moving its economy away from paper transactions toward digital transactions. Throughout the year 2021, it is reported that about 80% of payments in China were made electronically.

It has been reported that China had already begun limited trials of transactions using the digital yuan in the year 2020.[637] This resulted in the creation of over 120 million individual cryptocurrency wallets for use with the digital yuan. That is an impressive number, but when looked at closely it was found that the average sum in these wallets was only equal to about US$ 0.45. It is believed that the Chinese government had hoped that the digital yuan would be used more extensively. This was an indication that the Chinese population was not using the new digital currency enthusiastically.[638]

In response, the Chinese hoped to use the Winter Olympics of January 2022 to promote the digital yuan to the world. In the period preceding the Olympics, China hoped to double the number of digital yuan transactions. During the Games, the PBC reported that there was a daily average of about US$ 300,000 dollars' worth of digital yuan transactions. Although domestically, China's digital yuan payments are still relatively small compared to the digital payments transacted by the country's biggest digital payment companies, AliPay and TenPay, China's ambitions for the digital yuan in the international markets remain strong.[639]

One strategy to turn those ambitions into reality is to use the digital yuan as a tool for conducting financial transactions relating to China's foreign investment initiative in developing countries called the Belt and Road initiative (BRI). It is hoped that using the digital yuan in Chinese infrastructure projects in foreign countries will make a number of foreign countries comfortable with the digital yuan as a currency for transacting business. This could lead to strengthening the Chinese currency's position in world monetary markets. The BRI is projected to cost approximately a trillion dollars. If much of this investment is in the form of digital yuan, this makes the digital yuan a strong contender in international business.[640]

636. *Ibid.*
637. BBC News, online, February 2, 2022.
638. Sam Davidson, August 29, 2022.
639. *Ibid.*
640. *Ibid.*

[E] Do Non-government Cryptos Have a Future?

It is not clear whether the introduction and use of the digital yuan will lead to relaxation of the current Chinese ban on most private cryptocurrencies. If they are perceived as posing a threat to China's centralized control of its social and economic life, probably not. But if the digital yuan becomes so dominant both in China and internationally that its strength outweighs the impact of private digital assets in China, China may reopen its economy to private cryptocurrencies once again.

CHAPTER 7
Indian Law

§7.01 CRYPTO IN INDIA

The Indian government's reaction to the existence of private cryptocurrency has been largely negative.

In 2018, the Indian Prime Minister Narendra Modi commented that cyber currency posed a risk to Indian youth and that the government had a duty to introduce legislation to regulate cyber currency to reduce the chances for digital assets to provide avenues for money laundering and terrorist financing.[641]

Shortly thereafter, the Reserve Bank of India imposed the ban on trading of cryptocurrencies.[642] However, that was overturned in 2018 by the India Supreme Court.[643]

According to an article published in September of 2022, India had not yet passed any formal legislation on how cryptocurrencies should be regulated. However, planning to do so was underway.

At that time, it was reported that India was planning a law that will ban the use and trading of cryptocurrencies but would permit the use of the underlying blockchain technology. Blockchain technology can be used in many ways not related to cryptocurrency. The name of the bill that has been proposed to achieve this is called the Cryptocurrency & Regulation of Official Digital Currency Bill, 2021.[644]

---

641. Live Mint, "PM Modi Has a Warning for "Young" Crypto Users in India," updated November 18, 2021, online at: livemint.com.
642. Prohibition on dealing of Virtual Currencies (VCs), Circular No. RBI/2017-18 154.
643. *Internet and Mobile Association of India v. Reserve Bank of India Writ Petition (Civil)* No. 528 of 2018.
644. Rishi Batta and Karan, "India: Cryptocurrency: A Legal Perspective on a Misunderstood Technology," TATVA LEGAL, September 26, 2022, online at: mondaq.com.

According to a summary of the proposed bill, violators of the law against private cryptocurrency could be arrested without a warrant and held without bail pending their prosecution for a criminal offense.[645]

The ban will extend to all private crypto-related activities, including mining, generating, holding, selling, or dealing in "digital currencies as a medium of exchange, store of value or unit of account." Essentially, no private payments of any kind are to be permitted using privately issued digital currency.

However, prior to this proposed legislation becoming law, it was an open question as to whether cryptocurrency was an asset that was covered by existing legislation or require new legislation to treat it as a new type of asset.[646] Existing Indian legislation relating to currencies and the issue of what is "legal tender" include:[647]

- Reserve Bank of India Act, 1934 (RBI Act).
- Foreign Exchange Management Act, 1999 (FEMA).
- Payments and Settlement Act, 2007 (PSSA).
- Coinage Act, 2011.

Although none of the above specifically deal with digital currency or virtual currency, all relate to money and payments. It might be possible to interpret some of their provisions to apply to cybercurrency. However, the Indian government had not yet done that.[648]

There is also a question as to whether digital assets could be interpreted as "securities" under Indian law.

Despite the uncertain position of Indian law on digital assets, several cryptocurrency exchanges have been established in India. This has raised the question of whether digital assets could constitute a regulated investment. An additional factor in this consideration is that Initial Coin Offerings (ICOs) are available for purchase on cryptocurrency exchanges.[649] Might these be regulated in the same way that Initial Public Offering (IPOs) of company shares are regulated?

The definition of "securities" under India's Securities Contract (Regulation) Act 1956 does not expressly include digital assets such as cybercurrencies, tokens, or NFTs, but it is a broad definition and could be used to cover some digital assets.[650]

It is reported that at least one Indian court case has applied a test to define "investment" that could cover certain digital assets. In 2004, a case in a division of the Allahabad High Court[651] applied the "Howey Test" to decide whether a certain finance arrangement was an investment.

645. Aftab Ahmed and Nupur Anand, "Proposed India Bill Banning Crypto Payments Could Mean Jail for Violations—Document," Reuters, online, December 7, 2021.
646. Rishi Batta and Karan, September 26, 2022.
647. *Ibid.*
648. *Ibid.*
649. *Ibid.*
650. *Ibid.*
651. *Ibid.*, citing *Paramount Bio-Tech Industries v. Union of India (2004)* 2 Compl.J 446 All. The "Howey Test" was established by the U.S. Supreme Court in *SEC v. W.J. Howey Co.*, 328 US 293 (1946).

The *Howey Test* looks at whether a transaction satisfies the following four conditions:

(1) An investment of money.
(2) In a common enterprise.
(3) With the expectation of profit.
(4) To come significantly from the efforts of others.[652]

Commentators in different jurisdictions have reached the conclusion that applying an analysis of the type found in the Howey Test could find that a number of different digital assets, such as ICOs, do constitute regulated investment contracts.[653] That may be the ultimate conclusion under Indian law.[654]

India does expect to introduce an official digital currency according to reports.

Despite the fact that India appears to support the concept of digital currency to some extent by considering issuing its own government-sponsored digital "rupee," their refusal to allow private-issued digital currencies to become part of the Indian economy deals a heavy blow to the value and usefulness of the many private digital currencies that have been issued including Bitcoin.

India is one of the largest economies in the world, and now that private digital currency has been banned by China, a substantial portion of world economic activity has been barred to privately issued digital currencies. That could put downward pressure on the value of those currencies.

If a significant number of countries decide to go the route of issuing their own digital currencies and banning the use of private currencies, the values of privately issued cryptos may fall so far that they are eventually not used at all and may become valueless.

In fact, even if private digital currencies are not expressly forbidden, but significant numbers of countries issue their own digital currency, it seems likely that the use of government-sponsored digital currencies will become a more popular medium of exchange than the privately issued ones. The privately issued ones may be restricted to narrow areas of the world economy. Unfortunately, one of those areas may be the "dark web" and criminal activity if such currencies can still be used to purchase goods and services in those contexts.

§7.02 DIGITAL RUPEE

In early February of 2022, the Indian finance minister announced that India intended to issue a digital version of the rupee. However, it was also announced that any profits made from transactions in cryptocurrencies or NFTs would be taxed at India's highest tax rate.[655]

652. *Ibid.*
653. Nathan Reiff, Andy Smith and Michael Logan, "Howey Test Definition: What It Means and Implications for Cryptocurrency," Investopedia, August 11, 2022, online at: investopedia.com.
654. *Ibid.*
655. BBC News, online, February 2, 2022.

CHAPTER 8
Japanese Law

§8.01 CRYPTO REGULATION IN JAPAN

Regulation of financial services in Japan is overseen by Japan's Financial Services Agency (JFSA).

As of the start of 2022, there were no overall restrictions on the ownership or use of cryptocurrency in Japan. However, the JFSA was keeping a watching brief on the development and expansion of the use of cryptocurrency, and some digital assets did fall within regulation of Japanese financial market regulations.

In November of 2021, the JFSA published a paper entitled "The FSA Strategic Priorities July 2021-June 2022."[656] In section 2 of that paper, subsection 1, they included a discussion entitled "Promotion of Digital Innovation." In that section, they say:

> International discussions on the potential use of new financial technologies and how to respond to their risks are also underway, including how to handle global stable coins, with the aim of enhancing cross-border payments. In light of these moves, the study group on digital and decentralized finance, which was established by the JFSA in July of 2021 intends to seek optimal ways for financial institutions to adapt to the shift toward the digitalization of payment measures, securities products and others from the perspective of promoting innovation in the private sector and ensuring appropriate use of protection for financial services.

As of 2022, although there was no overall regulation of digital assets in Japan, that does not mean that they are entirely free of regulation. There are different categories of digital assets, and depending on their characteristics and uses, they can fall within regulation by different Japanese financial laws and regulations such as the Payment Services Act (PSA) or the Financial Instruments and Exchange Act (FIEA).

---

656. FSA, "The JFSA Strategic Priorities July 2021-June 2022," online, November 17, 2021.

For example, there are reported to be transactions in Japan in digital instruments that are called "security tokens." These are said to represent interests in shares, bonds, or funds. These are considered to be regulated under the FIEA because they constitute regulated "electronically recorded transferable rights." Those who are in the business of engaging in transactions for those rights can be required to register as Type I Financial Instruments Business Operators.[657]

Other categories of digital assets such as some cryptocurrencies or tokens (including Bitcoin or Ethereum, and some stablecoins) are regulated under the PSA as "Crypto Assets." Those who engage in transactions in Crypto Assets for the benefit of third parties are required to register as providers of Crypto Asset Exchange Services.[658]

A "Crypto Asset" is defined under the PSA as:

> "1. Proprietary value that may be used to pay an unspecified person the price of any goods purchased or borrowed, or any services provided and that may be sold to or purchased from an unspecified person (limited to that recorded on electronic devices or other objects by electronic means and excluding Japanese and other foreign currencies and currency denominated assets, ...) and that may be transferred using an electronic data processing system;"
>
> "2. Proprietary value that may be exchanged reciprocally for proprietary value specified in the preceding item with an unspecified person and that may be transferred using an electronic data processing system."[659]

In July of 2021, the JFSA established a Digital and Decentralized Finance Planning Office for the purpose of considering what laws and regulations should apply to stablecoins exchangeable for fiat currency.

NFTs are not thought to be within the coverage of the current financial regulatory system, but that may be changing.

§8.02 CONCLUSION

For those wishing to engage in the business of digital asset-related transactions in Japan is that there is in place a complicated and multifaceted financial services regulatory system that can apply to digital asset transactions or transactions related to digital assets such as derivative transactions relating to those assets. There are also likely to be more digital asset-focused regulations introduced as time goes on.

Consequently, engaging in businesses relating to digital assets in Japan will require advice from qualified advisors.

657. Takeshi Nagasse, Tomoyuki Tanaka and Takato Fukui (all with the firm of Anderson, Mori and Tomotsune), "Blockchain & Cryptocurrency Laws and Regulations 2022/Japan," Global Legal Insights, online at: globallegalinsights.com.
658. *Ibid.*
659. *Ibid.*

CHAPTER 9

South Korean Law

Cryptocurrency trading has become extremely popular in South Korea.

It is reported that about 10% of South Koreans have purchased cryptocurrencies. This enthusiasm reached a peak in 2021 when the prices of Bitcoin reached a high value.

It is reported that South Korea has become one of the top three cryptocurrency markets around the globe. Around 10% of total global cryptocurrency trading in August of 2021 was done in Korean currency. The Korean Won has been of the five top currencies used to purchase Bitcoin.

In 2021, cryptocurrency trading in South Korea increased more than ten times from the previous year and at one point exceeded the value of company shares being traded on the South Korean Stock Exchange.

§9.01 TAX AND REGISTRATION

The high interest in South Korea in trading cryptocurrencies has caused the South Korean government to issue regulations to control trading. These have included taxes on cryptocurrency and a requirement that providers of these kinds of "virtual assets" register with the South Korean Financial Intelligence Unit which is the anti-money laundering body of the Korean Financial Services Commission.

This registration had to be completed by September 24, 2021. Those registering had to include proof that the vendors of cryptocurrency were using actual bank accounts. However, many banks were unwilling to accept this business because of what they perceived to be the potential risks involved in cryptocurrency trading. As a result, many small cryptocurrency dealers were unable to find the bank support they needed and that caused them to either shut down or cut back on their business.

Crypto trading in South Korea seems to be particularly popular with young people. More than half of the newly registered users of the four biggest South Korean cryptocurrency exchanges are in their 1920s or 1930s. These young people may see trading in cryptocurrency as a way of helping them deal with rapidly rising housing prices in South Korea and problems young people are having finding jobs. Youth unemployment in South Korea is almost 10%. So, some young people are hoping that they can make a fortune from crypto.[660]

§9.02 BITHUMB EXCHANGE

Bithumb is a South Korean cryptocurrency exchange and reportedly, by trading volume, one of the most active exchanges in the world. One can trade 174 cryptocurrency tokens on the exchange. The exchange reportedly hosts about 75% of Bitcoin trading in South Korea and about 50% of South Korean Ethereum trading.

The trading volume on the exchange is huge. Trading sometimes reportedly equals more than US$ 300 million per day. On some days, Bithumb reportedly hosts more trading than any other crypto exchange in the world.

However, Bithumb has had problems. In June 2017, the personal details are more than 30,000 customers were put at risk due to a reported hack on the exchange. In a 2018 hack, it was reported that US$ 51 million in funds was stolen. A lawsuit was brought against the exchange which was reportedly ordered by the Seoul Central District Court to pay more than 1 billion Won (about US$ 760,000).[661]

[A] *The Bithumb* Case in Hong Kong

A subsidiary of South Korea Bithumb was reportedly sued in Hong Kong for criminal fraud and breach of contract. Top executives also faced criminal fraud charges. The central allegation was that the South Korean exchange had announced that it intended to establish a crypto exchange in Thailand. It is alleged that the announcement was false and was only a ploy to persuade investors to buy the South Korean exchange's BXA cryptocoins. At the conclusion of the case, the court reportedly ruled against Bithumb, ordering them to pay 100 billion Won (KRW) to investors (about US$ 70 million).[662]

[1] TerraUSD and Luna Crash Case

Do Kwon is the South Korean creator of Terra USD and Luna cryptocurrencies. Those cryptocurrencies suffered a crash in value in the spring of 2022. The circumstances surrounding that crash have prompted an investigation by South Korean regulatory authorities.

660. L. Yoon, "Cryptocurrency in South Korea—Facts and Statistics," Statista, online, September 24, 2021.
661. Amara Khatri, "Bithumb Ordered By Seoul District Court to Pay Reimbursements of More Than 1B Won," Crypto Daily UK, online at: cryptodaily.co.uk, February 11, 2021.
662. Sayantani Sanyal, "South Korea's Crypto Exchange Bithumb Sued for Fraud," Analytics Insight, online, October 6, 2021.

Some investors in those cryptocurrencies are reportedly claiming that they were defrauded by Do Kwon. South Korean regulatory authorities have been seeking to question Do Kwon, but in September of 2022, he was reportedly "on the run." He is reported to have been living in Singapore for some time but disappeared from there, and the South Korean authorities did not know where he was. Consequently, in September of 2022, the Seoul Southern District Prosecutors Office issued an arrest warrant for Kwon and others who worked on the cryptocurrencies and for Terraform Labs, a company of which Do Kwon was a cofounder. Frustrated prosecutors in South Korea reportedly asked Interpol to issue a "red notice" for Do Kwon that would allow any Interpol member to arrest him.[663]

Do Kwon issued a statement saying:

> We are in the process of defending ourselves in multiple jurisdictions—we have held ourselves to an extremely high bar of integrity and look forward to clarifying the truth over the next few months.[664]

[B] Regulation of Digital Assets

The activity in the digital currency markets in South Korea has stimulated the South Korean government to introduce a new regulatory framework which it intends to bring fully into effect in 2024. There is an intention to introduce the regulations in 2023 and to begin enforcement of them in 2024.

A national task force implementation plan has been created that proposes the introduction of the digital asset regulations in the form of a Digital Asset Basic Act to be introduced in 2023.[665] It will cover all digital assets, including digital currencies, NFTs, Initial Coin Offerings (ICOs) and digital tokens. The purpose of the legislation is to help to improve confidence and security for investors in digital assets. It will also expand South Korea's position as a significant market in the digital asset space.

[C] Digital Won

In August of 2021, the Bank of Korea (BOK) began a program to consider the implications of issuing a digital currency (Digital Won). Although no commitment has been made to issue a state digital currency, it is an example of how South Korea is moving toward a cashless society.

It is reported that in 2010 cash was used in 66% of payment transactions in Korea. By 2020 the percentage of transactions using cash had fallen to 34% as electronic payments increased. Because of the appearance of and interest in digital currencies around the world, BOK has joined the many other central banks around the world that are considering whether it makes sense to introduce a state-sponsored cryptocurrency.

---

663. Steven Zeitchik, "Disgraced Crypto Founder Says He's Not on the Run. But No One Knows Where He Is.," The Washington Post, online, September 20, 2022.
664. *Ibid.*
665. FINTECH GLOBAL, "South Korea to Introduce Digital Currency Regulatory Framework by 2024," May 18, 2022, online at: member.fintech.global.

It is expected by many in South Korea that a Digital Won will be introduced before the end of 2024.[666]

666. Troy Stangarone, Korea Economic Institute of America, "South Korea's Forward-thinking Digital Currency Pilot Program," EastAsiaForum, August 10, 2021, online at: eastasiaforu-m.org.

CHAPTER 10
Singapore Law

§10.01 CRYPTO IN SINGAPORE

Since the early days of its introduction, cryptocurrency has been relatively welcome in Singapore. Under Singapore financial regulations, it is legal to both own and trade cryptocurrency in Singapore.

Singapore has been making strong efforts to become a financial trading center. Without many natural resources but with an energetic and entrepreneurial population, Singapore's principal commercial resource is trade. They have made significant efforts to develop trading centers in a number of important commodities, including energy and precious metals. Recently, they have made efforts to expand into cryptocurrency.

In fact, the Monetary Authority of Singapore (MASP) has made efforts to introduce its own e-money, related to Ethereum. This was initially introduced in 2016 and labeled "Project Ubin."[667]

§10.02 MOVING FROM "PROOF OF WORK"

In Singapore, cryptocurrency is classed as "property," not as legal tender.

As property, cryptocurrency can be purchased from some banks and from cryptocurrency ATM machines in Singapore.

There has been considerable dissatisfaction with the cyber currency authentication process known as "proof of work" mining. One of the important problems which has been frequently mentioned in 2021 is the fact that the mining "work" required to produce cyber currencies such as Bitcoin consumes a tremendous amount of electricity.[668]

667. "Singapore Cryptocurrency Regulations 2021," Confirm, online January 14, 2021.
668. "Explained: Proof-of-work vs Proof-of-stake Mining and Why Ethereum Is Transitioning to Latter," CNBCTV18.com, online, December 15, 2021.

Because the cost of electricity in Singapore is relatively high, and cryptocurrency mining uses a lot of electricity, Singapore is not the most popular place to do cryptocurrency mining.

Cyber currencies can be classed as "financial securities" under Singapore law which can make their issuance and sale subject to a formal registration process. This can require registration of a prospectus, as is the case with other financial securities.

In 2017 the government of Singapore decided that the MASP would regulate "virtual assets" like cyber currencies when they were found to be the equivalent of financial securities.[669]

§10.03 SECURITIES AND FUTURES ACT

Initial offerings of cryptocurrency in Singapore known as ICOs are regulated by the Securities and Futures Act.[670] The offerings are categorized as regulated services, and anyone performing regulated services in Singapore must obtain a license as a Capital Markets Service.

The conditions for determining whether an initial coin offering (ICO) is a "financial securities offering" are set out in Chapter 289 of the Singapore Securities and Futures Act.

Cryptocurrency exchanges are allowed to operate in Singapore when they are licensed and regulated by the MASP. Licensing is required by the Payment Services Act of 2020.

A number of cryptocurrency exchanges are happy to operate in Singapore because of the low corporate tax (17%) and the fact that there is no capital gains tax in Singapore. Profits on the sale of cryptocurrencies are taxed under the ordinary Goods and Services Tax.

§10.04 PAYMENT SERVICES ACT 2019

The PSA[671] was intended to modernize, and make secure, payment services in Singapore.

It took notice of the growing importance of digital assets. An abridged selection of relevant definitions from the PSA is as follows:[672]

> "currency" means currency notes and coins that are legal tender in Singapore or a country or territory other than Singapore;
>
> "digital payment token" means any digital representation of value (other than an excluded digital representation of value) that—

669. "Singapore Cryptocurrency Regulations 2021," Confirm.com.com, online January 14, 2021.
670. Monetary Authority of Singapore, "A Guide to Digital Token Offerings" May 26, 2020, available in PDF form for review and download online at: mas.gov.sg.
671. Payment Services Act of 2019, Republic of Singapore Government Gazette, Acts Supplement, February 22, 2019, Singapore Statutes Online, online at: sso.agc.gov.sg
672. Please note that the PSA contains many other definitions that may be relevant to your particular situation.

a) is expressed as a unit;
b) is not denominated in any currency, and is not pegged by its issuer to any currency;
c) is, or is intended to be, a digital medium of exchange accepted by the public, or a section of the public, as payment for goods or services or for the discharge of a debt;
d) can be transferred, stored or traded electronically;
e) Satisfies such other characteristics as the Authority may prescribe

"e-money" means any electronically stored monetary value that—

a) is denominated in any currency, or pegged by its issuer to any currency;
b) has been paid for in advance to enable the making of payment transactions through the use of a payment account;
c) is accepted by a person other than its issuer; and represents a claim on its issuer,
d) but does not include any deposit accepted in Singapore, from any person in Singapore."

§10.05 DOES SINGAPORE HAVE A DIGITAL CURRENCY FUTURE?

There has been some evidence that the Singapore authorities may be cooling their enthusiasm about cyber currency. In November of 2021, the MASP issued a statement saying that cryptocurrency had been subject to "sharp speculative swings" and that investors in cryptocurrency were risking significant losses. The MASP also indicated that it was no longer in any hurry to develop its own digital currency for retail use.[673]

This cooling toward cryptocurrency was confirmed by a speech made by the Minister of Manpower in late 2021 entitled "Building Talent to Fuel the Future of Financial Services—Keynote Speech by Dr. Tan See Leng, Minister for Manpower, at the Institute of Banking and Finance Distinction Evening 2021 on 16 December 2021."

In his speech, he emphasized the strong interest of Singapore in developing banking and financial services and the importance of increasing digitalization in those areas. However, he made no mention of cyber currency having any importance in Singapore's financial services expansion.

For an entrepreneurial society like Singapore to cool off about cyber currency might be a signal that worldwide interest in this financial sector may be waning.

673. Abigail Ng, "Singapore's Central Bank Warns Against Crypto, Says Retail Investors Risk 'significant losses'," CNBC, online, November 9, 2021.

CHAPTER 11
Selected Other Countries

To give a good picture of how cyber currency is regulated around the world, the countries listed below are either countries that have a particular interest in cyber currency or countries among the fifty largest economies in the world by GDP that have not been described in their own chapter in this book. They are listed in alphabetical order.[674]

§11.01 ARGENTINA

There is no ban on owning or using cryptocurrencies in Argentina. They are subject to tax regulations. They are also subject to both anti-money laundering and anti-terrorist regulations.

There have been reports that crypto is becoming more popular in Argentina because of the volatility of the Argentina economy and periodic devaluations of the currency.[675]

An important component of the move to cryptocurrency seems to be public distrust of the government. People have memories of the financial crisis endured by Argentina in 1990 where, because of government intervention, people were prevented from using their bank accounts and devaluation of the currency caused people's savings to disappear.

There continue to be significant restrictions on financial transactions for Argentinians such as restrictions on foreign currency transactions. Consequently, some people in Argentina believe that cryptocurrency, such as Bitcoin, provides a more flexible alternative to official Argentine currency. Distrust of the government has encouraged the production and purchase of cryptocurrency in Argentina.

674. "Regulation of Cryptocurrency Around the World: November 2021 Update," Law Library, Library of Congress, online, accessed January 3, 2021.
675. Christine Ro, "Why Argentina Is Embracing Cryptocurrency," *BBC News*, online, April 22, 2022.

It is true that production of cryptocurrencies such as Bitcoin mining uses an enormous amount of electricity, but in Argentina, the cost of electricity is low compared to power prices in other countries. It is cheaper both to use computers to mine cryptocurrency and to run the cooling systems needed to keep them from overheating.

There have been reports pointing out that the excessive use of electricity which cryptocurrency mining requires may be damaging to the environment, but in Argentina financial issues are reported to be more important to many people than environmental concerns.[676]

§11.02 AUSTRALIA

There is no ban on cryptocurrencies in Australia. They are taxed under Australian tax law and are subject to both money laundering and anti-terrorist regulations.[677]

At the very end of 2021, Australia announced that it was taking a close look at cryptocurrency and would be introducing a new legal framework for cryptocurrency exchanges in 2022. It is reported they will be considering a licensing framework for such exchanges. The Australian Federal Treasurer Josh Frydenberg announced what he called a cryptocurrency asset "reform plan" which is intended to make Australia one of the leading countries in regulating and dealing with cryptocurrency. He said of these proposed reforms:

> It represents the most significant reforms to our payments system in 25 years.... Australia has an opportunity to be among the leading countries in the world in leveraging this new technology.

From such statements, it appears clear that the government of Australia is enthusiastic about exploring the possibilities for the use of cryptocurrency but is cautious about how these assets should be treated from a regulatory point of view.[678]

§11.03 AUSTRIA

There is no ban on owning or using cryptocurrency in Austria. They are not subject to VAT but are subject to other tax regulations. They are also subject to both anti-money laundering and anti-terrorist regulations.

§11.04 BANGLADESH

In Bangladesh, the Foreign Exchange Regulation Act has made crypto illegal. Anyone dealing with crypto could be subject to penalties under the Foreign Exchange

676. *Ibid.*
677. "Cryptocurrency in Australia—Statistics and Facts" statista, online at: statista.com
678. Marion Rae, "Treasurer Moves to Regulate Cryptocurrency," The New Daily, online, December 8, 2021.

Regulation Act, 1947; the Anti-Terrorism Act, 2009; and/or the Money Laundering Prevention Act, 2009. Cryptos are not subject to tax regulations. They are subject to both anti-money laundering and anti-terrorist regulations.
On September 15, 2022, the Bangladesh Bank issued a "FE Circular" that said:

> Any transactions made in/ from/to Bangladesh for obtaining virtual assets ... or it's subset—virtual currencies, are not permitted by the Bangladesh Bank.[679]

§11.05 BELGIUM

There is no ban on owning or using cryptocurrency in Belgium. They are subject to tax regulations, and subject to both anti-money laundering and anti-terrorist regulations. They are also subject to EU regulations.

In late November of 2022, it was reported that the Belgian Financial Services and Markets Authority (FSMA) had determined that major cryptocurrencies, Bitcoin and Ethereum, were not considered "securities" in Belgium.[680]

§11.06 BRAZIL

There is no ban on owning or using cryptocurrencies in Brazil. They are taxed under Brazilian tax law.

On November 30, 2022, it was reported:

> The Chamber of deputies of Brazil, a federal legislative body, legalizes cryptocurrencies as a means of payment throughout the country, boosting the adoption of digital currencies and the expansion of the ecosystem.[681]

§11.07 CANADA

There is no ban on the ownership or use of cyber currency in Canada. They are taxed in Canada. Cryptos are also subject to various state and federal regulations. Generally, they are classed as securities in Canada and subject to applicable securities laws.[682]

679. Managing Director, Sarwar Hossain, "Prohibition Regarding Virtual Assets, Virtual Currencies and Facilitating Their Exchange/transfer/trading," FE Circular No. 24, Foreign Exchange Policy Department, Bangladesh Bank, online at: bb.org.bd, September 15, 2022.
680. Brian McGleenon, "Bitcoin and Ethereum Are Not Securities, Belgium Declares," yahoo/finance, online at: uk.finance.yahoo.com, November 28, 2022. This report refers to a "Communication" published by the FSMA on November 22, 2022, entitled "Classification of Crypto-assets As Securities, Investment Instruments or Financial Instruments," online at: fsma.be.
681. Kathleen Marshall, "With the Latest Move, Brazil and India Embrace Cryptocurrency," Investopedia, online at: investopedia.com, November 30, 2022.
682. Murtuza Merchant, "A Beginner's Guide to Blockchain and Cryptocurrency Regulation in Canada," COINTELEGRAPH, online at: cointelegraph.com, accessed December 6, 2022.

§11.08 CENTRAL AFRICAN REPUBLIC

At the end of April in 2022, the Central African Republic (CAR) announced that it has approved Bitcoin as legal tender. This made them the second country to do so after El Salvador.[683] The country has been using the Central African Franc (CFA) as its official currency, which is a French-backed currency used in six central African countries. The introduction of Bitcoin is reported to highlight competition between France and Russia over influence in CAR. It is reported that Russian-backed mercenaries have been helping the government to fight rebels.

CFA is currently a very poor country, but the government says that the introduction of Bitcoin as legal tender puts CAR "on the map of the world's boldest and most visionary countries."[684]

What effect this move will have on the economy of the CAR remains to be seen.

§11.09 CHILE

There is no ban on owning or using cryptocurrency in Chile. They are subject to tax regulations and financial regulations under Chile's Financial Market Commission.

It was reported in November of 2022 that Chile implemented a new fintech law that:

> promotes the implementation of new technologies and innovation in the sector, improving financial conditions for consumers, promoting competition, delivering legal certainty, and, finally, aiming to democratize access to more personalized and lower-cost financial services.[685]

§11.10 COLUMBIA

There is no ban on owning or using cryptocurrency in Columbia. They are subject to tax regulations, as well as money laundering and anti-terrorist regulations.

In July of 2022, it was reported that Columbia's Congress had approved a new law to regulate cryptocurrency exchanges and was drafting new regulations to effectuate that.[686]

§11.11 THE CZECH REPUBLIC

The financial sector is supervised by the Czech National Bank (CNB). It licenses and regulates electronic money issuers. There is no ban on owning or using

683. "Bitcoin Becomes Official Currency in Central African Republic," *BBC News*, online, April 27, 2022.
684. *Ibid.*
685. "Everything You Need to Know About Chile's Fintech Industry," InvestChile Blog, online at: blog.investchile.gob.cl, November 7, 2022.
686. Sergio Goshenko, "Columbia Takes First Steps Toward Regulating Cryptocurrency Exchanges," *Bitcoin.com News*, online at: news.bitcoin.com, June 9, 2022.

cryptocurrencies in the Czech Republic. They are subject to tax laws. They are also subject to money laundering and anti-terrorist regulations.

However, the Czech Republic is considering additional crypto asset regulations. The CNB Financial Market Supervision Report for 2021 discusses a "Proposal for a Regulation on Markets in Crypto-Assets."[687] It says:

> The regulation sets out the rules for crypto-asset-related service providers and for crypto-asset issuers regarding, inter *alia*, their legal form, disclosure, governance arrangements and capital requirements.
>
> EU regulations apply in the Czech Republic.

§11.12 DENMARK

There is no ban on owning or using cryptocurrency in Denmark. They are subject to tax regulations. They are also subject to both anti-money laundering and anti-terrorist regulations. EU regulations apply in Denmark.

§11.13 EGYPT

Since 2018, trading in cryptocurrency has been forbidden in Egypt under Islamic law. However, that ruling is not legally binding, and under banking laws in Egypt, it is possible to deal in cryptocurrencies with a license from the Egyptian Central Bank. Dealings in crypto are difficult in Egypt but trading still goes on.[688] Crypto dealings are subject to both anti-money laundering and anti-terrorist regulations.

§11.14 EL SALVADOR

One of the more surprising developments in the world of cryptocurrency has been the decision of Nayib Bukele, the President of the small Central American country of El Salvador, in June of 2021, to adopt Bitcoin as a legal tender.

This required businesses to accept digital currency as payment for goods and services wherever possible. To smooth the introduction of the new currency, the government created a new "digital wallet" that included US$ 30 worth of Bitcoin given to every citizen of El Salvador.[689]

The president of El Salvador also announced in November of 2021 that he intended to build a "Bitcoin city" near a volcano in El Salvador, and he intended to finance the project with Bitcoin.[690]

687. CNB, "Financial Market Supervision Report 2021," "Proposal for a Regulation on Markets in Crypto-assets," pp. 17-18, online at: cnb.cz.
688. Sandali Handagama, "Egyptians Are Buying Bitcoin Despite Prohibitive New Banking Laws," CoinDesk, online at: coindesk.com September 14, 2021.
689. "IMF Urges El Salvador to Remove Bitcoin As Legal Tender" *BBC News*, online, January 26, 2022.
690. *Ibid.*

It was reported in January 2022, the Board of Directors of the IMF:

> urged the [El Salavador] authorities to narrow the scope of the Bitcoin law by removing Bitcoins legal tender status.

Among the risks highlighted by the IMF is that it would be more difficult for El Salvador to get a loan from the IMF. In addition, they pointed to the dangers to "financial stability, financial integrity and consumer protection" posed by El Salvador issuing government bonds backed by Bitcoin.[691]

Making Bitcoin legal tender entails a number of risks for El Salvador.

The volatility of Bitcoin is well known. If Bitcoin is legal tender in a country, citizens can pay taxes in Bitcoin. If thereafter the price of Bitcoin falls significantly, those could cause devastating financial losses to national finances.

US dollars are also legal tender in El Salvador. People could swap Bitcoin for dollars increasing the risks to El Salvador's Treasury. Companies and individuals may want to pay their obligations in Bitcoin, receive payments in dollars and keep their dollars.[692]

According to a well-known economic proverb known as "Gresham's Law"—"Bad money drives out good."[693]

Bukele tweeted:

> We must break the paradigms of the past. El Salvador has the right to advance towards the first world.[694]

On the first day that El Salvador officially began allowing Bitcoin to be used as legal tender (September 7, 2021), the price of Bitcoin collapsed by 15% to 20%, causing protestors to gather outside El Salvador's Supreme Court burning tires and setting off fireworks. One critic complained that this cost El Salvador US$ 3 million.[695] This was not good news in a country with fewer than 7 million people, a per capita income of less than US$ 8,500 a year, and a GDP below the top 100 in the world.

In the spring of 2021, the news from El Salvador got worse. In late March and early April of that year, more than eighty-five people were murdered. It was believed that they were shot at random by gang members with assault rifles to punish President Nayib Bukele for not having lived up to the terms of an agreement he allegedly made with gangs in El Salvador. In response, President Bukele imposed "emergency rule" on El Salvador and arrested approximately 3,000 people who the government believed may be associated with criminal gangs. He reportedly has been deliberately holding

---

691. *Ibid.*
692. Gian M. Volpicelli, "Ël Salvador Is Racing to the Future of Bitcoin," Wired, online, 30 June 2021.
693. After Sir Thomas Gresham, a prominent English merchant who in 1565 founded London's Royal Exchange, and who acted on behalf of English monarchs in financial transactions.
694. Katie Silver, "Bitcoin Crashed on First Day As El Salvador's Legal Tender," *BBC News*, online, September 8, 2021.
695. Katie Silver, September 8, 2021.

them in poor prison conditions which have led to objections from human rights organizations.[696]

These events have reportedly damaged El Salvador's reputation. It reportedly will make it harder for El Salvador to establish itself as a country with a stable economy where it would be a good place to conduct businesses relating to cyber currency. This situation has caused considerable doubt that President Bukele will be able to deliver on his key election promise to end gang violence in El Salvador.[697]

Almost a year later, Bitcoin has not transformed the economy of El Salvador in the way that President Bukele had hoped.[698] It was hoped that adopting Bitcoin as a national currency would put El Salvador on the cutting edge of a world financial revolution. The value of Bitcoin has declined approximately 60% since November of 2021. This means that any Bitcoin held by El Salvador has also suffered significantly.

Salvadorans have also significantly reduced their use of Bitcoin. Only about 10% of El Salvadorans have continued to use Bitcoin in regular transactions. The El Salvador Chamber of Commerce has reported that less than 15% of El Salvador's businesses have made Bitcoin transactions since it was introduced as a national currency in September of 2021.

President Bukele also urged Salvadorans in the United States to use Bitcoin to send money to their relatives in El Salvador, but the President's request has been largely ignored.[699]

The overall result is that El Salvador is running out of usable currency. President Bukele had hoped to raise additional funds from cryptocurrency investors, but these have not materialized to counterbalance the financial losses being suffered by El Salvador in the cryptocurrency market.[700]

However, President Bukele remains popular among El Salvadorans, and some feel that the introduction of Bitcoin has had a positive effect on El Salvador's image as a financially innovative economy. A negative impact on that image has been the fact that El Salvador's hope to attract Bitcoin-oriented businesses has not been realized. Some feel that the introduction of Bitcoin scared off financial market companies because they were worried about the impact of Bitcoin on the Salvadoran economy. President Bukele reportedly remains enthusiastic about Bitcoin. He has announced that the Salvadoran government has purchased approximately US$ 100 million worth of Bitcoin since September of 2021. At the end of June 2022, he is reported to have written on Twitter:

> Bitcoin is the future! Thank you for selling cheap.[701]

696. Stephen Gibbs, "El Salvador's 'Coolest Dictator in the World' Responds Ruthlessly to a String of Shootings," The Times, online, April 2, 2022.
697. *Ibid.*
698. Anatoly Kurmanaev and Bryan Avelar, "A Poor Country Made Bitcoin a National Currency. The Bet Isn't Paying Off," The New York Times, online, July 5, 2022.
699. *Ibid.*
700. *Ibid.*
701. *Ibid.*

Nevertheless, it is estimated that US$ 100 million worth of Bitcoin has lost approximately 63 million dollars in value recently. This is a problem for a country trying to subsidize increasing costs of food and fuel and trying to make national debt payments. To counterbalance these losses, public services have been slashed, including funding for local government, which has reduced public subsidies for scholarships and water supply. The Salvadoran government did announce that it was going to issue a government bond backed by Bitcoin worth US$ 1 billion. However, that project has reportedly been postponed indefinitely. Could the Bitcoin problems push all of Salvador into debt default? That remains to be seen. There is certainly concern that President Bukele made the wrong choice in backing Bitcoin as a national currency.[702]

§11.15 FINLAND

There is no ban on owning or using cryptocurrency in Finland. They are subject to tax regulations. They are also subject to both anti-money laundering and anti-terrorist regulations. Finland is also a member of the EU and implements relevant EU directives and regulations.

In July of 2019, the Finish Financial Supervisory Authority (FIN-FSA) issued regulations and guidelines for virtual currency providers to implement the Act on Virtual Currency Providers (AVCP).[703]

Under the AVCP, which took effect on May 1, 2019, the FIN-FSA acts as registration and supervisory authority for virtual currency providers. Among other things, the AVCP requires registration by:

- virtual currency exchange services;
- custodian wallet providers; and
- issuers of virtual currencies.

The above are required to comply with statutory requirements concerning such things as:

- whether they are fit and properly reliable;
- holding and protecting client money;
- segregation of client money and own funds;
- marketing of services; and
- compliance with relevant regulations.

Only those that meet statutory requirements will be able to carry on their activities in Finland.[704]

702. *Ibid.*
703. FIN-FSA, "Regulations and Guidelines 4/2019: Virtual Currency Providers" available for review and download at: finanssivalvonta.fi, accessed December 7, 2022.
704. FIN-FSA, "Virtual Currency Providers to be Supervised by the FIN-FSA Briefing for Virtual Currency Providers on 15 May," Supervision release April 26, 2019—17/2019, available for review and download at: finanssivalvonta.fi, accessed December 7, 2022.

§11.16 FRANCE

France is a member of the EU, and will implement EU directives and regulations, such as those to be brought in under MiCA.

However, France has already established regulations to consider, such as the regulation of electronic money (E-money).

Under French law, if one wishes to "issue, manage, or provide" electronic money one has to apply for an electronic money institution license.[705]

Before licensing an electronic money institution, the French regulator Autorité de contrôle prudentiel et de résolution (ACPR)[706] will review the following things:

- suitability of the legal form for the proposed activity;
- sufficient initial capital and level of prudential capital with respect to capital requirements;
- the program of operations, and technical and financial resources;
- description of the distribution network;
- identity and status of direct and indirect capital contributors, and where applicable, of their guarantors;
- central administration located in the same national territory as the registered office;
- sound governance arrangements including a clear organizational structure with a well-defined, transparent and consistent division of responsibilities;
- persons effectively running the undertaking, or the persons placed in charge of the electronic money activity in the case of hybrid institutions (institutions pursuing other commercial activities) must meet propriety, knowledge, experience and fitness requirements;
- effective risk detection, management and control procedures and an appropriate internal control system, including sound administrative and accounting procedures and appropriate arrangements to prevent money laundering and terrorist financing;
- protection of user funds;
- resources implemented to ensure the security of means of payment and general organization to ensure security, oversight of orderly operation and fraud prevention.

If the electronic money issuer expects that its volume of electronic money will be less than five million euros a month, there is an alternative option for registration "simplified electronic money institution."[707] In that case, both the initial capital requirements and the regulatory requirements are lighter, but the institution may not issue E-money in units larger than €250. Also, a simplified electronic money institution

705. Article L. 315-1 of the Monetary and Financial Code.
706. ACPR.
707. Article L. 526-19 of the Monetary and Financial Code.

is not eligible to operate its business in another EU Member States under the EU "passport" procedure.[708]

There is also a possibility that the ACPR will grant an exemption under limited circumstances:

> The College of the ACPR may, under very specific circumstances, grant a license exemption (art. L. 521-3 of the Monetary and Financial Code): an undertaking may issue and manage electronic money with a view to the acquisition of goods or services solely on the premises of the undertaking or, under a commercial agreement with it, within a limited acceptance network or for a limited range of goods or services, provided that the maximum amount that may be loaded on the electronic device does not exceed EUR 250.

When considering granting such an exemption, the ACPR will look particularly at:

- security conditions for the means of payment; and
- consumer protection arrangements.

§11.17 GERMANY

Germany is also a member of the EU and implements relevant EU directives and regulations.

Crypto assets are subject to German tax regulations.

In addition, Germany introduced new additional regulations on crypto assets in January 2020, under legislation supplementing the EU money laundering directives.[709] This legislation designates "crypto custody business" as a regulated financial service. This new regulated service includes the following:

- Custody.
- Administration.[710]
- Safeguarding.

of crypto assets.

These activities require a license under either the German Banking Act or the German Financial Supervisory Authority (BaFin), depending on whether one is entering the business as a "custody wallet provider" or is operating under already regulated business.[711]

708. ACPR, "Electronic Money Institution: Licensing Procedures and Review Times, Procedure for Extending Licensing to Payment Services, License Exemption Procedure," online, December 19, 2021.
709. "Act on the Implementation of the Amendment Directive to the Fourth EU Money Laundering Directive," which entered into force January 1, 2020. "German Law Aspects of Crypto Assets," The National Law Review, December 7, 2022, online at: natlawreview.com.
710. *Ibid.*
711. *Ibid.*

As to tokens, BaFin will decide separately in each case whether a token is a regulated financial instrument under either the German Securities Trading Act or the EU Financial Instruments Directive.[712]

§11.18 HONG KONG

Hong Kong is subject to Chinese political rule.
There is no ban on owning or using cryptocurrency in Hong Kong. They are subject to tax regulations. They are also subject to both anti-money laundering and anti-terrorist regulations.

The Hong Kong Monetary Authority (HKMA) has indicated an aim to introduce a new regulatory framework for stablecoins and other crypto assets in 2023 or 2024. The rapid growth of the crypto asset industry has made the HKMA aware that regulations will need to be adjusted for them to follow international standards and maintain monetary and economic stability. As a result, they have been focusing on three particular issues:

(1) stablecoins.
(2) investor protection relating to crypto assets; and
(3) the interface between regulated entities and crypto assets.

These examinations have made them aware that changes will need to be made to Hong Kong financial services regulations. It is thought that Hong Kong will introduce new regulations within the next two years.[713]

§11.19 ICELAND

Iceland is one of the most prosperous but most sparsely populated countries in the world. During the last twenty years, Iceland has come to the attention of the world during times of financial controversy. This may have something to do with the fact that Iceland privatized its banking sector in the early years of the twenty-first century, and its economy began to change from dominance by the traditional fishing and farming industries to an economy involved in investment banking and financial services on an international scale.

However, this booming business was severely hurt by the financial crisis of 2008, and this led to thousands of people leaving the country. In the years following the 2008 crisis, the country was led by a group of talented women who stabilized the economy by 2012.

However, during the cryptocurrency era, Iceland has once again come to the attention of the international community because of the unusual fact that electricity in

712. *Ibid.*
713. *See*, "Insight" by HKMA, "Crypto-assets and Stablecoins" online at: hkma.gov.hk, January 12, 2022.

Iceland is largely provided by relatively inexpensive geothermal and hydroelectric power. It is well known that the production or "mining" of cryptocurrency requires huge amounts of electricity. As a result, cryptocurrency miners have tended to establish themselves in places where they can get the needed electricity at the lowest price. Among the economically developed countries, Iceland provides electric power to its inhabitants at a relatively low price. In fact, Iceland became so popular with cryptocurrency miners by 2019; cryptocurrency miners were using more electric power in Iceland than was being provided to domestic homes.[714]

By December of 2021, Iceland's popularity with crypto miners began to be a problem. At that time, low hydro reservoir water levels meant that Iceland's principal electric company, Landsvirkjun, was unable to supply requested power to all customers. As a result, it reduced power to big industrial users, such as metal smelters. It also rejected supply requests from bitcoin mining companies that wanted to set up new operations in Iceland.[715]

§11.20 INDONESIA

There is no express ban on owning or using cyber currency in Indonesia, but they may not be used for payment. The county's constitution and currency legislation require that all payment transactions in Indonesia are to be conducted in the national fiat currency, the Rupiah.[716] Indonesia does not allow cryptocurrencies to be used for payments and instead treats them as commodities. They can be traded in the commodity markets as investments.[717]

At the end of November 2022, Bank Indonesia, Indonesia's central bank, published a "white paper" to discuss the introduction of a "digital rupiah" in the future. No specific timeline was given other than to say, "Digital rupiah will be implemented in stages ... ."[718]

§11.21 IRAN

There are various restriction bans on cryptocurrencies in Iran. They did permit and require licenses for crypto mining in 2019. However, after a period of electricity blackouts, they banned cryptocurrency mining for four months in May 2021. It is estimated that crypto mining in Iran was using about 2GW of electricity per day.[719]

714. Laura Mallonee, "Inside the Icelandic Facility Where Bitcoin Is Mined: Cryptocurrency Mining Now Uses More of the Nordic Island's Electricity Than Its Homes," Wired, online, November 3, 2019.
715. Ragnhildur Sigurdardottir and Mark Burton, "Iceland Cuts Power to Industry, Turns Away New Bitcoin Miners," Bloomberg, online December 7, 2021.
716. Constitution of the Republic of Indonesia (As amended, 2019), Article 23B: "The denomination and value of currency are regulated by law."
717. Stefanno Sulaiman, "Indonesia c. Bank Launches White Paper on Planned Digital Currency," REUTERS, online, November 30, 2022.
718. *Ibid.*
719. "Iran Bans Cryptocurrency Mining for Four Months After Blackouts" *BBC News*, online, May 26, 2021.

In December of 2021, Iran allowed a new Blockchain and Cryptocurrency Association to form. The belief of the government appears to be that cryptocurrency can help the economy of Iran.[720]

In the summer of 2022, it was reported that:

> Iran has officially approved the use of cryptocurrency for imports as a measure to circumvent US sanctions imposed on its finance and banking sector. ... [C]ryptocurrencies are not traded through normal channels such as banks and it is very difficult to track them.[721]

§11.22 IRELAND

There is no ban on owning or using cryptocurrency in Ireland. They are subject to tax regulations. They are also subject to both anti-money laundering and anti-terrorist regulations. There is yet no specific regulatory scheme for cryptocurrency.

In Ireland, the crypto business has been expanding in new and innovative ways.

Ireland, as a member of the EU, is subject to EU directives and regulations on crypto assets and other financial service businesses. The Government of Ireland has established a Department of Finance Fintech Working Group (FFWG) to integrate the EU Digital Finance Package into Irish policy and law. The FFWG held its first meeting on November 16, 2022.[722] Among the purposes it identified are the following:

- Provide strategic guidance on the state's industrial strategy for digital finance from an expert industry perspective.
- Act as a pre-consultation forum on policy and legislative developments related to digital finance.
- Act as a forum for private and public sectors to engage on key items of the European Commission's digital finance agenda.

The FFWG includes members from the tech and financial industries as well as government departments. Its brief is to provide direction and recommendations for Ireland's wish to responsibly expand business in the crypto assets sector. It will probably recommend the adoption of future legislation and regulations in the crypto asset sector.

[A] Crypto ATMs

In Dublin, Boinnex ATM machines, where one can buy or sell cryptocurrency, have been appearing around the city.

720. "Iran Launches New Blockchain and Cryptocurrency Association," The Times of India, online December 3,2021.
721. "Iran Approves Use of Cryptocurrency for Imports to Bust Sanctions," IRAN INTERNATIONAL, online at: iranintl.com, August 29, 2022.
722. Department of Finance, "Minister Fleming Holds Inaugural Meeting of the Joint Fintech Group" Press release, online at: gov.ie, November 18, 2022.

Boinnex is an Irish company based in Cork. Their intent is to make it easier for members of the public to access crypto.[723]

§11.23 ISRAEL

There is no ban on owning or using cryptocurrencies in Israel. They are subject to tax regulations. They are also subject to both anti-money laundering and anti-terrorist regulations.

The Bank of Israel (BOI) is aware of the necessity of regulating digital assets as necessary to maintain financial stability. The BOI is likely to expand its supervision of this area. Toward that end, the Israel Ministry of Finance published a proposal in November of 2022 for a new regulatory system for crypto assets. This would include:[724]

- licensing and supervision for issuers of digital assets.
- supervision by the BOI to protect financial and monetary stability.
- an inter-ministerial committee to regulate decentralized autonomous organizations (DAOs); and
- taxation of crypto assets held overseas.

The Israeli government is also considering the implications of the introduction of a digital central bank currency, an "e-shekel."[725]

§11.24 ITALY

There is no ban on cyber currency in Italy. They are not taxed under VAT regulations but are taxed under other Italian tax laws.

Italy is also a member of the EU and implements relevant EU directives and regulations.

Italy is planning to strengthen its regulation of digital assets and increase taxation of crypto transactions starting in 2023.[726]

Italy has not had a comprehensive regulatory scheme for crypto assets, but a decision of the Italian Supreme Court in November of 2022 may change that.[727] The court ruled that initial offers of cryptocurrencies, so-called ICOs, are financial products subject to Italian regulations of financial services. Failure to comply with those regulations can be a criminal offense. The court noted that the virtual currencies

723. "ick Webb," "Inside Track: John and Daniel Gleason Make Deposits at Boinnex Bitcoin Cash Machines," The Times, online, June 20, 2021.
724. Elizabeth Napolitano, "Israel's Ministry of Finance Proposes New Guidelines for Regulating Digital Assets," CoinDesk, online at: coindesk.com, November 29, 2022.
725. BOI, "Report of the Team to Examine the Issue of Central Bank Digital Currencies," section 3 (e-Shekel), online for review and download, November 2018.
726. Marco Bertacche and Anna Irrera, "Italy Plans to Tax Crypto Trading Gains, Expand Disclosure," Bloomberg, online, November 30, 2022.
727. Angelo Messore, Francesco Dagnino and Carlo Giuliano, "Crypto-assets and Financial Products: The Italian Regulatory Landscape After the Recent Ruling of the Supreme Court," LEXIA AVOCATI, online at: lexia.it, November 29, 2022.

involved can be purchased for investment purposes rather than as a means of exchange. The court found that the essential elements of an investment were satisfied:

- The purchasers invested their own capital.
- In order to gain a financial return.
- And accepted the risk to their investment.[728]

§11.25 MALAYSIA

There is no ban on owning or using cryptocurrency in Malaysia. They are subject to tax regulations. They are also subject to both anti-money laundering and anti-terrorist regulations. The Securities Commission of Malaysia reportedly wishes to provide a regulatory framework that safely allows finance as part of the Malaysian capital market.[729] To this end, certain digital currencies and tokens can be classified as securities if they meet certain conditions indicative of a regulated investment under the Capital Markets and Services (Prescription of Securities, Digital Currency and Digital Token) Order 2019.[730] Traders in these assets will be subject to Malaysian financial services regulations.

§11.26 MEXICO

Since June of 2021, cryptocurrency has been banned in Mexico. A statement from the Mexican financial regulatory authority said:

> The country's financial institutions are not authorized to carry out on offer to the public operations with virtual assets, such as bitcoin, Ether, XRP and others in order to maintain a healthy distance between them and the financial system.[731]

Crypto asset transactions are subject to money laundering regulations in Mexico.

§11.27 THE NETHERLANDS

There is no ban on owning or using cryptocurrencies in the Netherlands. They are not subject to VAT but are subject to other tax laws. They are also subject to money laundering and anti-terrorist regulations.

728. *Ibid.*
729. Chin Wei Min and Azrina Azmel, "Developing a Facilitative Ecosystem for Digital Innovation in the Malaysian Capital Market," *Nomura Journal of Asian Capital Markets*, Autumn, 2017, Vol. 2, No. 1, Malaysian Securities Commission, online at: sc.com.my, accessed December 7, 2022.
730. Capital Markets and Services Act 2007, Capital Markets and Services (Prescription of Securities (Digital Currency and Digital Token) Order 2019, Malaysia Securities Commission, online at: sc.com.my.
731. Andres Engler, "Mexico's Finance Minister Confirms Cryptos Are Banded from Financial System," yahoo/finance, online at: finance.yahoo.com, June 28, 2021. The Mexican financial regulatory authority is the National Banking and Securities Commission (Comision Nacional Bancaria y de Valores) (CNBV).

The Netherlands is a member of the EU and implements EU directives and regulations relating to crypto assets.

The financial markets in the Netherlands are regulated by the Dutch Authority for the Financial Markets (AFM).[732]

§11.28 NEW ZEALAND

There is no ban on owning or using cryptocurrencies in New Zealand. They are subject to tax laws. They are also subject to anti-money laundering and anti-terrorist regulations.

Financial regulation in New Zealand is the responsibility of the Financial Markets Authority (FMA).

Many crypto assets are considered regulated "securities" in New Zealand. If the provision of these securities does fall within the category of a regulated financial service, then the provider will need to be registered on the Financial Service Providers Register.[733]

§11.29 NIGERIA

There are a number of financial regulators in Nigeria.[734] For crypto assets, the most relevant are Central Bank of Nigeria (CBN) and the Securities and Exchange Commission (SEC).

In early 2021, the CBN:

> Directed all banks to desist from transacting in and with entities dealing in cryptocurrency. The CBN also directed banks to close accounts of persons or entities involved in cryptocurrency transactions within their systems.[735]

In October of 2021, the CBN justified its negative stance on cryptocurrency by citing a number of problems including the volatility of crypto and its role in illegal activities.[736]

In February of 2021, the CBN:

> renewed its directives to [banks], non-bank financial institutions and other regulated financial institutions on the existing prohibition from dealing in cryptocurrencies or facilitating payments from cryptocurrency exchanges. Although

732. The Dutch AFM supervises the conduct of the entire financial market sector: savings, investment, insurance, loans, pensions, capital markets, asset management, accountancy and financial reporting. *See* AFT online at: aft.nl.
733. NZ FMA: "Crypto Asset Service Providers," FMA, online at: fma.govt.nz., accessed December 8, 2022.
734. "Full List of Financial Regulatory Bodies in Nigeria," Nigerian Infopedia online at: nigerianinforpedia.com.ng, accessed December 8, 2022.
735. Ademola Bakare, "Cryptocurrency Trading: CBN Orders Banks To Close Operating Accounts," CNB online at: cbn.gov.ng, accessed December 8, 2022.
736. CNB, Financial Markets Department, Annual Activity Report 2020, Box 1 "CBN Stance on Crypto-currencies," p. 25, accessed December 8, 2022.

the Bank did not ban cryptocurrencies in Nigeria, it prohibited regulated institutions from enabling or participating in cryptocurrency-based transactions. The Bank further mandated all regulated financial institutions to identify and close all accounts of cryptocurrency traders and exchanges nationwide.[737]

§11.30 NORWAY

There is no ban on owning or using cryptocurrency in Norway. They are subject to tax regulations. They are also subject to both anti-money laundering and anti-terrorist regulations.

The principal financial service regulator in Norway is the Financial Supervisory Authority (FSA).

The Norwegian government's Financial Markets Report 2021 notes:

> The market for virtual assets and currencies has grown rapidly in the last few years, thereby giving rise to regulatory issues. In the autumn of 2020, the European Commission published a proposal for joint regulation of virtual assets ('Markets in Crypto-Assets', MiCA). The proposal forms part of a strategy to support digital finance innovation and competition. Norway is not a Member of the EU, but the government will consider Norwegian implementation when the regulations have been enacted, and it's monitoring decentralized finance developments in general.[738]

They also note that a "regulatory sandbox" had been established which permits selected businesses to test their solutions. At that time, three projects had successfully applied to be admitted.[739]

§11.31 PAKISTAN

The ownership of crypto assets has not been totally banned in Pakistan, but the State Bank of Pakistan (SBP) has been supporting such a ban, and in 2018 the SBP issued the following restrictions:[740]

> "General Public is advised that domestic and international payment and money transfer services in Pakistan are regulated by SBP under the applicable laws. In this regard, no entity is currently licensed or authorized by SBP to offer money remittance services and products in Pakistan using Virtual Currencies /Coins/Tokens. Persons using Virtual Currencies/Coins/ Tokens for the purpose of transferring value outside Pakistan are subject to prosecution as per the applicable laws.

737. CNB, Financial Markets Department, Annual Activity Report 2021, section 7.4 "Prohibition on Crypto-currencies in the Banking System," p. 44, accessed December 8, 2022.
738. Meld. St. 31 (2020-2021), Financial Markets Report 2021, "Digitization and Financial Technology," online at: regjeringen.no, accessed December 8, 2022.
739. *Ibid.*
740. SBP, "Public Notice: CAUTION REGARDING RISKS OF VIRTUAL CURRENCIES," p. 1, April 6, 2018, available for review or download online at sbp.org.pk, accessed December 8, 2022.

"In view of the above, the General Public, in their own interest is advised to be cautious of and refrain from indulging in activities relating to mining, trading, exchanging, transferring value, promoting and investing of Virtual Currencies/Coins/Tokens to avoid any potential financial loss and legal implications."

Nevertheless, Pakistanis continue to buy and hold crypto assets.[741]

§11.32 IS CRYPTO FORBIDDEN BY ISLAMIC LAW?

About two years later in 2020, the SBP issued a bulletin on Islamic Law that said, in relation to crypto:

> The CBB (Central Bank of Bahrain)[742] introduced a Regulatory Sandbox that allow startups, fintech firms to provide innovative banking and financial solutions, in addition to issuance of crowdfunding regulations for both conventional and Shariah compliant services. In 2018, the regulations on cryptocurrency and robo-advisors were issued. Shariah compliant crypto exchange, RAIN, became the first crypto exchange that was established by virtue of the sandbox and received Shariah compliance certification from Shariah review Bureau.[743]

§11.33 THE PHILIPPINES

There is no ban on owning or using cryptocurrency in the Philippines. However, Philippines regulators have developed a series of detailed regulations relevant to crypto asset transactions in the Philippines.

The Philippines has a number of financial regulators which include the central bank of the Philippines (Bangko Sentral ng Pilipinas (BSP)) and the Securities Exchange Commission (SEC).

The Bangko Sentral has issued a number of crypto regulations to protect citizens. The issuance of these regulations was intended to help citizens who dealt with crypto assets to require entities that provided such assets to engage in legitimate cryptocurrency trading and to prevent citizens from becoming involved in criminal activity.[744]

Anyone who engages in security transactions or solicits investment, as defined by the securities regulation code, is required to register with the SEC.[745] Consequently,

741. Jordan Tuwiner, Buy Crypto & Bitcoin in Pakistan, Chapter 1: "Bitcoin & Cryptocurrency Trading in Pakistan," online at: buybitcoinworldwide.com.
742. SBP, "Country Model: Kingdom of Bahrain," Islamic Banking Bulletin, April-June 2020: "The Kingdom of Bahrain has long been recognized as one of the global leaders in Islamic finance, because the country is home to a number of global standard-setting organizations and it hosts the largest concentration of Islamic financial institutions in the Middle East," p. 8.
743. *Ibid.*, p. 9.
744. Jay Astillo, Mary Caroline Castro, Kathia Chanyee, Ingrid Corrine Chua, Laura Aurea De los Santos, Betty Belle Fabe, Gillian Ruth Grancho, Yveza June Gmentiza, Missy Maree Martinez, Jessalyn Púerin, "A Report on Blockchain and Cryptocurrency," online at scribd.com, February 20, 2019, p. 3, accessed December 8, 2022.
745. Jay Astillo, et al., cited above, pp. 12-13.

cryptocurrencies that are treated as securities must be registered with the SEC prior to any offering to the public.[746]

In 2017, the BSP issued guidelines for virtual currency exchanges which required obtaining a certificate of registration to operate remittance and transfer companies, money changers, or foreign exchange dealers.[747]

In 2016, the BSP has also issued a Manual of Regulations for Non-Banking Financial Institutions that requires the registration of virtual currency exchanges after they have completed the requirements for registration as remittance, transfer companies, money changers or foreign exchange dealers.[748]

In 2021, the BSP issued guidelines for virtual asset service providers (VASP), which amended both of the above publications, expanded regulation, and established that the directors and officers of VASP could be personally liable for regulatory violations.[749]

Crypto service providers are subject to both anti-money laundering and anti-terrorist regulations.

§11.34 POLAND

The Polish financial market regulator is the Financial Supervision Authority (KNF).

Poland is a member of the EU and implements EU directives and regulations.

Poland does not prevent use of cryptocurrency, believes there may be future benefits for the Polish economy and is trying to create a regulatory environment that will comply with Polish law and encourage the development of a crypto assets market.[750]

There is no ban on owning or using cryptocurrencies in Poland. They are subject to tax laws. They are also subject to money laundering and anti-terrorist regulations.

§11.35 PORTUGAL

There is no ban on owning or using cryptocurrencies in Portugal.

In early 2022, Portugal was being identified as a particularly "crypto friendly" jurisdiction.

An Ethereum conference was held in Lisbon in October of 2021, and a crypto art festival was held in May of 2021. In October of 2021, a crypto exchange, Crypto Lohja,

746. *See*, SEC Advisory on Initial Coin Offering, January 8, 2018, online: sec.gov.ph.
747. BSP, Guidelines for Virtual Currency Exchanges, Circular No. 944, February 7, 2017, online at bsp.gov.ph.
748. *See*, BSP Manual of Regulations for Non-Banking Financial Institutions (Volume 2), March 31, 2016, online at bsp.gov.ph, accessed December 8, 2022.
749. BSP Guidelines for Virtual Asset Service Providers (VASP), January 21, 2021, online at: law.upd.edu.ph, accessed December 8, 2022.
750. Helen Partz, "Poland Financial Regulator Issues Public Warning About Binance," COINTELEGRAPH, July 8, 2021, available online at: cointelegraph.com, accessed December 8, 2022.

was licensed by the Central Bank of Portugal and trades over ninety cryptocurrencies in euros. It is even possible to make purchases in Portugal with a crypto visa card.[751]

They are subject to tax laws, but cryptocurrency is reportedly treated like any fiat currency, and individuals are not charged vat or capital gains tax on crypto sales and purchases. However, businesses that deal in cryptocurrency pay capital gains tax between 28% and 35%.

It is also possible to purchase real estate with cryptocurrency in Portugal.[752]

In May of 2022, the first purchase of an apartment in Portugal with Bitcoin, without conversion to euros, was reported.[753]

Cryptocurrencies are subject to money laundering and anti-terrorist regulations.

§11.36 ROMANIA

In Romania, the financial services industry is regulated and supervised by the Romanian FSA (Autoritatea de Supraveghere Financiara (ASF)).

There is no ban on owning or using cryptocurrencies in Romania. They are subject to tax laws. They are also subject to money laundering and anti-terrorist regulations.

Romania is a member of the EU and implements EU directives and regulations.

On November 18, 2022, the ASF reiterated a warning about crypto assets originally published in March of 2022 which included the following:[754]

> You should be aware of the specific risks of cryptoassets and related products and services and carefully assess whether the risks are acceptable, given your preferences and financial situation. These include:
>
> - The risk losing all the money invested;
> - The risk of prices falling and rapidly rising over short periods;
> - The risk of becoming a victim of fraud, deception, operational errors or cyber attacks;
> - The risk that you are unlikely to have rights to protection or compensation if problems arise.

§11.37 RUSSIA

In January of 2020, the Russian central bank proposed to ban the mining, issuance, trading and other uses of cryptocurrencies. Their concern was that crypto posed a danger to the stability of the Russian ruble and the Russian financial system.[755]

751. Lara Silva, "Crypto in Portugal: A Guide to the Crypto-Friendly Country" online at: Portugal-.com, February 10, 2022.
752. *Ibid.*
753. Katarina Lukac, "Meet Europe's Crypto Paradise," online at: linkin.com, May 10, 2022.
754. ASF, "Warning Issue by EU Financial Regulators on the Risks of Cryptoassets," November 18, 2022, online at: asfromania.ro, accessed December 9, 2022.
755. Lawrence Carrel, "Russian Central Bank Proposes Banning Crypto Mining, Trading," Forbes, online, January 20, 2022, accessed December 9, 2022.

However, serious financial sanctions against doing business in Russia or with Russian entities have been implemented:

> The West has imposed an unprecedented package of sanctions on Russia, its top companies and businesses and political elite in response to Moscow's invasion of Ukraine.[756]

§11.38 SAUDI ARABIA

In Saudi Arabia, the Saudi Central Bank, also known as the Saudi Arabian Monetary Authority (SAMA), is the financial regulator charged with regulating and supervising banking and foreign exchange, monetary policy, the growth and stability of the financial system and finance companies.[757]

The legal status of crypto in Saudi is not clear. It has been declared illegal, but transactions reportedly take place.

On August 8, 2018, SAMA issued the following statement:

> The standing committee[758] ... assured that virtual currency for example, but not limited to, the Bitcoins are illegal in the kingdom and no parties or individuals are licensed for such practices.[759]

However, it has been reported since then:

> [T]he official stance taken by the SAMA mentions no legal sanctions, punishments or fines for using cryptocurrencies. The Saudi government doesn't seem to actively enforce its crypto prohibition and buying or selling Bitcoin and other cryptocurrencies isn't really a problem in Saudi Arabia.[760]

There are reportedly crypto ATMs in the country. Because crypto is technically illegal, the tax situation is unknown. However, it would be subject to both money laundering and anti-terrorist regulations.

§11.39 SOUTH AFRICA

The financial markets in South Africa are regulated by the Financial Sector Conduct Authority (FSCA).[761]

There is no ban on owning or using cryptocurrency in South Africa.

756. "Factbox: Western financial Sanctions on Russia," Reuters online, May 13, 2022, accessed December 9, 2022.
757. The Saudi Central Bank website is found at: sama.gov.sa.
758. Standing Committee for Awareness on Dealing in Unauthorized Securities in the Foreign Exchange Market.
759. C. Edward Kelso, "Bitcoin Illegal: Saudi Arabia Monetary Authority" Bitcoin.com, online at: news.bitcoin.com, August 15, 2018, accessed December 9, 2022.
760. Mark Kitney, "Saudi Arabia Crypto & Blockchain Guide," *Mena Digital News* online at: *mena news*, February 24, 2021, accessed December 9, 2022.
761. FSCA online at fsca.co.za.

A crypto asset is a regulated financial product in SA.[762] It is (with certain exemptions) subject to financial regulatory and licensing requirements.[763] They are subject to tax regulations. They are subject to money laundering and anti-terrorist regulations.

§11.40 SPAIN

As a member of the EU and Spain implements EU directives and regulations.

Financial markets in Spain are under the regulation of the Bank of Spain (Banco de Espana) and the SEC, known as the Commission Nacional de Mercado de Valores (CNMV).

There is no ban on owning or using cryptocurrency in Spain.

On February 9, 2021, the Bank of Spain and the CNMV issued a joint press statement[764] on cryptocurrency investment risks that included the following:

> From a legal standpoint, cryptocurrencies:
> - are not considered a means of payment,
> - are not backed by a central bank or other public authorities, and
> - are not covered by customer protection mechanisms such as the deposit guarantee scheme or the investor compensation scheme.

Cryptocurrencies were identified as a "high risk investment" ... "that may not be appropriate for small scale savers."

In January of 2022, the CNMV was given the power to regulate crypto advertising.[765]

Crypto asset transactions are also subject to tax and money laundering and anti-terrorist regulations.

§11.41 SWEDEN

As a member of the EU, Sweden implements EU directives and regulations.

The financial market regulator of Sweden is the Swedish Financial Supervisory Authority, called the Finansinspektionen (FI). The direct trade of crypto assets has little regulation in Sweden. However, when financial instruments have underlying crypto

762. FSCA, General Notice 1350 of 2022, "Declaration of a Crypto Asset as a Financial Product Under the Financial Advisory and Intermediary Services Act" October 19, 2022, online for review and download at: fsca.co.za, accessed December 9, 2022.
763. FSCA, "Policy Document Supporting the Declaration of a Crypto Asset as a Financial Product Under the Financial Advisory and Intermediary Services Act," October 19, 2022, online for review and download at: fsca.co.za, accessed December 9, 2022.
764. Banco De Espana, CNMV, "Joint Press Statement by the CNMV and the Banco De Espana on Cryptocurrency Investment Risks," February 9, 2021, online for review and download at: cnmv.es, accessed December 9, 2022.
765. Daniel Dombey, Joshua Oliver, and Sam Fleming, "Spain Leads European Crackdown on Crypto Promotions," Financial Times online, January 17, 2022, accessed December 9, 2022.

assets, there are some regulations that apply.[766] Offerors will need to assess the suitability of these products for the target market. Those who provide investment recommendations will need to make sure that advice on these products is objectively presented. Market abuse regulations will apply, and reporting regulations will require compliance with reporting requirements.

Sweden intends to cooperate with other trading partners to create stronger crypto asset regulation in future.

There is no ban on owning or using cryptocurrency in Sweden. They are subject to tax regulations. They are also subject to both anti-money laundering and anti-terrorist regulations.

§11.42 SWITZERLAND[767]

In Switzerland, the financial markets are regulated by the Swiss Financial Market Supervisory Authority (FINMA).

There is no ban on owning or using cryptocurrency in Switzerland. Numerous cryptomarket companies operate in Switzerland. Both crypto exchanges and Virtual Asset Services Providers (VASPs) can operate legally in Switzerland if they are licensed and regulated by FINMA. Mining is also permitted. ICOs are regulated as financial securities.

Crypto assets are subject to income tax regulations. They are also subject to both anti-money laundering and anti-terrorist regulations.

The Canon of Zug in Switzerland is known as "Crypto Valley " Swiss residents there can pay lower taxes on cryptocurrencies including Bitcoin.

§11.43 THAILAND

There is no ban on owning or using cryptocurrency in Thailand. They are subject to tax regulations. They are also subject to both money laundering and anti-terrorist regulations.

The Bank of Thailand is the overall financial market supervisor:

> The Bank of Thailand discourages the adoption of digital assets as a means of payment for goods and services. A wide scale replacement of the Thai bot by digital assets would create a new unit of account and adversely affect the public and the economy in several aspects namely:
>
> Cost and security of both payers and receivers
> Payment system stability

766. FI Supervision Report Number 21, "Financial Instruments With Crypto-assets as Underlying Asset," February 22, 2021, available online for review or downloading at: fi.se, accessed December 9, 2022.
767. Coinfirm, "Switzerland Crypto Regulations: KYC, Taxes and FINMA" available online at: confirm.com, accessed December 9, 2022.

Financial stability and management of domestic financial conditions.[768]

The Bank of Thailand has been reviewing the growth of the crypto markets and the responses of other regulatory jurisdictions. It intends to introduce its own regulatory regime which it intends will be:

> a flexible supervisory regime with no significant regulatory burdens on financial service providers. A supervision framework that is adequately flexible for service providers to adapt and utilize new technology and digital infrastructure to enhance financial services.[769]

§11.44 TURKEY

There is no specific ban on owning or using cryptocurrency in Turkey, but some restrictions have been imposed by the Central Bank.

They are subject to income tax regulations, but not VAT. They are also subject to both money laundering and anti-terrorist regulations.

In January of 2022, the Turkish government drafted a bill to change the capital markets law to include a framework for crypto assets. Among its provisions, the bill intended to ban payments in crypto assets.

In April of 2020, prior to the enactment of the proposed bill, the Central Bank of Turkey issued a regulation on the use of crypto assets. The regulation prohibited the use of crypto assets in making payments and/or providing services to enable payments in crypto assets. Also, payment institutions and electronic money institutions were banned from acting as intermediaries on platforms for the sales, storage, transport or export of crypto assets. However, the regulation continued to permit purchases and sales of crypto assets between private parties or through exchanges.

There was considerable criticism of this unilateral imposition of regulations on crypto assets by the Central Bank.[770]

§11.45 UNITED ARAB EMIRATES

There is no specific ban on owning or using cryptocurrency in the UAE. But there are some implicit restrictions.

Both the Abu Dhabi Securities Exchange and the Dubai Financial Market operate under the UAE Securities and Commodities Authority.[771] They are subject to tax regulations. They are also subject to both anti-money laundering and anti-terrorist regulations.

768. Bank of Thailand, "Repositioning Thailand's Financial Sector for a Sustainable Digital Economy," online for review and download at: bot.orth, February 2022, accessed December 9, 2022.
769. *Ibid.*
770. Kayahan Cantekin, "Turkey: Regulation Bans Use of Crypto Assets in Payments," Library of Congress, May 12, 2021, online at loc.gov, accessed December 9, 2022.
771. UAE, Information and services, "Financial Markets" online at u.ae, accessed December 9, 2022.

Recently the UAE has been trying to attract crypto business:

> The UAE has picked a bad time to embrace crypto currencies. The chaotic calamity of the crypto exchange FTX has potentially imperiled the very future of an already volatile industry. This comes as MENA[772] was the world's fastest growing crypto market in 2022 and the UAE has moved aggressively to attract crypto companies to the country. ... Despite this crypto calamity, the UAE doesn't appear to be backing off from broader ambitions to become an industry hub.[773]

§11.46 VENEZUELA

There is no ban on owning or using cryptocurrency in Venezuela. It is not clear whether they are subject to tax regulations.

Certain Venezuelan individuals and entities have been subject to U.S. sanctions in recent years. Venezuela's economy, suffering from the effects of sanctions and rampant inflation, has caused people and businesses in the country to use cryptocurrency (such as Bitcoin) to hedge against devaluation of the national currency. Crypto usage has been so great that in 2020, Chainalysis, a group that reviews blockchain transactions, ranked the country third in its Global Crypto Adoption Index.

In 2017, the government introduced a not very popular petro-based crypto.[774]

§11.47 VIETNAM

There is no specific ban on owning or using cryptocurrency in Vietnam. They can be bought, sold, owned and traded. However, their use is restricted. The government does not consider them legal tender or a legal means of payment. The government is considering what further regulatory action it should take with respect to crypto assets.[775] The extent to which they are subject to tax regulations is not yet clear. They are subject to both money laundering and anti-terrorist regulations.

§11.48 OTHER COUNTRIES

Other countries are considering different approaches to digital currencies as interest in them continues to expand despite the volatility of crypto markets and the FXT crash.

Arguments are being made that digital currencies would offer benefits of faster payments and might make financial services easier for people with low incomes to access.[776]

---

772. Middle East and North Africa. Often used to describe stock and commodity exchange operating tin the region.
773. Samuel Wendel, "UAE's Cryptocurrency Ambitions to Continue Despite FTX Crash" AL-MONITOR, online at: al-monitor.com, November 30, 2022.
774. AlJazeera, "With Venezuela's Economy in Crisis, Cryptocurrency Fills the Gaps" June 22, 2021, source: Reuters, online at: aljazeera.com, accessed December 9, 2022.
775. A.K. Qadir, "Cryptocurrency Regulations in Vietnam," CoinPedia, online at: coinpedia.org, June 8, 2020, accessed December 9, 2022.
776. Callum Jones, June 12, 2021, cited above.

CHAPTER 12

Financial Service Regulation

Which regulatory authority should regulate cyber currency? As an editorial in *The Times* put it in late December in 2021:[777]

> Cryptocurrency has slunk into our lives and no one knows what to do about it. Is it an investment, a currency or a giant con? It's certainly a massive risk to the economy, so it's time regulators decided and did something about it to protect the vulnerable.

There is a question of regulatory jurisdiction. This question has become considerably more complicated in the era of the Internet. Because cyber currency is passed from party to party electronically, on the Internet, it is technically available to anyone that has a connection to the Internet. Does this then give jurisdiction to any regulatory authority in any jurisdiction in which a cyber currency is accessible over the Internet?

If a financial product is deliberately offered on the Internet with an understanding by the offeror that it will be accessible to anyone with an Internet connection, is there any limit to the jurisdiction that may be exercised by a regulatory authority in a jurisdiction where the cyber currency in question is accessible by people within that jurisdiction?

That is a question that has been considered many times by regulatory authorities and courts around the world. Taking a look at how this issue has been resolved in major jurisdictions, we find the following:

> This issue is still being settled as various cases that have come to court in countries around the world. However, the general legal rule that is being adopted is that local courts can exercise jurisdiction over any Internet postings that are accessible within their jurisdiction. In other words, in any country where Internet postings can be accessed, the law of that country can apply. The extent to which it will apply may vary, and may be uncertain.

777. James Coney, "Time to Wake Up to the Threats Posed by Cryptocurrency," The Times, online, December 28, 2021.

A considerable amount of thought has been given to the question of what jurisdiction applies to "financial instruments" offered Internet platforms. So, it is useful to consider the extent to which cyber currencies would fall within the accepted definition of "financial instruments."

A generic definition of financial instruments is provided by Investopedia. That definition says:

> Financial instruments are assets that can be traded, or they can also be seen as packages of capital that may be traded. Most types of financial instruments provide efficient flow and transfer of capital all throughout the world's investors. These assets can be cash, a contractual right to deliver or receive cash or another type of financial instrument, or evidence of one's ownership of an entity.[778]

§12.01 REGULATED INVESTMENT

On a number of occasions issues have been raised about whether cybercurrencies constitute "investments" and whether they should be regulated as investments.

This has not been clear because "regulated" or "controlled" investments are usually specifically identified in applicable legislation or regulations. For example, under UK regulation (which, at this writing, is still in compliance with EU investment regulations), specifies about twenty-two different investments that come with in financial services regulation.[779]

There is no specific reference to cybercurrencies. However, UK legislation also contains an instrument called the RAO. Article 9B of the RAO specifies "issuing electronic money" as a "regulated activity."

This may apply to those that are offering cyber currencies for trading or sale in the United Kingdom and require them to be authorized and regulated by the UK's principal financial regulator, the FCA.

Because of the possible regulatory implications, the people issuing, dealing in or advising on cryptocurrency may not be clear about the exact nature of cryptocurrency. Is it a medium of exchange or an investment opportunity? Depending on what the answer to that question is, the regulatory status of the cryptocurrency in question is going to be different.

Because there are so many cryptocurrencies and other crypto assets on offer, it is difficult to understand how they can all be considered currency or "mediums of exchange." That would depend on whether or not there are merchants who will accept payments in crypto for goods and services and whether governments will permit those that need to make tax or other payments to governments to pay in crypto on a level comparable to the official local currency.

For example, there is a website operating out of Australia called "Mining Store." They offer those that are interested an opportunity to benefit from their research on the

778. Will Kenton, reviewed by Marguerita Cheng, fact checked by Katrina Munchiello, "Financial Instrument, Investopedia," online, updated August 29, 2021, accessed December 20, 2021.
779. Financial Services and Markets Act 2000 (Financial Promotion Order) UK Statutory Instruments 2005 1529.

thousands of cryptocurrencies available and to learn about those that they consider their "Top 3 crypto picks ... [for the year]" for the year. In describing the nature of cryptocurrencies they make it quite clear that they consider them to be "investments." They say:

> Like any financial market, there are good eggs and bad eggs, so it is essential that investors do their own research and understand the investment before putting their funds at risk.[780]

> Can that really be a valid regulatory philosophy in the modern world? That seems to be simply a restatement of the age-old investment cliche: "*caveat emptor*: let the buyer beware."

At least since the stock market crash of the 1920s, many governments around the world have adopted a view that laws and regulations should be put in place to protect the investing public from being persuaded to put their money at risk with unregulated and unsupervised promoters, or without having adequate information to judge the nature of the risks they are taking on.

Allowing market participants to regulate themselves has been tried but has not been a consistently successful method of preventing the greed of certain market participants from engaging in activities that can cause systemic damage to financial systems and losses to members of the investing public. The top directors of the well-known investment company Berkshire Hathaway have been clear in stating that they believe that financial markets need careful sensible regulation.

As a result of the financial market turmoil of 2008 and the years immediately afterward, fingers were pointing at different reasons for the problem. Some said it was the fault of the banks and investment companies, others said it was the fault of the financial instruments being bought and sold, such as "derivatives" and others said it was the result of outrageous frauds such as the Bernie Madoff Ponzi Scheme. However, Charlie Munger, the Vice-Chairman of Berkshire Hathaway, said:

> Our problem is that our commercial banks and our investment banks have been regulated with a combination of permissiveness and stupidity. ... The government regulatory system has utterly failed us.[781]

This view is consistent with other expert analyses. Following the financial crisis of 2008, The United States government established a Financial Crisis Inquiry Commission (FCIC) to examine the causes of the turmoil. In January of 2011, that Commission released a 662-page Financial Crisis Inquiry Report[782] in which the following was one of its principal conclusions:

> We conclude this financial crisis was avoidable. The crisis was the result of human action and inaction, not of Mother Nature or computer models gone haywire. The

780. "Free Report Reveals.... Mining Store's Top 3 Crypto Picks for 2021," MiningStore.com.AU, online, December 26, 2021.
781. "Buffett Sees No Wrongdoing in Goldman Case," *NBC News*, online May 2, 2010.
782. The Financial Crisis Inquiry Report: The Final Report of the National Commission On The Causes of the Financial and Economic Crisis in the United States, January 2011, online at fcic-static.law.stanford.edu.

> captains of finance and the public stewards of our financial system ignored warnings and failed to question, understand, and manage evolving risks within a system essential to the well-being of the American public. Theirs was a big miss, not a stumble. While the business cycle cannot be repealed, a crisis of this magnitude need not have occurred. To paraphrase Shakespeare, the fault lies not in the stars, but in us."[783]

In hearings in the U.S. Congress during the crisis, the Chairman of the U.S. House of representatives, Henry Waxman, expressed his criticism of the fact that the Federal Reserve, the SEC, and the U.S. Treasury because they had consistently agreed with "the prevailing attitude in Washington ... that the market always knows best."[784]

This criticism may sound harsh, but it was not unjustified. Even the regulators who were targets of the criticism at one point admitted that regulation had been too weak. For example, in October of 2008, in the middle of the crisis, Alan Greenspan the former Chairman of the Federal Reserve admitted that the financial turmoil was more than anything he could have imagined and that he was wrong to trust that banks and financial institutions could regulate themselves. He is quoted as saying:

> I made a mistake in presuming that the self-interest of organisations, specifically banks and others, was such that they were best capable of protecting their own shareholders.[785]

Since the crisis of 2008 and the years following, additional regulatory protections for market participants and the public have been put in place. However, in the face of the creation of new digital products such as cyber currency, NFTs, and tokens, it is not clear whether regulators will apply them to these new products or the extent to which they will be applied.

Some regulators have taken a very strong position. For example, China has banned privately created cyber currency although it will apparently introduce its own digital currency in the near future.

Countries such as El Salvador have gone to the other extreme and both adopted Bitcoin as a national currency and allowed Bitcoin companies to both manufacture and install physical Bitcoin dispensing machines within their borders.

Other regulators have fallen somewhere in the middle and appeared to be considering whether cyber assets can be properly regulated in the same way as other financial products such as securities, bonds, and financial derivatives are regulated.

Despite all the information that has been published both by government and by private commentators about the reasons and causes of the financial crisis of 2008 and the years following, some financial regulators seem not to be paying much attention to what was learned from that crisis.[786]

---

783. *Ibid.* at p. xv.
784. Alan Beattie and James Politi, "'I made a mistake', admits Greespan," Financial Times, online, October 23, 2008.
785. *Ibid.*
786. If one does not want to read the serious reports generated about the 2008 financial collapse, it may help to watch the films *The Big Short* or "*Margin Call.*"

This is surprising; it should be recognized that the situation with digital assets bears some striking parallels to the way that over-the-counter (OTC—off-exchange) financial derivatives were treated between 1990 and 2008, which led to the 2008 financial collapse. This was the result of a law case that concluded in 1990,[787] and caused a great deal of disturbance among financial institutions and international conglomerates that were trading various financial and commodity derivatives, OTC, between themselves assuming they were not regulated. However, the U.S. District Court for the Southern District of New York decided they were regulated under the U.S. Commodity Exchange Act (CEA).

In the trading on North Sea Oil (technically, fifteen-day Brent System Blend Crude Oil—"Brent"), some major oil companies assumed that they were exempt from U.S. regulation under the CEA because the contracts they used called for physical delivery, the market was in North Sea oil and the trading was centered in London. However, in the case of *Transnor (Bernuda) Limited. v. B.P. North America Petroleum, et al., 738 F. Supp.1472 (S.D.N.Y. 1990)*, the U.S. Federal District Court for the Southern District of New York disagreed. The trading of Brent was found to be within U.S. legal jurisdiction because much of the trading was done in the US. Brent could be delivered to satisfy the Light Sweet Crude Oil contracts traded on the New York Mercantile Exchange. But more significantly, the Court found that the OTC trading of Brent was subject to subject to the CEA because, despite the fact that the contracts called for physical delivery, they were actually "futures contracts" under the CEA, and subject to the regulation of the U.S. Commodity Futures Trading Commission (CFTC):

> In *Transnor*, the District Court held that the mere opportunity to offset, coupled with an expectation and common practice of offsetting, is sufficient to deem a transaction a futures contract and not a "forward" (where physical delivery as expected). Because most fifteen-day Brent oil contracts did not result in delivery, and offsetting was facilitated by the high degree of standardization of the terms, the court held that the investors, most of whom were institutional, used the contracts for speculative purposes without contemplating delivery. Thus, the court found that Brent oil contracts were futures contracts.[788]

The *Transnor* ruling appeared to require financial and commodity companies trading in contracts where physical delivery was rare to execute their trades in these "futures" contracts on authorized futures exchanges (such as the Chicago Board of Trade, the London Petroleum Exchange, etc.) under the regulation and rules of the exchanges and government futures contract regulators such as the U.S. CFTC.

Large financial institutions and companies objected strenuously and urged the U.S. legislators to change the law to permit large financial institutions and trading companies (the "Big Boys") to conduct less formal party-to-party, off-exchange

787. *Transnor (Bernuda) Limited. v. B.P. North America Petroleum, et al.*, 738 F. Supp.1472 (S.D.N.Y. 1990). The author of this book was attorney for Transnor in that case.

788. Rebecca Leon, "The Regulation of Derivative and the Effect of the Futures Trading Practices Act of 1992," *Journal of Law and Policy*, 1994, Volume 3, Issue 1, online, accessed March 25, 2022, pp. 333-334.

trading, known as "over-the-counter" (OTC) trading between themselves, which would not be permitted to the general public. In 1992, the "Big Boys" got their wish:

> The Futures Trading Practices Act of 1992 authorized the Commodity Futures Trading Commission (CFTC) to permit less regulated "professionals only" (OTC) futures trading in the United States. For this purpose, professionals are considered to be entities and individuals with assets that tend to exclude the general public from participation. In 1993, the CFTC exempted a number of "professionals only" markets from its regulatory structure, including the over the counter (OTC) derivatives markets.

In response, over the next fifteen years, the trading of all kinds of OTC contracts (by then popularly known as "derivative contracts") expanded in many international markets at "an unprecedented rate"[789] until they covered many monetizable transactions, including the notorious subprime mortgage bonds. All kinds of things were traded by OTC derivatives, which are a very flexible financial instrument, defined by at least one commentator as:

> Derivative instruments are financial contracts which allow or obligate the investor to buy or sell underlying assets such as stocks, commodities, stock indexes or currencies.[790]

But the use of derivatives expanded to cover many more kinds of assets including the subprime mortgages. This flexible definition expanded to the point where it is probably fair to say that a derivative there's nothing more than the "sale of a promise."

Although it may be true to say that the value of the underlying asset can affect the value of the contract, the thing that has the biggest impact on the value of the contract is the financial strength of the promisor. If the promissor cannot deliver on its promise, the value of the underlying asset is not going to be very much help because the promisee may never get the asset or its monetary value.

The promissor may never have owned the promised asset at the time the promise was made, and the promisor may have been unwilling or unable to acquire the asset prior to the time a delivery, or unable to make a compensating payment, at the time of fulfillment of the promise became due.

In other words, derivatives are a very conceptual product. Their existence is embodied in a promise that may or may not be fulfilled. That is not significantly different today from the existence of cyber currencies which also have an intangible digital existence. Consequently, it is not impossible that cryptocurrencies may have the same impact on the financial system that derivatives had on the financial markets in 2008.

Following the collapse of 2008 regulators were motivated to place a number of restrictions on the derivatives markets in order to make them more transparent and the derivative promises more likely to be fulfilled.

---

789. Leon, p 321.
790. *Ibid.*, p. 322.

Therefore, would it not be sensible to impose, on the latest conceptual financial product, cyber assets, at least the same level of protections that have been found important for derivatives?

The intangibility of the digital instruments in question seems to puzzle some regulators enough that they feel that they do not know how and when to regulate them. This is may a serious mistake. One hopes that the regulators will recognize this before disruptions of the financial markets as great as the ones that occurred following the 2008 problems occur again.

Following the financial problems of 2008 regulators around the world imposed additional regulations on derivatives trading, and particularly on over-the-counter derivatives trading in order to provide regulators with more information about the exposure of regulated institutions and the state of the market.

These regulations consisted, among other things, of:

- regulatory capital requirements that required financial institutions to limit the number and types of derivative contracts they could have on their books in any particular risk category;
- reporting requirements so that both regulators and the public knew who was trading what numbers of particular financial instruments; and
- clearing requirements which required the insertion of a third party between the buyers and sellers of different categories of financial instruments who were in a financial position to guarantee the performance of the contracts entered into by buyers and sellers in markets.

Regulations of this type had often been applicable to financial contracts including futures, forwards and options that had, prior to 1992, been traded on regulated exchanges. However, because of the loosening of regulations that followed the decision in the *Transnor* case, similar regulations did not apply in the same way to many categories of OTC derivatives until after 2008.

Following the 2008 problems, it was thought by many commentators that the application of "light touch" regulation, that was largely dependent on large institutional market participants regulating their own risk, had been a key cause of the financial problems of 2008 and the following years.

There is an excellent question as to whether the cyber currency markets are not facing a similar situation today. Some regulators have appeared reluctant to apply similarly strict regulatory requirements to participants in the cryptocurrency markets. Could this lead to another disastrous financial collapse because regulators are once again asleep at the wheel? The world can certainly hope not.

§12.02 THE CRYPTOCURRENCY BUSINESS

Crypto businesses often describe themselves as entities where one can easily and safely buy, sell, and manage up to thousands of cryptocurrencies.

They may offer secure storage of the "money" in customer accounts.

They may have hesitation about describing the cryptocurrencies as a new form of "money."

They may provide investment advice.

They sometimes provide loans and debit cards, and may offer interest or dividend payments.

These appear to be the kinds of businesses that are strictly regulated when performed by banks, investment advisors, investment funds, etc.

Consequently, one of the oddest things about cryptocurrency business is that it is not yet more strictly regulated by more financial service regulators around the world.

The cryptocurrency business clearly appears to be within the category of financial instruments that financial services regulation wishes to control.

The issuing of electronic money is clearly a specific regulated activity under EU and UK law. In addition, the extraordinary number of cryptocurrencies that have come into the market over the last 15 years or so do not all seem to be effective "mediums of exchange." That is, they are not really "money" or actual "currency." The reason this appears to be so is that, given that number of cryptocurrencies that have been created, there will be some that are not accepted by many or perhaps not any merchants in exchange for goods or services.

If they are not an acceptable medium of exchange, then their status seems to be that they are purely instruments for investment. In other words, their purchasers must be buying them in the hope that their value will increase significantly in the future. At least some issuers of cryptocurrencies are marketing them on the basis that they provide investment opportunities that may appreciate significantly in the future.

Given the fact that the sale purchase and trading of investments is usually a heavily regulated industry, it is extraordinary that issuers of cryptocurrency are not required to register as authorized persons with both the financial services regulators in their home country and the financial services regulators in countries in which these cryptocurrencies are accessible for purchase.

Although this seems to be an area which has been somewhat neglected, it appears that at least some cryptocurrencies are coming in for criticism and/or regulatory punishment for crossing the line into unregulated "investments."

§12.03 TOKENS

A particularly puzzling category of digital assets is a group of offerings called "tokens."

Digital tokens can be described in a number of different ways, but one definition that probably covers them adequately is the following:

> A digital token is a code which stands as a representation of certain token owner's "rights." Digital tokens can represent entitlement to certain benefits including such things certain goods, services or rewards.[791]

791. *See* Chapter 17 for more discussion of Tokens.

[A] Tokens and Football

[1] SEC Regulation

So-called Non-Fungible Tokens (also called NFTs) are apparently regulated by the U.S. SEC. On May 3, 2022, the SEC published a press release that said:

> The expanded Cyber Assets and Cyber Unit [of the SEC] will leverage the agency's expertise to ensure investors are protected in the crypto markets, with a focus on investigating securities law violations related to
>
> – non-fungible tokens (NFTs) ...[792]

§12.04 INVESTMENT LAW

Investment law covers many different kinds of investments. These include securities, commodities, and derivatives.

Crypto assets constitute a new category of financial product. Usually, they have no physical existence and are dependent upon computers and the Internet to provide their digital life. An exception is that cryptocurrency AFTs provide physical evidence of token ownership in some cases.

Crypto assets have come into existence within the last twenty years or so and having become well known only since about 2015. A question that many governments and regulators have had to wrestle with is whether these new crypto assets constitute financial instruments that come within the definitions of regulated investments.

Of course, each legal jurisdiction has its own laws and regulations as to what kinds of financial instruments need to be regulated and how they need to be regulated. In some jurisdictions, such as the United States, different kinds of investments are regulated by different regulatory agencies and under different regulatory statutes.

There can also be a division of that regulation between federal and state governments. This adds another layer of regulation and supervision for those that may be engaged in regulated activities.

A key question is always going to be what constitutes regulated investment activity within any particular jurisdiction. There is no universal definition of investment activity accepted throughout the world, but, in general terms, there are particular characteristics that most jurisdictions agree on.

As discussed above, cyber assets share certain characteristics with OTC derivatives. The UK hosts the world's largest trade in OTC derivatives. So, it may be useful to look at UK regulation.[793]

---

792. Securities Exchange Commission, "SEC Nearly Doubles Size of Enforcement's Crypto Assets and Cyber Unit," Press Release, 2022-78, May 3, 2022, online at: sec.gov.
793. Statista, "Financial markets in the UK—Statistics and Facts," online at: statista.com, February 7, 2022.

[A] United Kingdom

In the United Kingdom, "regulated activity" is a business of a particular kind that relates to a specified investment or property of any kind.[794]

No person or entity is permitted to carry on a "regulated activity" or purport to do so unless they are authorized or exempt. This is referred to as the "general prohibition" and is found in section 19 of the UK Financial Services and Markets Act (FSMA). Violating this prohibition is a criminal offense, and agreements made as a result of such activity may be unenforceable.

Specifically, what constitutes a regulated activity or a specified investment is set out in a regulation called the Regulated Activities Order (RAO).[795]

How these regulations relate to cybercurrency is a complex question that has not yet been completely explicated in the United Kingdom, but the relevant regulators there are making efforts to sort that out. There are basically six regulators in the UK whose jurisdiction will come into play when determining the regulatory status of cybercurrency.[796] They are as follows:

(1) The Treasury, which bears the ultimate responsibility for the UK financial system.
(2) The Bank of England, which is responsible for financial stability.
(3) The Financial Policy Committee, which assists the Government in maintaining financial responsibility.
(4) The Prudential Regulation Authority (PRA), which regulates banks, insurers and large investment firms.
(5) The FCA, which supervises the conduct of most financial services firms, and the functioning of the financial markets.

As previously mentioned, cybercurrency touches on nearly every aspect of the financial services sector:

- it a medium of exchange;
- it may be a form of money;
- it may be a commodity;
- it may be considered an investment;
- it raises questions of its effects on financial stability;
- there are issues of fraud and other crimes associated with cybercurrency;
- it often has a purely digital existence;
- it is principally created and issued by nongovernment persons and entities;
- it is international, and its movements are not limited by borders;
- the transfer and ownership of cybercurrency can be untraceable;

794. section 22 of the Financial Services and Markets Act 2000 (FSMA).
795. Financial Services and Markets Act 2000 (Regulated Activities) Order 2001 (SI 2001 2001/544)(RAO).
796. Simon Morris, Financial Services Regulation in Practice (Oxford: Oxford University Press, 2016), pp. 122-123.

- it can be traded in markets where there are no records;
- it can be traded privately, one-to-one.

By the summer of 2022, the price of cryptocurrencies and other digital assets had fallen so much (approximately 70%) that one official of the Bank of England, Sir John Cunliffe, the Bank's Deputy Governor for Financial Stability, was expressing concern that the entire digital asset industry could collapse unless they were willing to accept governmental financial regulation. He expressed the view that such a step was necessary so that the risks of owning digital assets could be reduced and "the benefits of technological change can be secured." He suggested that it would be wise for financial regulators around the world to create an international rule book for this sector because "to be successful and sustainable, technologically driven innovation needs regulation."[797]

The article quoted did not detail what Sir John expected "the benefits" of the digital assets industry to be, But there have been reports that the UK, among other countries, is considering introducing its own digital currency to supplement or replace the physical fiat currency currently issued and supported by the British government.

Considering the losses sustained by purchasers of digital assets in 2021-2022, it is not clear why Sir John implies that the industry should be given a choice as to whether to "embrace" financial regulation for the digital asset industry. It seems more logical that regulators around the world should insist on imposing international regulations on an industry which has shown itself to be a threat to both the financial stability of individuals and nations where cryptocurrency and other digital assets are being widely used and "invested" in.

As to what "benefits" the innovative digital asset industry offers to society as a whole, that is not completely clear. Certainly, the introduction of cryptocurrency has benefited criminal hacking groups, tax evaders, sanction evaders, and others who wish to avoid government scrutiny as to their possession and use of this new "money." But it is hard to know what benefits such inventions have offered to law-abiding citizens outside of an opportunity to invest in a very risky asset, from which they can profit only if they find someone who is willing to pay them more for the digital asset than they paid themselves (a "greater fool"?).

797. Ben Martin, "Crypto Sector 'Could Crash' Without Regulation," The Times, online, July 13, 2022.

CHAPTER 13
Crypto Crime

One of the major problems with cryptocurrency is its association with crimes of various kinds. These include money laundering, ransom attacks, fraud, market abuse, financing terrorism, sanctions avoidance and even more ordinary financial crimes such as insider dealing and tax avoidance.

It is believed that the existence of cryptocurrency makes all of these crimes easier to execute, more difficult to detect, and more attractive to criminals.

These problems have caused some countries to severely restrict cryptocurrency, such as China, or to try and dominate the market by introducing nationally sponsored cryptocurrency or to strictly regulate how cryptocurrency can be bought and sold within their jurisdiction.

§13.01 MONEY LAUNDERING

The purpose of money laundering laws and regulations is to prevent criminals from profiting from the gains from illegal activity and to prevent the financing of terrorist activities.

Most nations have put anti-money laundering laws and regulations in place. Also, there has been a general recognition that the illegal activities that need to be prevented are, to a significant extent, international in scope and, therefore, international treaties and conventions have been agreed to restrict the movement of illegally gained or used funds around the world.

The purpose of this section will be to summarize the major international conventions and treaties that have been agreed with respect to money laundering and financing terrorist activities, and to review the anti-money laundering laws (AML).

Generally, all businesses need to comply with AML regulations, and these will also cover transactions in cybercurrency.

§13.02 INTERNATIONAL MONEY LAUNDERING REGULATION

[A] Financial Action Task Force on Money Laundering

In 1989, a number of major nations formed the FATF on Money Laundering. The members of FATF include the following:

- Argentina
- Australia
- Austria
- Belgium
- Brazil
- Canada
- China
- Denmark
- Finland
- France
- Germany
- Greece
- Hong Kong (China)
- Iceland
- India
- Ireland
- Israel
- Italy
- Japan
- Korea
- Luxembourg
- Malaysia
- Mexico
- The Netherlands
- New Zealand
- Norway
- Portugal
- Russia
- Saudi Arabia
- Singapore
- South Africa
- Spain
- Sweden
- Switzerland
- Turkey
- United Kingdom
- United States.

FATF calls itself "the global money laundering and terrorist financing watchdog."[798]

FATF sets international standards that aim to prevent these illegal activities and the harm they cause to society. As a policy-making body, the FATF works "to generate the necessary political will to bring about national legislative and regulatory reforms in these areas."[799]

FATF publishes a number of documents describing problems and suggested solutions for combatting money-launder activities and countering terrorist financing (MLA/CTF) and listing countries they consider to be "high-risk countries."

Their most comprehensive publication is *International Standards on Combatting Money Laundering and the Financing of Terrorism & Proliferation: The FATF Recommendations*. They were originally adopted in 2012, and have been (as of this writing) updated to October 2021.[800]

The FATF Recommendations provide advice on the following:

(1) Assessing risks and applying a risk-based approach.
(2) National cooperation and coordination.
(3) Money laundering offenses.
(4) Confiscation and provisional measures.
(5) Terrorist financing offenses.
(6) Targeted financial sanctions related to terrorism and terrorist financing.
(7) Targeted financial sanctions related to proliferation.
(8) Nonprofit organizations.
(9) Financial institution secrecy laws.
(10) Customer due diligence.
(11) Record keeping.
(12) Politically exposed persons.
(13) Correspondent banking.
(14) Money or value transfer services.
(15) New technologies.
(16) Wire transfers.
(17) Reliance on third parties.
(18) Internal controls and foreign branches and subsidiaries.
(19) Higher-risk countries.
(20) Reporting suspicious transactions.
(21) Tipping-off and confidentiality.
(22) Customer due diligence.
(23) Other measures.

798. FATF, "Who we are," online at ftaf-gafi.org.
799. *Ibid.*
800. FATF, online at ftaf-gafi.org.

[B] EU Anti-money Laundering Legislation

Directive (EU) 2015/849 is the EU's principal legislation against money laundering and terrorist financing. Under the Directive, banks and other businesses intimately involved with finance are required to be especially vigilant in their business relationships and transactions, particularly those that involve "high risk" countries.

Since 2015, the Directive has been strengthened by a number of other directives and regulations that enhance the anti-money laundering powers of law enforcement agencies within the EU.

Regulation (EU) 2015/847 was enacted to make transfers of funds more transparent to assist law enforcement authorities in tracking transactions involving terrorists and criminals.

Since 2015, the Directive has been expanded by additional money laundering Directives that gave authorities greater scope in detecting and preventing money laundering.

The fifth Anti-Money Laundering Directive of June 19, 2018 (Directive (EU) 2018/843), introduced amendments to improve money laundering prevention including:[801]

- additional transparency regulations that set up with for certain legal businesses such as companies and trusts;
- additional powers for the EU financial intelligence units that allowed them access to more financial information;
- additional restrictions on anonymity with respect to cyber currency and wallet providers and to prepaid payment cards;
- establishment of central bank account registries for all Member States;
- improved requirements for cooperation and information exchange between anti-money laundering supervisors, financial regulatory supervisors and the ECB.

More recent developments have included EU adoption of a report on September 16, 2020, on whether Member States have fully implemented the obligations of Directive (EU) 2015/849 that required Member States to identify trusts and trust-like legal arrangements that were created within those Member States.

Previously, on May 7, 2020, the EU proposed a comprehensive action plan against money laundering and terrorist financing based on the following six principles:

(1) Effective implementation of existing rules and regulations.
(2) A single EU rulebook.
(3) EU-level supervision.
(4) A support and cooperation system for Member State financial intelligence units.

801. *See*, "Factsheet on the Main Changes of the 5th Anti-money Laundering Directive," download online at ec.europa.eu, Anti-money laundering and countering the financing of terrorism.

(5) Stronger enforcement of criminal law based on available information.
(6) Stronger EU international cooperation.

The implementation of the plan came into effect in early 2021.[802] These measures were intended to correct what was seen as inconsistency of rules, differences in supervision among Member States and limitations that interfered with cooperation between EU financial intelligence units.

On July 24, 2018, the Commission issued a communication entitled "Toward Better Implementation of the EU's Anti Money Laundering and Countering the Financing of Terrorism Framework." This was accompanied by four reports that made suggestions for the improvement of EU anti-money laundering regulations.

On June 26, 2017, the Commission issued a "Supranational Risk Assessment Report" and in it reviewed the vulnerability of financial products and services to money laundering and terrorist financing risks.[803]

To improve the ability of EU members to counter money laundering and terrorism financing, the Commission undertook to identify what they categorized as "high risk" third countries that had legal deficiencies that diminished the effectiveness of their anti-money laundering and anti-terrorist financing efforts. The purpose of this identification was to protect the EU financial system from the damaging effects of dealing with inadequate protective systems in countries that were not EU members.[804] In aid of promoting protection against the "deficiencies" in the anti-money laundering and anti-terrorist funding (AML/CFT) efforts of such countries, the EU has published a list of more than twenty countries it has identified as "high-risk third countries."[805] These are:

- Afghanistan
- The Bahamas
- Barbados
- Botswana
- The Democratic People's Republic of Korea (North Korea)
- Ghana
- Iran
- Iraq
- Jamaica
- Mauritius
- Myanmar
- Nicaragua
- Pakistan
- Panama
- Syria

802. *Ibid.*
803. *Ibid.*
804. *Ibid.*
805. European Commission, "EU policy on High-risk Third Countries," online, ec.europa.eu.

- Trinidad and Tobago
- Uganda
- Vanuatu
- Yemen
- Zimbabwe.

On that site, the European Commission has also published "Revised EU Methodology for the Identification of High-Risk Third Countries."[806]

In terms of AML/CFT efforts, banks are identified as the principal "gatekeepers." Banks are usually the destination for criminals to place the proceeds of their illegal activities. Having deposits in well-known, heavily regulated banks lends a respectability to the money deposited there.

§13.03 FRAUD

The years 2021 and 2022 saw a dramatic rise in the number of people that claimed to be victims of fraud relating to cryptocurrency. It was reported that there were over nine thousand reported cases of alleged fraud relating to cryptocurrency investments in the year 2021. This was nearly double the number of reported cases in the previous year.[807]

A significant part of the problem is that cryptocurrencies are often heavily promoted as opportunities to "get rich quick." Many unsophisticated investors become persuaded that this is a golden opportunity to get a lot of money quickly from buying cryptocurrency which they believe may quickly appreciate in value.

There are currently thousands of cryptocurrencies on offer. At the beginning of their existence, cryptocurrencies tend to sell for relatively low prices. To the unsophisticated, this can seem a better opportunity to profit from rapid appreciation of a cryptocurrency than investing in already well-established and popular cryptocurrency such as Bitcoin or Ethereum.

However, the fact that a relatively unknown cryptocurrency is available on an established cryptocurrency exchange or is being sold online by an appealing salesperson who claims that they have made substantial profits from investing in "new" cryptocurrencies does not mean that the currency is being promoted by a person of honest or neutral intentions. As the famous and successful investor Warren Buffett has advised: if someone knows of a way to earn a great deal of money quickly, why are they telling you about it?

One of the common fraud scams is called the "rug pull," where a promoter of a cryptocurrency persuades potential investors to buy the product and, when the promoter believes they have accumulated a substantial amount of other people's money, he simply takes their money and disappears. These kinds of promotions frequently appear on social media sites fronted by appealing salespeople who claim

806. *Ibid.*
807. Tom Howard, "Crypto Fraud Soars as More Fall for Get-rich-quick Scams," The Times, online March 28, 2022.

that they have already made significant profits from investment in certain cryptocurrencies.[808]

An example of a notorious "rug pull" has been the Quadriga Canadian crypto exchange scam. It has been the subject of several published articles,[809] and in the spring of 2022, Netflix offered a documentary about it entitled "Trust No One: The Hunt for the Crypto King."[810]

Quadriga CX was founded in about 2015 by two men, one of whom, a young man named, Gerald Cotten, was the smiling, charming public face of the company. Cotten was the CEO, and ran the company himself. Quadriga became known as Canada's most prominent Bitcoin exchange where people were told they could purchase crypto in exchange for standard currency. People were charmed by Quadriga and Cotten's trust-inducing pitches and placed hundreds of millions of dollars worth of crypto and cash on the exchange, being told they would never have to worry about their crypto accounts and they could always easily exchange their crypto for standard currency. Then, in 2018, Cotten was reported to have died from complications of a gastro problem in India. It was then reported that no one had the "keys" to accessing the crypto or currency accounts held on Quadriga—that information had died with Cotten. This caused outrage from Quadriga's customers, at least one of whom had his entire life savings on deposit at Quadriga.

The Quadriga collapse triggered several investigations, unofficial by Quadriga customers, and official by Canadian regulatory authorities. At first, there was considerable doubt that Cotten was actually dead. His wife and others connected to Quadriga also came under suspicion. Ultimately, his death was accepted, and no wrongdoing was found attributable to his wife, but a lot of unexpected information was revealed about Cotten. Apparently, he had been involved in scams since he was about 15 years old, and may not have been the charming, harmless person he seemed to be. Detailed forensic accounting by Canadian regulatory authorities revealed that Cotten was operating Quadriga as a Ponzi scheme. When customers deposited funds with Quadriga, Cotten credited their accounts with crypto coin purchases. But those purchases were fake. Rather than using customer money to purchase crypto on their behalf, Cotten was taking customer money and investing it for his own account with other crypto exchanges. At first, when customers asked to draw money from their Quadriga accounts, Cotten would pay them with other customer money. But when the price of crypto fell significantly, many customers asked to withdraw money from their accounts, and Cotten could not pay them all. That is when he disappeared, and reportedly died in India.

Quadriga was a classic Ponzi scheme: paying early investors false "profits" with money from later investors.

---

808. *Ibid.*
809. For example, Dr. Katie Spalding, "Inside the Strange Tale of Quadriga, The $215 Million Bitcoin Ponzi Scheme," online at iflscienc.com, accessed 31 March 2022, and "Nathaniel Rich, 'Ponzi Schemes, Private Yachts and a Missing $250 Million in Crypto: the Strange Tale of Quadriga,'" Vanity Fair, online, 2019, accessed March 31, 2022.
810. Netflix, online, accessed March 30, 2022.

However, the forensic accounting showed that Cotton did not have access to enough money to pay his customers the balances alleged to be in their Quadriga accounts. Despite the boom in crypto, Cotton had managed to lose at least US$ 190 million of his customers' money with his own trading. There was no money left in the Quadriga accounts.

Unfortunately, because so many people are investing in cryptocurrencies or are tempted to invest in them, fraudulent promotions are increasing. The cryptocurrency market has been reported to have expanded by over 500% in the last year with over US$ 15 trillion worth of cryptocurrency being bought and sold. The UK FCA has reported that over 2,000,000 persons in the UK have purchased cryptocurrency. However, the crypto data group, Chainalysis, has reported that around US$ 14 billion worth of cryptocurrencies have been deposited in the accounts of known criminal groups.[811]

[A] Bonnie and Clyde

An indication of how big a problem money laundering has become within the crypto crime space was given by the arrest in the United States of a couple called the "Bitcoin Bonnie and Clyde"[812] in February of 2022, Heather Morgan and Ilya Lichtenstein were arrested by the FBI in their Wall Street apartment and charged with having US$ 4.5 billion in stolen Bitcoin. The U.S. government claims this is the largest financial seizure in U.S. history. Lichtenstein and Morgan presented themselves as entrepreneurs in the tech world. However, their biggest entrepreneurial move was hacking Bitfinex, a Hong Kong cryptocurrency exchange and stealing almost 120,000 bitcoins which were worth about 4.5 billion U.S. dollars. They then opened a series of bank accounts under false names. Using thousands of very small transactions, they moved the money to purchase such things as gold and NFTs. They contacted criminals about fake passports and were apparently considering fleeing to Ukraine or Russia. Government agents unlocked an encrypted file of Lichtenstein's and found the keys to about 2,000 cryptocurrency addresses containing more than US$ 3.6 billion worth of stolen Bitcoin.

If the couple are convicted of the crimes they are charged with, they are facing a possible twenty-five years in jail. Their lawyers have said that Morgan, who sometimes called herself "the crocodile of Wall Street," was an "unwitting bystander" to the crimes charged.

Deputy Attorney General Lisa O. Monaco said:

> Today's arrests, and the Department's largest financial seizure ever show that cryptocurrency is not a safe haven for criminals. In a futile effort to maintain digital anonymity, the defendants laundered stolen funds through a labyrinth of cryptocurrency transactions. Thanks to the meticulous work of law enforcement, the

811. The Chainalysis 2022 Crypto Crime Report, available for download at: go.chainalysis.com.
812. "Social Media Glitz Masked Crimes of the Bitcoin Bonnie and Clyde." The Times, online, February 12, 2022."

Department once again showed how it can and will follow the money, no matter what form it takes.[813]

[B] San Diego Ponzi Scheme

In February of 2022, federal prosecutors in San Diego indicted a person named Satish Kumbhani, who is reportedly identified as the founder of BitConnect. Kumbhani is accused of running a US$ 2.4 billion global Ponzi scheme. The scheme is allegedly a misleading cryptocurrency lending program. Investors were reportedly told that they could earn substantial sums by "lending" crypto to program which Kumbhani claimed profited from following cryptocurrency exchange markets. However, the Justice Department alleges that the scheme was essentially paying early investors with money obtained from later investors rather than from investment profits. Kumbhani and others involved in the scheme are alleged to have made over US$ 2 billion from the scheme.[814]

§13.04 PUMP AND DUMP SCAMS

A number of commentators have pointed out that the weakness in the value of cryptocurrencies is that their value is dependent on what investors are willing to pay for them. Because they may exist only digitally, and, as an investment, they do not have any connected "productive" function, they do not have any independent value other than how potential investors regard them.

In contrast, stock market shares often represent ownership interests in companies that perform service functions or produce goods that are produced separately from the share value of the organization producing those goods and services. The desirability of the goods and services produced to the using public provides a separate intrinsic value that helps support the share price of the company producing them.

That additional value is not present in cryptocurrency. The value of cryptocurrency is usually how valuable potential purchasers think it is. Some commentators call this the "greater fool" paradigm. That is, an owner of crypto's hope to profit from the future sale of their crypto purchases depends on finding a purchaser who is a "greater fool" than the seller was, someone who has a stronger belief in the value of the crypto than the seller.

§13.05 CONCERN WITH INFLUENCERS

There is also a controversial group of so-called cryptocurrency "influencers" who are reported to publish information about Bitcoin price increases. These "reports" are

813. U.S. DOJ, "Two Arrested for Alleged Conspiracy to Launder $4.5 Billion in Stolen Cryptocurrency" online at justice.gov, February 8, 2022. For further details, *see* "Statement of Facts" for DOJ Case: 1:22-mj-00022, downloadable PDF on DOJ website.

814. Ramishah Manuf, "BitConnect Founder Charged With Orchestrating $2 Billion Ponzi Scheme," CNN Business, online, February 27, 2022.

allegedly published in order to create a positive public view of the advantages of investing in Bitcoin, but which are allegedly intended to create profits for these "influencers" and their friends.[815]

Some of these incidents do rise to the level of criminal fraud or Ponzi schemes. At that level, there may follow criminal investigations and prosecutions. Some may not rise to that level but may still violate financial trading and investment regulations and can be subject to investigations and penalties imposed by financial regulators such as the SEC, the IRS or the CFTC (and/or equivalent regulators in non-US jurisdictions).

[A] Elon Musk

One of the major influencers in the cryptocurrency market has been the industrial billionaire Elon Musk who has been called the world's richest person.

[1] Musk Sued for US$ 258 Billion for Alleged Crypto Pyramid Scheme

In June of 2022, a lawsuit seeking US$ 258 billion in total damages was filed in the U.S. Court for the Southern District of New York in Manhattan,[816] alleging that Elon Musk operated a "pyramid scheme" to support a digital currency named Dogecoin. The lawsuit alleged that Musk knew that "Dogecoin had no value" but operated a pyramid scheme to support it "for profit, exposure and amusement." In June of 2022, the market value of Dogecoin had fallen from a high of US$ 0.74 in May of 2021 to a trade price of just under US$ 0.06 in June of 2022.[817]

[2] Musk and Bitcoin

In January of 2021, Musk reportedly indicated that he had invested about 1.5 billion U.S. dollars in Bitcoin and was going to accept Bitcoin as a purchasing medium for Tesla cars.

According to news reports in June of 2022, Mr. Musk's fame and his historical associations with cryptocurrency have put him in the unfortunate position of having his name and image used by cyber criminals to promote fraudulent cryptocurrency scams on sites such as YouTube. BBC News reported that:

> Every few days, it was reported, hackers changed the name and picture of dozens of YouTube channels to make them look like official Tesla channels, the electric car manufacturer of which Mr. Musk is chief executive.[818]

---

815. Concoda, July 9, 2021.
816. *Johnson v. Musk, U.S. District Court, Southern District of New York*, No. 22-05037.
817. Jonathan Stempel, "Elon Musk Sued for $258 Billion Over Alleged Dogecoin Pyramid Scheme," Reuters, online, June 17, 2022.
818. Joe Tidy, "YouTube Accused of Failing to Tackle Fake Elon Musk Livestream Scams," *BBC News*, online, June 10, 2022.

[B] Influencers Push Crypto

One of the things that appears to boost the value of a cryptocurrency is endorsement by a respected or popular celebrity or "influencer." However, endorsement by a person well known to a significant portion of the public does not necessarily guarantee that the value of a particular cyber currency is stable or that the creation and trading of that cyber currency are conducted in compliance with applicable laws and regulations. Also, it may not be made clear whether the celebrity or influencer in question is being paid for the use of their name, image or opinion by persons selling the cryptocurrency to the public.

[C] Influencer Problems: Mayweather, Pierce, Kardashian

In January of 2022, a lawsuit was launched against defendants, including three well-known figures: the boxer Floyd Mayweather junior, the basketball player Paul Pierce and the media celebrity Kim Kardashian, alleging that they worked with a cryptocurrency seller, EthereumMax, to "misleadingly promote and sell" the cryptocurrency. It is reported that EthereumMax has no business or legal connection with Ethereum which is one of the more popular cryptocurrencies on the market.[819]

The multi-plaintiff class action, which was brought in the Central District Court of California, claimed "the company's executives, collaborating with several celebrity promoters," were responsible for "false or misleading statements to investors about EthereumMax, through social media advertisements and other promotional activities."[820]

The previously mentioned three celebrities were reportedly involved in promoting EthereumMax in the following ways:

- Paul Pierce, a former professional basketball player, reportedly published a post on Twitter "praising EthereumMax's ability to make money for him."
- EthereumMax was reportedly promoted by Mr. Mayweather at a cryptocurrency conference and EthereumMax used a Mayweather boxing match to promote its crypto.
- Kim Kardashian reportedly told her 250 million Instagram followers, "this is not financial advice but sharing what my friends tell me about the EthereumMax token."[821]

Charles Randall, the head of the UK FCA, later suggested that the Kardashian post might have been the "financial promotion with the single biggest audience reach in history."

Mr. Randall, who in September of 2021 was speaking at the Cambridge International Symposium on Economic Crime, reportedly said that Kardashian had "asked her

819. "Kim Kardashian Sued in Crypto 'Pump and Dump' Case," *BBC News*, online, January 12, 2022.
820. *Ibid.*
821. *Ibid.*

250 million followers to speculate on crypto tokens" by touting a promotion for EthereumMax. Randall allegedly described EthereumMax as a "speculative digital token created a month before by unknown developers." Randall reportedly said that Kardashian and other "influencers" were promoting "delusions of quick riches."[822]

The defendant promoters reportedly claimed that investors could make "significant returns" from purchasing "E-Max tokens." This allegedly caused a significant rise in the market price of EthereumMax because investors were reportedly buying these tokens at "artificially inflated prices." This allowed the promoters to sell their E-Max tokens to these investors at a profit. The promotion campaign reportedly increased the value of this crypto by more than 1300%. However, the price then crashed causing many investors to lose significant amounts of money.[823]

In its investigation, the SEC found that Kardashian had been paid US$ 250,000 to tout the cryptocurrency and that she had not disclosed this fact to her followers. At the beginning of October 2022, Kardashian agreed to pay a penalty of US$ 1.26 million to settle the charges brought against her by the SEC.[824]

A classic "pump and dump scheme" follows a pattern whereby:

- A person whose opinions about investment are influential is either used or cooperates with the promoter of an investment.
- To advertise the strong profit potential of a particular investment.
- If the "influencer" is respected enough, this will cause potential investors to buy the investment in question.
- Which will usually cause the investment's market value to rise.
- The promoter, who has purchased or otherwise owns significant amounts of the investment in question before the influencer states their confidence in the future profits that may be made from the investment, takes advantage of the rise of value to sell or offload their holdings in the investment to the influenced investors.
- Making the promoter, and perhaps the influencer (who may be given a quantity of the investment or be paid in cash), a substantial profit.
- Then, as is often the case, shortly afterward, the market will lose confidence in the investment in question and its price will fall dramatically, causing significant losses to the influenced investors.
- In short, the promoter and the influencers have "pumped" up perceptions of the future value of an investment and "dumped" their own holdings on new investors, at a profit, without being concerned about whether the investment has any significant underlying value.

822. "Kim Kardashian Crypto Ad Singled Out by Financial Watchdog," *BBC News*, online, September 6, 2021.
823. *Ibid.*
824. Siladitya Ray, "Kim Kardashian Agrees to Pay $1.26 Million to Settle SEC Cryptocurrency Promotion Charge," Forbes, online, October 3, 2022.

[D] Promising Money for Gaming?

Another crypto-related situation which tempted a number of people to try it out was the online game Axie Infinity which reportedly seemed to offer players the opportunity to earn money while they were playing the game. The game involved players controlling digital creatures called, "Axies" that battled each other. When a player won a battle, the player could earn digital tokens that could be traded like cryptocurrency. There was also a market for "Axies" as well.

These features reportedly allowed players to earn some money, and some players reportedly hoped playing the game could become a full-time job. However, the price of the token fell dramatically by June of 2022, and the game attracted fewer players, which meant fewer earning opportunities. By that time, the operators of the game were downplaying its earning potential, reportedly saying things such as, "We've been trying to warn people, even when prices were high, don't expect this to be a stable source of income." [825]

[E] Insider Dealing

[1] Coinbase Insider Dealing Charges

As with any investment, the public offering of digital assets on crypto exchanges, such as Coinbase, combined with the volatile price fluctuations of such assets, offered opportunities for "insider dealing," and some "insiders" are alleged to have taken advantage of that to earn illegal profits.

In July of 2022, the U.S. SEC issued the following announcement:

> The Securities and Exchange Commission today announced insider trading charges against a former Coinbase product manager, his brother, and his friend for perpetrating a scheme to trade ahead of multiple announcements regarding certain crypto assets that would be made available for trading on the Coinbase platform.
>
> ***
>
> [I]n breach of his duties Ishan [Wahi—a former Coinbase product manager], repeatedly tipped the timing and content of upcoming listing announcements to his brother, Nikhil Wahi, and his friend, Sameer Ramani. Ahead of those announcements, which usually resulted in an increase in the assets prices, Nikhil Wahi and Ramani allegedly purchased at least 25 crypto assets, at least nine of which were securities, and then typically sold them shortly after the announcements for a profit. The long-running insider trading scheme generated illicit profits totaling more than $1.1 million.[826]

The SEC filed their complaint in the Federal District Court in Seattle, Washington.

825. Joshua Brustein, "A Billion-Dollar Crypto Gaming Startup Promised Riches and Delivered Disaster," Bloomberg, Businessweek, online, June 10, 2022.
826. U.S. SEC, Press Release, 2022-127, "SEC Charges Former Coinbase Manager, Two Others in Crypto Asset Insider Trading Action," online at: sec.gov, July 21, 2022.

Coinbase had not yet been registered with the SEC as an exchange for the trading of regulated securities.

[F] Coinbase: Illegal Trading of Unregistered Securities

In addition to its probe as to whether Coinbase officials have been guilty of insider trading, the SEC was also investigating whether Coinbase was permitting trading of digital assets that should have been registered as securities with the SEC. In July of 2022, a report of the SEC's investigations contributed to a drop in Coinbase's share price of more than 20%.[827]

In late July of 2022, it was reported:

> The US Securities and Exchange Commission scrutiny of digital currencies that are listed on Coinbase global Inc is igniting concerns that a major crackdown for the rest of the industry is imminent.[828]

§13.06 OVERALL CRIME STATISTICS

Annual crypto crime reports are provided by a blockchain data company called "Chainalysis."[829]

They claim:

> Our data powers investigation, compliance and market intelligence software that has been used to solve some of the world's most high-profile criminal cases and grow consumer access to cryptocurrency safely.[830]

Their 2022 Cryptocurrency Crime Report showed that illegal transactions in cryptocurrency had increased by almost 80% to around US$ 14 billion. Fortunately, the Report also showed that legitimate transactions had grown over 560% which meant seven times as many legal transactions were concluded as criminal transactions.

In the full year 2021, about US$ 7.8 billion worth of cryptocurrency was reportedly stolen in scams. About one-third of that resulted from "rug polls" where promoters of crypto projects take investors' money and disappear without providing the goods or services promised. Unfortunately, huge growth was reportedly shown in using digital assets to illegally launder money. That activity increased by almost 2000%![831]

---

827. Allyson Versprille and Lydia Beyoud, "Coinbase SEC Probe on Crypto Listings: Shares Tumble," Bloomberg, online at: bloomberg.com, July 26, 2022.
828. Lydia Beyoud and Allyson Versprille, "Coinbase Faces SEC Probe Into Listed Tokens Has Crypto Traders Rattled," Bloomberg, online at: bloomberg.com, July 27, 2022.
829. Their website can be found online at: chainalysis.com.
830. *Ibid.*, accessed September 9, 2022.
831. Chainalysis, "The 2022 Crypto Crime Report: Original Data and Research into Cryptocurrency-based Crime," February 2022, available for download online at: chainalysis.com, accessed September 9, 2022.

§13.07 BITCOIN PONZI SCHEMES

In March of 2022, the CFTC reportedly filed enforcement actions in the U. S. District Court for the Eastern District of New York, charging that four defendants solicited US$ 44 million and misappropriated millions in connection with Bitcoin Ponzi schemes.[832] Three of the charged individuals were in the United States and one was in India. They were named as Duane Golden of Florida, Jatin Patel of India, Marquis Edgerton of North Carolina, and Gregory Aggesen of New York.

The complaint charged that the defendants operated various websites (Empowercoin, Ecoinplus and JetCoin) that solicited more than US$ 44 million in Bitcoin from customers. They promised their customers that professionals would trade their Bitcoin and provide profits which would be paid to customers on a daily basis. It is alleged that, in classic Ponzi scheme fashion, these so-called profits were paid from the funds provided by other customers. It is also alleged that the defendants misappropriated US$ 17 million for themselves.[833]

§13.08 CRYPTO THEFT

[A] State-Sponsored Theft

[1] North Korea

One of the more notable developments in crypto crime has been the rise of state-sponsored cryptocurrency theft by rogue nations such as North Korea.

In February of 2022, it was reported that North Korea has assembled a sophisticated and highly skilled hacking corps to steal cyber currency and utilize it through the employment of highly evolved money laundering techniques in order to evade international financial sanctions and provide money to help it develop the nuclear weapons it wants to threaten other countries. They are reported to have stolen hundreds of millions of dollars' worth of cryptocurrency in hacking attacks on crypto exchanges aiming particularly at the more liquid currencies such as Bitcoin.

They have been successful at disguising the source of the cryptocurrency they inject into the market using techniques that allow them to transfer and sell the stolen cryptocurrencies anonymously.

It is reported that the principal thieves in North Korea's crypto robbery cabal are called the Lazarus Group. They are reported to have been successful in a number of spectacular hacks, including an attack on the Central Bank of Bangladesh.[834]

832. "CFTC Charges Four Operators for $44 Million Bitcoin Ponzi and Misappropriation Schemes," online at cftc.gov, March 8, 2022, accessed April 20, 2022.
833. *Ibid*. As of April 21, 2022, this matter was not reported to be resolved.
834. Richard Lloyd Parry, "Kim Jong-un Steals Crypto to Make a Bomb: An Army of Skilled Cybercriminals Is Undermining Sanctions and Arming the North Korean Regime With Spectacular Success.," The Times, online, February 22, 2022.

What is particularly remarkable about this activity is that North Korean citizens are not generally allowed any access to the World Wide Web. However, North Korea's Reconnaissance General Bureau sponsors an ongoing campaign by hackers such as Lazarus to find cryptocurrency to steal to allow that country to develop the weapons it wants.

International financial and economic sanctions have made it difficult for North Korea to earn foreign currency. They are employing cryptocurrency theft and blockchain technology to allow them to replace this lost income with stolen cryptocurrency. The effectiveness of North Korea's crypto theft efforts has caused the Center for a New American Security, a Washington research group, to say:

> The Pyongyang-led cybercrime organization known as Lazarus Group has transformed from a rogue team of hackers to a masterful army of cyber criminals and foreign affiliates capable of compromising major national financial networks and stealing hundreds of millions of dollars' worth of virtual assets.

The use of criminal activities to earn foreign currency is not new for North Korea. It is reported that since the 1970s, North Korean diplomats have used illegal tactics such as selling tax-free alcohol and cigarettes. Since then, North Korea has been accused of being involved in a wide variety of criminal activities, including making and selling drugs, counterfeiting currency, selling fake luxury goods, money laundering and trading in banned items such as rhino horn, ivory, and a variety of armaments. It is reported that they sometimes smuggled illegal drugs, including heroin, opium and crystal meth amphetamines, in diplomatic bags. In order to further these activities, they are reported to have worked with Japanese and Russian criminal gangs, IRA terrorists and poachers in Africa.

In order to develop a variety of clever hacking techniques, North Korea has reportedly used the facilities of a special unit called Laboratory 110 at Mirim University in Pyongyang. Originally, their hacking targeted South Korean companies, but more recently they have reportedly moved on to hacking financial entities and crypto exchanges in more than thirty countries around the world which has reportedly earned them up to US$ 2 billion.

One of the most successful early hacking attacks, reported to have been originated in North Korea,[835] was the WannaCry attack of 2017 which encrypted the data on computers around the world and allegedly earned the hackers hundreds of millions of dollars in ransom payments.

Encouraged by their revenue-gathering success, hackers in North Korea have reportedly continued to find ways to steal cyber currency using the international Internet.

In 2018 Lazarus was reported to have stolen more than US$ 200 million in different kinds of cyber currency, including Bitcoin, Ethereum and Dogecoin, from a Chinese exchange called "Gate.io exchange." In 2019 US$ 7 million was taken from the Singapore-based DragonEx. These thefts were reportedly carried out by sending an

835. "Cyber-attack: US and UK Blame North Korea for WannaCry," *BBC News*, online December 19, 2017, accessed February 25, 2022.

email containing a malicious program to exchange employees which, when opened, provided access to "digital wallets" where cryptocurrency was held.[836]

One of the factors that made it easier for hackers to steal cryptocurrency from these sites was reportedly that the cryptocurrency on those exchanges was stored in the digital wallets of individuals rather than in a central holding facility which made it easier for the hackers to anonymously transfer cryptocurrency to themselves.

The total cryptocurrency that was reportedly stolen by North Korea in 2019 added up to around US$ 400 million. This money is reported to support, in one way or another, North Korea's nuclear and ballistic missile projects.[837]

[B] A British Expert in North Korea

[1] Overall Crime Statistics

In a surprising article published in April of 2022, it was reported that a cryptocurrency expert from Britain Was facing a possible £1 million fine and twenty years in jail in the United States for breaching sanctions against North Korea. The 30-year-old tech expert is alleged to have spoken at a conference in the North Korean capital advising on "cutting edge crypto currency."[838]

He was apparently invited to the conference by a Spanish businessman and allegedly told those attending the conference:

> I'm sure a lot of people in this room who work within the banking system will understand how predominantly the United States controls the way in which money moves around the world and this can be very, very unfair.[839]

[C] Fraud

A less exotic, but unfortunately, all too common, kind of crypto crime is fraud. Several examples have been described in other chapters of this book. But as one example here, there is FTX, a crypto exchange, once valued at US$ 32 billion, that filed for bankruptcy in November of 2022. In December of 2022, the founder and former CEO of FTX, Sam Bankman-Fried, was arrested in the Bahamas at the request of U.S. authorities. U.S. prosecutors have reportedly said:

> From the founding of his cryptocurrency exchange FTX in 2019, Mr. Bankman-Fried engaged in widespread fraud, the federal authorities charged on Tuesday, and used his customer deposits to finance his political activities, buy lavish real estate and invest in other companies ... . [H]e he repeatedly lied to customers,

836. Parry, February 22, 2022.
837. *Ibid.*
838. David Brown, "British Cryptocurrency Expert Christopher Emms Facing £1 Million Fine on Cyber Charge," The Times, online, April 27, 2022.
839. *Ibid.*

investors and lenders about the structure of his business empire and how he handled the billions of dollars in funds that crypto users deposited in his exchange.[840]

840. David Yaffe-Bellamy, Mathew Goldstein and Emily Flitter, "Prosecutor Announces Charges Against FTX Founder," The New York Times, online, December 13, 2022.

CHAPTER 14
NFTs and Fan Tokens

In the area related to cryptocurrency is the explosive growth of the sale of "crypto tokens" (sometimes known as NFTs) by a variety of issuers from art sellers, to celebrities, to football teams.

§14.01 NFTS IN THE ART WORLD

It is reported that digital images, constituting "art works," are being sold by artists as digital videos or one-of-a-kind digital images described as "non-fungible tokens (NFTs)." Some are sold for large sums, sometimes for millions of dollars. These unique NFTs exist only in digital form but contain a unique code that attests to their authenticity as one-of-a-kind digital assets.[841]

[A] Melania Trump

In what some may consider a particularly strange development in the developing "token market," Melania Trump, the former U.S. First Lady, announced in December of 2021 that:

> [S]he will sell her first [?] non-fungible token this holiday season. Titled "Melania's Vision" digital asset ... features watercolor art that "embodies Mrs. Trump's cobalt blue eyes, providing the collector with an amulet to inspire."[842]

841. Jade Cuttle, "NFTs and Multi-million Dollar JPGs: The Rise of Digital Art," The Times Online, March 24, 2021.
842. Emma Nolan, "Melania Trump Launches NFT For Sale Called 'Melania's Vision.'" Newsweek, online, December 16, 2021. Apparently, more amulets to inspire can be expected in the future.

The situation became murkier when *Bloomberg* reported:

> The source of funds for the winning bid that Melania Trump's first NFT auction appears to be the creators of the project themselves.[843]

It was reported that:

> "It seems that aspiring NFT artist Melania Trump has been bested at her own game. The former first lady minted her first NFTs, the *Head of State Collection*, on January 11, and put it up for auction, where it's sold for $180,000 dollars (1,800 Solana). A month later, it looks like she bought it herself.
>
> "Public records at the Solana (SOL) blockchain indicate that the auction winner is the same address that minted the piece—albeit through a very convoluted process. Solana is a public blockchain, like Ethereum and Bitcoin this means that anybody with Internet access can follow where the NFTS are sold."

[B] Donald Trump NFT "Trading Cards"

In December of 2022, it was reported that Donald Trump had announced the sale of NFT "trading cards" that consisted of a series of photographs connected with his life and career ("amazing ART of my Life & Career"). These were reportedly sold for 99 dollars each and proved very popular, making Mr. Trump over US$ 4 million. It was additionally reported that a secondary market in these tokens was offering them for much higher prices.[844]

§14.02 SPORTS CURRENCIES (FAN TOKENS)

[A] UK

[1] Football

An area that has grown to be a concern for government authorities in a number of countries has been the sale of "fan tokens" marketed to fans of football clubs.

For example, it has been reported that football teams in the UK are aiming to make hundreds of millions of pounds by selling "fan tokens." It is reported that twenty-four football clubs across Europe have begun issuing such tokens. It is estimated fans have spent over £250 million on them so far.

843. Misyrlena Egkolfopoulou, "Money That Won Melania Trump NFT Came From Melania Trump Wallet," Bloomberg online, February 16, 2022. The article said, "[S]ome actors ... simultaneously buy and sell the same asset and—in some cases—artificially raise its price. The process is known as wash trading." Newsweek subsequently reported a denial by Mrs. Trump that she bought her own NFT for $185,000. *See*, Emma Nolan, "Melania Trump Denies Buying Her Own NFT for $185,000," "[Mrs. Trump's] office confirmed then that she planned to release more NFTs at 'regular intervals'... ." Newsweek online February 17, 2022.

844. Josh Taylor, "Donald Trump's Digital Trading Card Collection Sells Out in Less Than a Day.," The Guardian, online December 17, 2022.

In addition, it is reported that some football clubs such as Manchester United are issuing souvenirs in the form of NFTs.

Most clubs are reported to be buying these tokens from a firm called Socios.com.[845] Socios apparently organize the initial sale and further trading of these tokens, as do other token platforms such as Binance and Bitci. However, to buy such tokens from Socios, potential purchasers reportedly must first purchase a cryptocurrency issued by Socios called "Chiliz."

[2] Regulation as Investments?

There are a number of troublesome aspects to this trade. One is that it is not clear whether these tokens are being advertised as having any intrinsic value or being described as potential "investments." If the latter is the case, then there are financial services regulation issues that need to be considered including whether the issuers of these tokens need to be regulated by the national financial regulators of the home countries of these sellers as "authorized persons" eligible to market investments.

It is not a small matter. Socios has reported that by itself it has sold in the region of £300 million worth of these tokens.

Those producing and trading in fan tokens may feel that being associated with a very popular sport, such as football, lends crypto additional credibility.

A number of famous teams and well-known players have become associated with cryptocurrency in one way or another. In 2021, there was a transaction that involved both. David Barral, a striker for Real Madrid, moved to DUX International de Madrid, and his move was reportedly paid for with Bitcoin.[846] The football teams that are reported to be selling the largest number of tokens are Lazio, Manchester City, Porto and Santos.[847]

Increasingly, international football teams are becoming known to be associated with cryptocurrency in one way or another. Obviously, their ownership must feel that this is a way of earning additional revenue and, possibly, attracting additional interest to the team among fans and non-football fans who are interested in cryptocurrency.

[3] Arsenal FC

An example that was reported in late 2021 is the case of "tokens" that were being promoted by the popular English professional football club, Arsenal FC, in partnership with Socios.com (Socios).[848]

---

845. "BE MORE THAN A FAN" online at socios.com.
846. Andrew Michael, "What's The Score With Football and Crypto," Forbes, online, February 4, 2022.
847. Joe Tidy and Edwin Lane, "Football Fans Spending Millions on Club Crypto-tokens," *BBC News*, online, December 10, 2021.
848. "Arsenal's Cryptocurrency Ads Breached Rules," The Times, online, December 22, 2021, also *see*, Chris Vallance, Arsenal fan token posts broke advertising rules, says watchdog", BBC online, 22 December 2021.

In Arsenal's partnership with Socios, the tokens had to be bought using the cryptocurrency "Chiliz."

The UK Advertising Standards Authority (ASA) reportedly alleged that Arsenal breached rules on social responsibility, financial products, and misleading advertising. Arsenal denied wrongdoing, but an ASA ruling reportedly upheld the complaints.

The Authority was specifically concerned with the issue of whether the tokens were being sold as "investments," saying:

> We told Arsenal to ensure that future ads did not trivialize investment in crypto assets [and that Arsenal should have made] clear that capital gains tax could be due on crypto asset profits. ... We told them to ensure they made sufficiently clear that the value of investments in crypto assets was variable and crypto assets were unregulated. ... .[849]

The Authority was apparently concerned about the fact that has been an increasing number of deals between crypto platforms and British football clubs relating to the sale of crypto-related products. The top English Football League, the Premier League, was reported to have promised to look into partnerships between member football clubs and what is described in *The Times* as "an unregulated financial industry."[850] Crypto token purchasers are not protected from losses by the UK Financial Services Compensation Scheme.[851]

[4] Expansion of Tokens and Football

In countries where football is a big sport, the teams and the game are usually governed by an overall regulatory body known as a "Football Association" (FA). The reaction of these governing bodies to the sale of NFT tokens by member teams has been mixed. However, Socios has been effective informing "partnership" arrangements in twenty countries, including with some governing football associations such as Argentina Football Association (AFA).

In May of 2021, the AFA reportedly agreed to a deal with Socios to sell tokens to football fans according to reports on the cryptocurrency information site CoinGecko Argentine.

However, these "partnerships" have not always been trouble-free. In January of 2022, it was reported that Socios sued the AFA for ending its agreement with Socios and making a similar agreement with Binance. The Argentine commercial court issued a preliminary injunction against the AFA, but the AFA is reported to have appealed.[852]

With respect to another football club, Manchester City, *The Times* reported that Manchester City had suspended a partnership with a Seychelles crypto company called

849. *Ibid.*
850. Chris Vallance, "Arsenal Fan Token Broke Advertising Rules Says Watchdog," BBC online, December 21, 2021.
851. Charles Randell, "The Risks of Token Regulation," FCA, online, September 9, 2021.
852. Andres Engler, coindesk.com, online, January 27, 2022.

3Key Technologies after it was reported that five people named as company executives appeared not to exist.[853]

In 2018, an investment trading operation named eToro was reported to have established a relationship with seven English football teams: Newcastle United, Tottenham Hotspur, Cardiff City, Brighton and Hove Albion, Leicester City, Crystal Palace and Southampton, which eToro described as "the first step in bringing the opportunity offered by Bitcoin and crypto assets to football."[854]

And football connections have also reportedly been made in other countries. The Italian team, Rimini FC, became partly owned by a blockchain company, Kuanto Coin, which reportedly purchased a 25% interest in the club with cryptocurrency.

AZ Alkmaar, a team in the Netherlands, reportedly plans to pay its team members in Bitcoin.[855]

Glasgow Rangers, Manchester City and Juventus (JUV) are reportedly marketing team-related NFTs.[856] Reportedly all twenty UK Premier League clubs have considered selling NFTs to their supporters.[857]

A top Italian team, JUV, reportedly permits token holders to decide the song to be played when JUV scores a goal.[858]

Token schemes have reportedly proved very popular with major international football clubs. They now are offered by, in addition to the clubs mentioned above, Paris St. Germain, Athletico Madrid, Inter Milan, Arsenal and AC Milan.

The prices of the tokens vary between US$ 2 and US$ 15. It is reported that the Socios scheme may have earned clubs a total of about US$ 300 million in revenue.[859]

Some fan tokens, such as the Argentine ARG, have come to be regarded as a tradeable investments. CoinGecko provides a variety of information about ARGs which appears similar to the kinds of information that is provided about traditional tradeable investments such as company shares. The information on CoinGecko includes the U.S. dollar price for ARGs (US$ 1.52), including an indication of whether the price is rising or falling, a market cap (US$ 1,995,445); A twenty-hour hour trading volume figure (US$ 73,700); A circulating supply figure (1,325,548) and a total supply figure (20,000,000), and a calculator function that allows a user to calculate the current value of ARGs in a number of cryptocurrency and other values: (Bitcoin, etc.); a large number of national fiat currencies (including U.S. dollars, Russian Rubles and Euros); and the prices of silver and gold. CoinGecko provides similar information for Arsenal, JUV, and

853. Martyn Ziegler, "3Key Technologies: Manchester City Back Out of Mysterious Cryptocurrency Partnership" The Times online, November 20, 2021.
854. *Ibid.*
855. *Ibid.*
856. *Ibid.*
857. Sam Cunningham, "All 20 Premier League Clubs Are Looking At Launching NFTs to Sell to Fans, Crypto Expert Claims," innews.co.uk, online January 27, 2022.
858. Andrew Michael, "What's the Score With Football and Crypto," Forbes, online, February 4, 2022.
859. *Ibid.*

Paris Saint-Germain (PSG) fan tokens, and probably others—the four above are the only football fan tokens searched on CoinGecko for this book.[860]

[5] Football Clubs as Authorized Persons?

From a financial regulatory point of view, where do football teams stand by getting involved with crypto in these ways?

In addition to the national laws of each country that regulate financial instrument dealings, national laws also impose criminal sanctions on such things as fraud, misrepresentation, and theft, etc.

Although, in their case before the UK Advertising Authority, Arsenal strenuously argued that fan tokens were not being sold as an investment vehicle and there was no implication that money could be made from them,[861] the fact that there is a growing market for football fan tokens around the world seems to confirm that fan tokens can be an investment vehicle and that they can be seen as a money substitute. For example, it is reported that the international football star Lionel Messi is accepting fan tokens as part of his compensation payments from PSG.[862]

The Socios arrangement with the Argentine Football Association Fan Tokens (ARGs) reportedly led to these tokens being both tradeable and convertible to national currency on the crypto trading platform Coinbase.[863]

Consequently, arguments that football fan tokens are not really investments, or any real form of currency, appear very weak. It seems likely that there will be increasing financial services regulation of fan tokens and other forms of cryptocurrency until they are eventually on the regulatory level of other kinds of investments and currencies.

[6] Sport Governing Body Reactions

Football teams are also governed by national and international sporting associations.

In England, the FA governs the rules and competitions of the game. There are also various leagues within English football, such as the Premier League, a collection of the most competitive teams, that have their own governing bodies.

The involvement of English football teams with crypto and digital "non-fungible tokens" (NFTs) appears to be making those teams more attractive to potential investors. A group of U.S. investors is reported to be interested in purchasing an

860. CoinGecko says that it aggregates data for over thirteen thousand crypto assets across more than five hundred crypto exchanges around the world, with data going back for more than eight years. coingecko.com. online, March 10, 2022.
861. ASA (UK), "ASA Ruling on Arsenal Football Club plc," online, December 22, 2021.
862. Jon Boon, "SOCIOS PATH Arsenal Sell Them, While Messi Was Paid in Fans' Token in His PSG Deal ... It's the Cryptocurrency Changing Football." The Sun, online August 19, 2021.
863. "Argentine Football Association Fan Token to British Pound (1ARG equals £1.23 GBP)," Conbase.com, online, accessed March 9, 2022.

English football team and using, "advanced analytics and non-fungible tokens (NFTs) to create a new model of sports team ownership."[864]

The investors group is called WAGMI United, and reportedly used cryptocurrency as a major source of funding for the purchase of the UK League Two football club Crawley Town.[865]

The view of the football regulators on teams under their supervision has been relatively accepting that it is a sensible thing for teams to sell digital products such as tokens and NFTs. The body that governs European football, Uefa, recognizes that teams have lost billions of dollars in revenue as a result of the COVID-19 epidemic and that they need to find ways to replace that lost revenue. UEFA reportedly accepts that the sale of digital products is a way to recover from some of those losses.[866] Going even further than that, UAFA has reportedly entered into a partnership with Socios, naming Socios as its "first official fan token partner." The arrangement is due to last until 2024.[867]

The Socios arrangement with Union of European Football Associations (UEFA) has reportedly provoked some backlash among fans. *USA Today* reported that the Football Supporters Europe said:

> Is this an attempt to monetize football's responsibility to properly engage with representative fans groups and their concerns? Since Socios began monetizing fan engagement through fan tokens they have reportedly met strong opposition from fans groups.[868]

Socios has been effective in forming "partnership" arrangements in twenty-five countries, including with some governing football associations.

Binance has also become involved in the fan token business in both motorsport and football. It does not boast as many "partnerships" as Socios, but its website claimed fan token arrangements with the BWT Alpine F1 Team and three Portuguese football clubs: S.S. Lazio, FC Porto, and Santos FC.[869] One difference from Socios fan token purchase appears to be that with Binance, one can buy a fan token without needing to buy a cryptocurrency to buy the tokens. Binance says:

> The Binance Fan Token Platform provides multiple ways for users to buy and sell finance fan tokens ... . Once a launchpad ends, you will be able to buy Binance Fan Tokens with fiat using a linked bank account, [or] bank card ... .[870]

864. Rick Maese, "U.S. Group Eyes English Soccer Club, Saying Crypto and NFTs Can Change the Game," The Washington Post, online, December 16, 2021.
865. *Ibid.* and BBC, "Crawley Town: US cryptocurrency investors WAGMI United, complete takeover of club", BBC online, 07 April 2022.
866. Andrew Michael, "What's the Score With Football and Crypto," Forbes, online, February 4, 2022.
867. Jamie Crawley, "European Soccer's Governing Body Signs Up Socios.com as Token Partner," CoinDesk, online, February 16, 2022.
868. "Fan Groups Slam UEFA Crypto-Token Champions League Sponsor," USA Today, online, eu.usatoday.com, February 15, 2022.
869. Binance.com, online, accessed March 11, 2022.
870. "Fiat" is a conventional central bank-issued currency such as: US Dollars, Pounds Sterling or Euros.

CHAPTER 15

Economic Impact

Over the last few years, there has been an awful lot of information over the Internet, in the written media and in visual media about cryptocurrency. As a result, many people have decided to try investing in it. This has led to the creation of over 10,000 digital currencies. Some have become well known such as Bitcoin and Ether; others have much smaller or even tiny followings. The attraction of any of them seems to be that their volatility means that it can rapidly change value. Those that buy them, of course, hope they will go up dramatically, such as Bitcoin has done from time to time, and this could earn those that purchase them extraordinary amounts of money.

It appears that investors have paid less attention to the fact that cryptocurrencies, even the most prominent, can rapidly go down in value, costing owners of those currencies significant losses very rapidly.

The economic impact of cryptocurrencies has become huge, and appears to have taken national financial regulators, including central banks, by surprise. By early November of 2021, the value of the cryptocurrency market surpassed US$ 3 trillion. The price of Bitcoin rose beyond US$ 65,000.[871] But by August of 2022, the market had lost more than two-third of its value:

> The crypto crash is, in one sense, a story as old as time: an easy money scheme that has left a lot of people with nothing. The thing that is different is how it has been sold: the vague, grander "purpose" that one was supposed to be buying into. Was it all just a hill of magic beans, sauteed in techno Babble? In the midst of a $2 trillion meltdown, it is hard to argue otherwise.[872]

One of the reasons for crypto's rapid worldwide rise in popularity and the slowness of many national regulators to respond to it was the fact that it was to some

871. Will Feuer, "Cryptocurrency Market Passes $3 Trillion in Value as Bitcoin Surges," New York Post, 08 November 2021, accessed August 22, 2022.
872. Danny Fortson, "How Crypto Finally Cracked," The Sunday Times, Magazine, August 21, 2022.

extent a reaction to the financial crash of 2008 (sometimes called the "Great Recession"). There arose a feeling that cryptocurrency offered a new path to financial stability and freedom from restrictive and inadequate regulation:

> [I]t tapped into the underlying conceit of much of crypto, which is that the "system"—Wall Street, the City, regulators—is unfair or corrupt and that software-based money that no one controls would rebalance the scales.[873]

However, it is not only investors that have jumped on the cryptocurrency bandwagon. The interest in these products has caused other businesses to try to make money out of their existence without necessarily purchasing any of them. For example, news organizations, such as CNN, have started offering specialized reports that provide information about market movements, the types of cryptocurrencies available, news stories relating to them and advice from financial advisors about whether investing in crypto is a good decision. CNN's program is called "Crypto 101" and claims to offer:

> Everything you need to know about Bitcoin, blockchain, and NFTs and more. Plus, the latest cryptocurrency news, interviews and investing guides.[874]

The attention that crypto has been receiving in the media has attracted not only those in the financial world but also investors who are well-known people in other sectors such as media and sports. For example, it was recently reported that Serena Williams, who for many years has been a top tennis player, has raised over US$ 100 million to set up an "early-stage venture capital fund that will focus on diversity." Among the investments targeted by this fund are cryptocurrencies including bitski and nestcoin.[875]

§15.01 CHANGES TO INVESTMENT BEHAVIOR

Just one example of the power of crypto assets is how they have contributed to changes in investment behavior in large economies.

Traditionally, investment in India has focused on precious physical items such as gold and later on the trading of company shares. However, the emergence of cryptocurrency has made a significant impact in India, particularly with younger investors.[876]

During the COVID-19 pandemic, India, among other countries, saw an enormous increase in trading cryptocurrency. This is despite the fact that Indian governmental authorities have been negative about cryptocurrency for a number of years.[877]

---

873. *Ibid.*
874. CNN Business, Crypto 101, online, accessed March 4, 2022.
875. "Serena Williams' Fund Aims to Prove Point," The Times, online, March 2, 2022.
876. Diksha Madhok, "Crypto 'superpower?' India's Young Investors Prefer Bitcoin to Gold and 'Boring' Stocks," CNN Business, online, March 3, 2022.
877. *See* Chapter 7 for information about the legal status of cryptocurrency in India.

By February of 2022, it was being reported that a number of younger investors in India preferred to invest in cryptocurrency rather than traditional investments such as precious metals and company shares. Some reportedly believed that India has the potential to become a "crypto superpower" because Internet use is huge in the country with about 750 million users and the potential that hundreds of millions more will become users.

It is reported that only Vietnam is ahead of India in cryptocurrency investment. It is estimated that there are more than 20 million cryptocurrency investors in India.[878]

As indicated throughout this book, there is no question that cryptocurrency could have a significant aspect on many aspects of economic life. It could aid or destabilize countries and aid cybercrime and cyber war. It could weaken the powers of national central banks over control of a nation's currency. It could compete with other "investments" that investors can choose.

§15.02 CRYPTO INFILTRATION OF RETAIL GOODS MARKETS

On the most basic level, crypto is beginning to affect the way that ordinary consumers can choose to purchase their goods and services and the ways in which retail businesses buy and sell goods and services.

It was announced some time ago that Elon Musk said that the carmaker, Tesla, would accept Bitcoin in payment for its products. He then went on to say that Dogecoin would be accepted for some Tesla products.

In May of 2022, Gucci stores joined that trend by agreeing to take a variety of cryptocurrencies, including Bitcoin, Ethereum and Litecoin in payment at its stores. The method that will be employed is that customers will be emailed a QR code to complete the transaction with a digital asset wallet. They will be able to transact business on mobile devices. This policy has initially been introduced in the United States, but Gucci reportedly plans to introduce it in all its North American stores soon.[879]

§15.03 CRYPTO CRASHES

The popularity of cryptocurrency and the fact that it has become regarded as a sensible financial asset to invest in by so many individuals and organizations throughout the world economy has raised an issue as to how fluctuations in the value of various digital assets can affect wider national and international economic systems.

As a result, concern about the impact of digital assets on financial systems has become more widespread among financial regulators. As an example, in the autumn of 2021, the Deputy Governor of the bank of England warned that the dramatic rise of the

878. Disha Madhok, above, citing an October 2021 report in Chainalysis.
879. "Gucci Stores to Accept Cryptocurrencies in the US," *BBC News*, online, May 6, 2022.

market prices of cryptocurrencies in October of 2021 could lead to a price collapse which could impact beyond the digital asset markets:[880]

> As crypto has shifted from the fringes of global finance to the mainstream, its status as a largely unregulated space has magnified concern among policymakers worldwide. Its rising prominence has posed questions about the impact of future corrections. Would they be contained within its realm? Or would they unleash shockwaves into the wider financial system?[881]

In fact, in some ways, the crypto economy is more worrisome than the subprime mortgage market was before the financial crash of 2008. It is reported that the total value of the subprime mortgage market in 2008 was about US$ 1.2 trillion. By the autumn of 2021, the value of digital assets was reported to total about US$ 3 trillion.[882] So, it is entirely possible that a serious crash in the digital assets market could cause an even bigger disruption to the worldwide financial markets than the subprime mortgage crash of 2008.

One important difference is that most investments in the subprime mortgage market were held by large financial institutions, whereas exposure to the digital assets market appears to be less concentrated in important financial institutions. However, whether this offers better protection to the worldwide financial system remains to be seen. It is worth noting that by June of 2022 the overall value of the digital asset market had fallen to just over US$ 900 billion. One impact of this fall is that major digital asset businesses such as Coinbase and crypto.com had laid off hundreds of employees. The hope that so-called stablecoins would offer better protection against the volatility of other kinds of cryptocurrency was dashed in 2022 when terraUSD, which was promoted as a "stablecoin" that was "pegged to the US dollar," crashed in value.[883]

As mentioned previously in this book, promises that "stablecoins" were backed on a one-to-one basis by less volatile assets such as fiat currencies or precious metals have often turned out not to be true and have led to prosecution and fines of some crypto entrepreneurs that promoted certain "stablecoins."

In June of 2022, another "stablecoin," Magic Internet Money, also ended its peg to the U.S. dollar causing its value to fall rapidly. These stablecoin problems reportedly caused market-wide repercussions.

As the comedian John Oliver is reported to have said, cryptocurrency combines everything people do not understand about money with everything people do not understand about computers.[884]

By the middle of June 2022, the price of Bitcoin, the most popular cryptocurrency had fallen by more than 70% since November of 2021. The second most popular, Ethereum, had fallen by 78%. It is reported that two key reasons for this decline in the

880. Callum Jones, "Could the Next Crypto Crash Engulf the Entire Financial System?" The Times, online, June 18, 2022.
881. *Ibid.*
882. *Ibid.*
883. *Ibid.*
884. *Ibid.*

cryptocurrency market were price inflation and rising interest rates. These things made less money available for people to invest in riskier investments such as digital assets.[885]

Further concern was expressed that crypto owners who had borrowed money to purchase their holdings would seek to sell off their crypto leading to further declines in the market.

There is also not much confidence that investors who have experienced substantial losses in the crypto markets will be entitled to any compensation for their losses. In an interview, the chief executive of the UK FCA, Nikhil Rathi, was negative on the possibility of compensation being available for losing investors:[886]

> The value of many crypto assets is exceptionally volatile if you are considering putting any of your money into these products, you need to be ready to lose the entire amount. ... We need to be quite clear that there won't be compensation available for losses. It wouldn't be reasonable for healthy financial firms and their consumers to be paying for losses from these assets.

§15.04 WEB THREE THEORY

In discussions about the nature and importance of digital assets, there is a theory being expressed that the creation and popularity of digital assets are reflective of an evolution in the Internet described as "Web Three." This is differentiated from the previous versions of the Internet as follows.[887]

"Web One" was created at the beginning of the Internet. Its main feature was that it allowed users an opportunity to find and review data online. However, the data available was only that placed there by "content" providers. Those were private companies, such as America Online (AOL), government agencies or universities. Individual users could not really contribute to the web. They were only permitted to use it to electronically view the information that had been put on the Internet by others. Web. One was not genuinely "interactive."

"Web Two," in the early 2000s, changed things. It became more interactive, allowing the contribution of user-created content. Several large platforms such as Facebook, Twitter, and YouTube allowed individuals to post their thoughts and messages. However, the popularity of sites such as these led to centralization of the web. The largest and most popular sites became rich and powerful through advertising and in some cases selling information that they gathered about their user's preferences and activities on their sites—"selling clics."[888]

Although usage on these sites may not have involved any upfront costs to users, the users were ultimately paying a price to these large platforms by viewing adverts and providing saleable personal information. This led to problems such as use of customer

885. Emma Powell, Tracey Boles, "Bitcoin Drops Below $20,000 as Losses Hit $900bn," The Times, online, June 20, 2022.
886. Lily Russell-Jones and Rachel Lavin, "Cryptocurrency Gamour Turns to Huge Losses," The Times, online, May 21, 2022.
887. Thomas Stackpole, "What is Web3?" Harvard Business Review, online at: hbr.org., May 10, 2022.
888. *Ibid.*

information to understand users' personal and political views and to be able to target them to try and influence important political elections in countries such as the United States.

Web Two also created ways for individuals to have an impact on users and make money for themselves. This was through the creation of "influencers" who posted content appealing enough to attract vast numbers of "followers" who influencers tried to persuade to use or purchase goods and services. The online attention that search influencers attracted could persuade producers of such goods and services to pay for an influencer's endorsement.

"Web Three" is now being presented as a way of correcting what are considered to be the problems that have arisen on Web Two.[889]

Web Three is promoted as a move away from centralization of networks and content which enhances individual freedom through the use of blockchains, cryptocurrency, NFTS, etc. Web Three allegedly brings more "democracy" to the Internet.

The pro-Web Three argument is that individuals have an opportunity to create, "mine," promote and sell unlimited quantities of valuable products, by means of digital technology on the Internet, verify and protect their ownership with "blockchains" and instantly promote and distribute them worldwide.

This supposedly gives individuals the opportunities to have valuable "ownership" stakes in the universe of online commerce and ideas. It supposedly takes control of value out of the hands of centralized networks and government agencies.

However, there is serious skepticism about whether the "benefits" of Web Three will ever be enjoyed by a large percentage of online users. For example, a large percentage of the supply of crypto assets is owned by a tiny percentage of holders (27% of Bitcoin is reportedly owned by 0.01% of holders).[890] Also, Web Three opens users to approaches by scam artists, hackers, abusers and terrorists that would have found it harder to reach the public in the past.

Will Web Three turn out to be just an unregulated, dangerous and destructive "Wild West." There are already serious problems (FTX, Crypto Queen, etc.). Will these eventually overwhelm the benefits?[891]

Do the so-called advantages of this new digital democracy really exist? It is certainly true that there is very little control over who can create, own or control digital assets. However, the principal advantage of cryptocurrency, so far, seems to be that it allows financial transactions relatively free from government scrutiny. The principal beneficiaries of this advantage are criminals who want to avoid taxation or want to be paid for their criminal activities with difficult-to-trace mediums of exchange. The only possible benefit to the average citizen is that if they buy cryptocurrency, there is a possibility that someone may be willing to pay more to buy that crypto from them in the future. Maybe they can benefit from "the greater fool" who is willing to pay more for a certain crypto than was paid by the seller.

889. *Ibid.*
890. *Ibid.*
891. U.S. Congressional Hearing on Crypto Regulation, CNET, online, June 22-23, 2022; Hearings to Examine Cryptocurrencies, 117th Congress (2021-2022), online at: congress.gov.

However, as the volatility of the crypto markets has shown us, that benefit can be illusory.

So exactly, what does this democratization of Web Three really mean?

Perhaps all it provides is an opportunity for a greater number of computer users to create digital products (generously described as "assets") and say to their fellow users on the World Wide Web, "Give me your relatively stable fiat currency, and I will give you my marvelous crypto-asset." Some people will gain financial or other advantages from these exchanges, but how many? The value of any nonproductive investment will only increase if greater and greater numbers of buyers are found who are willing to pay more for it than the original sellers.

Perhaps the most solid economic future for cryptocurrencies rests on the fact that a number of major economies such as China, the US, Great Britain, and Germany are considering whether to replace "paper" fiat currencies with digital versions of their relatively respected fiat currencies. If this happens, digital currencies will be more widely used, be more respected and be less volatile.

The same is true of other digital assets such as NFTs and digital tokens. When they were rare, there were some buyers that were willing to pay high prices for them. However, because digital assets are relatively easy to create, this is a kind of democratization because more people have an opportunity to own them. However, as they become more common, it seems likely that they will become less expensive and less valuable, and, perhaps, creators will have less incentive to create them.

CHAPTER 16

Crypto in War

One of the more sinister advantages of cryptocurrency is that it gives nations with little wealth or few natural resources and opportunity to create an international currency with little more than computing power and access to significant amounts of electricity. Given the other characteristics of cyber currency such as its untraceability and the difficulty of knowing who the currency actually belongs to, cyber currency provides a very useful tool for rogue states who would find it useful to increase their power to harm other states that they consider to be their enemies.

It has been reported that North Korea is stealing cyber currency to support its ballistic missile development and to allow it to create more nuclear warheads. This has been revealed in a report to the UN Security Council.[892]

In order to support these and other aggressive activities, North Korea is reported to have stolen around US$ 2 billion in cryptocurrency in 2019 and about US$ 400 million in 2021. These thefts are reported to be an important source of revenue for North Korea. The currency is stolen from several sites, including cryptocurrency exchanges in America, Europe and Asia.[893]

§16.01 RUSSIAN CYBERWAR AND CRYPTO SUPPORT OF WAR

In February of 2022, Russia began an invasion of Ukraine. In addition to the physical military attacks, Russia reportedly used cyberattacks on Ukrainian financial services and banks to complement its military strikes.

It is also to be reported on the other side that cryptocurrency is being used to fund Ukraine's defense:

892. Richard Lloyd Parry, "North Korea Stealing Cryptocurrency to Develop Missile Programme, UN says," The Times, online, February 6, 2022.
893. *Ibid.*

> Cryptocurrency payments to military and hacktivist groups in Ukraine aimed at countering Russian aggression against the country spiked sharply in the second half of 2021, according to cryptocurrency tracing and blockchain analysis firm Elliptic, crowdfunded payments to those organizations in bitcoin, litecoin, ether and other cryptocurrencies the company tracks reached a total value of around 550,000 last year … .[894]

Unfortunately, the nature of cryptocurrency has proved to be a significant aid to Russian dictator Vladimir Putin and his cronies during the invasion of Ukraine in February of 2022. In the wake of what was allegedly "a premeditated and unprovoked" attack on Ukraine, a significant number of the world nations including the United States, the United Kingdom and the EU imposed a number of punitive financial restrictions on dealings by and with Russia. Among other things, these caused the Russian stock market to close down and the Russian ruble to lose 30% of its value against major foreign currencies such as the US. dollar. In order to evade these sanctions, Russian banks and oligarchs reportedly turned to cryptocurrencies to protect the value of their assets:

> Cryptocurrencies could be providing Russian oligarchs and banks with an escape route as the country becomes economically isolated from the rest of the world.[895]

For some time prior to the invasion of Ukraine, other nations have been threatening Russia with severe economic sanctions if it went ahead with the invasion. Of course, Russia did, and it is reported that trading in various cryptocurrencies such as Bitcoin, Tether and Dogecoin shot up from the day that Moscow launched its attack on Ukraine. Russian institutions and individuals or apparently trying to escape the impact of the devaluation of the ruble. Shortly after the invasion, the value of Bitcoins rose from US$ 35,000 to more than US$ 44,000.

It was reported at the beginning of October 2022 that:

> Pro-Russian groups are raising funds in crypto currency to prop up paramilitary operations and evade U.S. sanctions as the war with Ukraine rages.[896]

These were reported to have raised more than US$ 400,000 since the start of Ukraine invasion. Telegram, an encrypted messaging service, is reportedly a popular vehicle to gather and send funds to Pro-Russian groups working to aid the invaders in their war against Ukraine.[897]

One group reportedly raising production funds is called "Task Force Rusich" which has been described by the U.S. Treasury as "a neo-Nazi paramilitary group that has participated in combat alongside Russia's military in the Ukraine." This group has been sanctioned by the U.S. Treasury Department. They were reportedly trying to use

894. Andy Greenberg, "Cryptocurrency Is Funding Ukraine's Defense—and Its Hacktivists," WIRED, online, February 8, 2022, accessed February 25, 2022.
895. Ben Martin, "Bitcoin Surges as Russians Seek to Avoid Sanctions," The Times, online, March 2, 2022.
896. Arjun Kharpal, "Pro-Russian Groups Are Raising Funds in Crypto to Prop Up Military Operation and Evade U.S. Sanctions," CNBC online, October 3, 2022.
897. *Ibid.*

the money they were raising to purchase useful military equipment such as thermal imaging hardware and radios.[898]

Another group named "Novorossia Aid Coordinating Center" raised about US$ 21,000, mostly in Bitcoin for the purpose of purchasing drones.[899]

It is believed by cryptocurrency market experts that groups like these, trying to circumvent sanctions, terrorist financing and anti-money laundering regulations, were able to do so because there are reportedly exchanges which do not comply with laws preventing these activities from allowing shadowy groups like these two transfer funds they raise in cryptocurrency into fiat currency.

It is reportedly possible to do such illicit exchanges but not on a very large scale. Very large transactions would attract too much attention from financial and other government regulators who are trying to prevent cryptocurrency from being used for illegal activities.[900]

It is not only those that are trying to avoid sanctions connected to the Ukrainian invasion that are seeking to raise cryptocurrency. Ukraine is also working to raise donations to its war efforts in cryptocurrency.[901]

It is well known that digital assets such as cryptocurrencies are decentralized, not controlled by national central banks, can cross borders, and are lightly regulated or unregulated. They also provide those buying and selling cryptocurrencies with a significant degree of anonymity.

Using cryptocurrency to avoid international financial sanctions is not unprecedented. Iran reportedly has used Bitcoin mining to avoid financial sanctions. North Korea is also engaged in a program of stealing cryptocurrency to help it avoid international sanctions:[902]

> Digital assets exist only as strings of computer code and are decentralized, unlike traditional money controlled by a central bank. Their status as borderless, unregulated currencies could prove attractive to those seeking to put assets out of reach of sanctions.[903]

However, experts point out that cryptocurrency will not provide Russia with the financing needed in order to be able to finance the invasion of Ukraine or run their economy. There is not enough cryptocurrency in circulation to allow Russia to replace the ruble. Also, those that deal in cryptocurrency will need to be cautious in their dealings because if they are aware that their counterparties maybe those subject to sanctions, these dealers will want to avoid being possibly found guilty of the criminal offense of assisting sanctioned parties in avoiding sanctions.

Finally, although cryptocurrency does provide a degree of anonymity, the Ledger function of blockchain technology means that no transactions can be entirely anonymous. This was shown to be true when the U.S. government recovered billions of

898. *Ibid.*
899. *Ibid.*
900. *Ibid.*
901. *Ibid.*
902. *Ibid.*
903. *Ibid.*

dollars in cryptocurrency stolen in a hack of Bitfinex and when the U.S. government arrested two people in New York for allegedly trying to launder a large amount of stolen cryptocurrency.

It is known that financial authorities in the countries that have imposed sanctions on Russia will be examining the cryptocurrency markets for possible attempts to avoid sanctions. The U.S. government has reportedly asked cryptocurrency exchanges to make sure they are not involved in sanction avoidance. The U.K. government has reportedly said that those that try to avoid sanctions will be subject to enforcement actions.

§16.02 CRYPTO WAR

One unfortunate consequence of the growth of crypto assets is that they have made it possible to change the nature of cyberwar into an unfortunate hybrid where crypto assets can assist in the prosecution of cyberattacks and can make it more possible to support physical war as well.

CHAPTER 17
The Future of Cryptocurrency

§17.01 A REGULATORY GAP?

[A] Compensation Issues

Most cryptocurrencies are not regulated by financial regulators and are not eligible for financial compensation schemes that may be in place to protect investors in more traditional assets and financial products.[904]

One line of thought that is emerging is that Banks that deal in cryptocurrencies must be prepared to cover the risks they pose.

[1] Basel BIS View

One of the international regulators that sets banking rules around the world, the Basel Committee on Banking Supervision, a division of Basel's Bank for International Settlements (BIS), has pointed out that because of the risks that digital currencies pose to world banking stability, banks that hold cryptocurrencies should have 100 times as much capital to protect against possible dramatic decline in the value of cryptocurrency.

A "risk weighting" for cryptocurrencies of 1250% has been proposed for every dollar of exposure to cryptocurrencies.[905]

However, this large risk weighting will apply only to be privately produced digital currencies and not to digital currencies that may be produced by central banks and tied to the value of traditional currencies such as the Pound Sterling or the Dollar.

---

904. "Cryptocurrencies Boom as Punters Throw Caution to the Wind," The Times, online June 18, 2021.
905. Patrick Hosking, "World's Banks Must Cover Risk of Bitcoin, Says Regulator," The Times, online June 11, 2021.

So-called stablecoins, if they were genuinely sufficiently "tied" to respected fiat currencies (or other assets of ascertainable value), would continue to operate under the same rules as applied to existing national currencies.[906]

There is little doubt that there will be a range of developments with respect to digital currencies as time goes on.

§17.02 RISKS MISUNDERSTOOD

However, despite the risks that have been described in the volatility the cryptocurrencies have shown, their popularity as an investment vehicle has continued to expand.

It was reported in June 2021 that the number of cryptocurrency buyers had expanded by about 400,000. This rise in ownership was occurring despite what was found to be the public's misunderstanding of the nature of cryptocurrency assets. It was also worrying to regulators that a significant portion of investors in crypto were borrowing money to buy them.

Since cryptocurrency's introduction, there have clearly been different and sometimes contradictory reactions to it from individuals, private companies, government organizations, of course, hackers and criminals. Some have been enthusiastic about it, and others have been wary or opposed.

§17.03 THOUGHTS ON CRYPTO

Since cryptocurrency was first created and used sometime after 2008, there have been several narratives published extolling the potential virtues of digital currency and predicting that not only it will become an accepted medium of exchange but also it might eventually replace state-created paper currencies.

However, these positive predictions appear not to be coming true.[907]

Cryptocurrencies appear to have become mostly a medium of wild speculation in which some people make a lot of money and others lose a great deal.

As a result, as shown above, financial regulators and other government agencies have moved to restrict or forbid their use.

One of the principal myths that has grown up around cryptocurrency is that it eliminated the centralization of currency creation.

It was argued that anyone could acquire the electronic means to create Bitcoins and other cryptocurrencies. The truth has been quite different; four or five firms have dominated cryptocurrency creation.

For example, it has been reported that nine Chinese companies controlled 79% of the Bitcoin mining network.[908]

---

906. Patrick Hosking, June 11, 2021.
907. Concoda, "We Are About to Witness the Great Cryptocurrency Reset," medium.com, online, July 9, 2021.
908. *Ibid.*

However, one thing is quite clear, the frenetic activity generated by interest in cryptocurrencies is changing the world of finance in a way that may be permanent.

For a long time, national governments have been considered the only legitimate creators of acceptable currency.

Prior to that, currencies had been issued by private banks and other private commercial groups. However, as over time, some of these went broke, and nations turned to central banks as the sole legitimate issuers of acceptable currency.

The centralization of money issuance also allowed central banks to step in at times of financial crisis and loan or inject money where needed to prop up important financial institutions in times when their collapse would have damaged the entire financial system and put the assets of individual citizens at risk of loss or devaluation.

Now the power of central banks is being threatened by a digital method of creating cryptocurrencies.

Initially, confidence in these cryptocurrencies was created by the fact that blockchain technology supposedly restricted their creation and use in highly restricted ways that would defeat attempts to counterfeit, manipulate or steal them.

Many people saw value in having a payment method that allowed them to engage in transactions free from the interference of government-regulated financial systems.

These developments have changed the world's view of how instruments of value can be created and have led to the creation of several different kinds. One of these is of course cryptocurrencies of which Bitcoin is the best-known example. Another is stablecoins, a kind of enhanced digital currency. A third kind is the types of electronic payment methods provided by tech companies. One has been created by Facebook called "Diem."

The public does not seem to be bothered by the fact that their "old-fashioned" electronic payments are only guaranteed by their commercial banks and not by a central government bank. But at least these commercial banks that are backing those electronic transactions are regulated by central government financial regulations.

Old-fashioned cash also has advantages. One of the reasons that people like to use cash is that it provides them with a certain level of privacy in their financial transactions.

If all financial electronic go electronic, how secure will the data surrounding them be?[909]

§17.04 IS THIS THE END OF CRYPTO?

Crypto has rapidly spread around the world, and a few countries have even adopted cryptocurrency as a legal tender of payment of debts.

On the other side, cryptocurrency has been volatile, has been involved in many frauds, literally hundreds of cryptocurrencies have flooded the market, and crypto has been criticized as a "non-productive" asset.

909. Simon Nixon, "State-backed Digital Currencies Are a Gamble that Might Not Pay Off," The Times, on line July 22, 2021.

It is the case that between November of 2021 and May of 2022 the value of cryptocurrencies has fallen by about half. However, it has been reported that respected investors still regard crypto as a desirable investment. The venture capital company Andreessen Horowitz is reported to be thinking that May of 2022 was a "Golden era for crypto":[910]

> A Silicon Valley venture capital giant has raised $4.5 billion to invest in blockchain technology via the largest cryptocurrency fund to date. Andreessen Horowitz hailed a golden era for "Web 3" technology products underpinned by blockchains, the shared ledger systems used by cryptocurrencies as it announced its fourth crypto fund. The firm said it had decided to "go big" and place an unprecedented bet on the sector's role in the future of the internet, which it believes will be powered by blockchain-based platforms and tools.

There are clearly different views about the value of digital assets, and their future will not be settled for some time to come. There seems little doubt that the virtual, digital world will increasingly be a more important part of our lives over the coming decades. The invention of digital computing and the Internet has opened a vast, largely unexplored world of possibilities for obtaining information, expanding communication, diversifying entertainment, changing the nature of work, and radically reorganizing commerce. Digital assets will undoubtedly play an important role in these changes. But the extent to which cryptocurrency will become recognized as the dominant medium of exchange and who will control it is unsettled.

It does seem inevitable that paper, fiat currency, will ultimately be replaced by digital currency. But it is not clear what limitations if any will be placed on issuing and trading search currency. Will it, like fiat currency, become a monopoly of the state?

Since the beginning of time, the role of private individuals in issuing "money" has always been troublesome. Counterfeiting and adulteration were problems that always troubled financial markets. Consequently, government increasingly took the role of monopolizing the issuance and regulation of money.

Because of the numerous problems that the private issuance of cryptocurrency has presented, including theft, frauds perpetrated on the public, and the danger of permitting competition with government-controlled financial systems, it is not unreasonable to expect the control of digital assets will increasingly fall to the government and that private digital assets will be heavily restricted and, in some cases, banned.

[A] The FTX Collapse

FTX was a cryptocurrency exchange that allowed customers to purchase cryptocurrencies. It was once valued at US$ 32 billion. In November of 2022, FTX filed for bankruptcy, and clients were unable to withdraw funds. Sam Bankman-Fried, the founder and chief executive, resigned and was arrested in the Bahamas on 12 December and deported to the U.S. to face criminal and civil proceedings.

910. Callam Jones, "'Golden Era' for Crypto as Andreessen Horowitz Bets $4.5bn on Blockchain" The Times, online, May 26, 2022.

Damian Williams, U.S. attorney for the Southern District of New York, said that the operation of FTX was one of the "biggest financial frauds in American history."[911]

John Ray, an executive who was tasked with liquidating Enron, was appointed as administrator and CEO of FTX. He is reported to have said:

> Never in my career have I seen such an utter failure of corporate controls at every level of an organization, from lack of financial statements to a complete failure of internal controls or governance whatsoever.

FTX is a serious failure, but its collapse may only have a temporary financial impact on the expanding crypto asset business around the world.

However, it will undoubtedly inspire some financial market regulators to make regulatory changes to regulate the crypto asset business more strictly.

But, at this point, we do not know when those changes are going to happen and how extensive they will be.

One issue that has been of particular concern to governments is what impact cryptocurrency will have on the economies of various countries.

By the end of 2021, this was reasonably difficult to know. This is partly due to the fact that the ownership of cryptocurrency is so concentrated. Apparently less than one-tenth of 1% of cryptocurrency investors hold more than a quarter of the total amount of cryptocurrency in circulation.[912] It is reported that about 10,000 investors have 5 million of the 19 million Bitcoins in circulation. Their holding is worth about US$ 230 billion. This has turned out to be a matter of considerable interest not only to governments and regulators but also to the general public. There are websites that concentrate on providing the names and addresses of the largest holders of Bitcoin.

From a regulatory policy point of view, it is useful for economic regulators to understand who is likely to benefit the most from rises and falls in the values of cyber currency. It is well known that cyber currency has been very volatile and that changes in the perception of its value, which might be triggered by statements of well-known influencers or changes in government attitudes toward cyber currency, can lead to rapid and dramatic changes in the market value of cryptocurrencies.

One of the striking things about the cryptocurrency market is that competition between them to sell units has become so intensive that promoters of various cryptos have undertaken huge advertising campaigns not only with "influencers" as spokespeople but also using internationally famous celebrities and sports figures to promote sales and trading.

In the first half of 2022, an article in *The New York Times* highlighted the extent to which cryptocurrencies have been intensively advertised using well-known celebrities and pointing out that falls in the value of cryptocurrencies have become

911. Kattie Prescott and Callum Jones, "FTX 'Is One of the Biggest Financial Frauds in History': Exchange's Former Chief Sam Bankman-Fried Faces Extradition to America.," The Times, online, December 14, 2022.
912. "Tiny Bitcoin 'Rich List' Holds Huge Proportion of Cryptocurrency," The Times, online, December 21, 2021.

something of an embarrassment to the celebrities who participated in these marketing campaigns:[913]

> "Enthusiasm for crypto from Hollywood celebrities and top athletes reached a fever pitch over the past year. On social media, during interviews and even in music videos, they portrayed virtual currency as a world with its own hip culture and philosophy—one that was more inclusive than traditional finance and that involved the chance to make loads of money. The Super Bowl of 2022 was nicknamed the "Crypto Bowl" this year because so many ads—which cost as much as $7 million for 30 seconds—featured the industry several of them starring boldfaced names."
>
> But after investors watched hundreds of billions of dollars disappear in a sell off this month [May 2022] those famous boosters now face intensifying criticism that they helped drive vulnerable fans to invest in crypto without emphasizing the risks.[914]

In a follow-up article, John Reed Stark, former chief of the Internet enforcement at the SEC, is quoted as saying:

> You have this shameless profiteering from celebrities and others, who aren't at all disinterested or impartial. There is a lot of potential for harm.[915]

A particular promotion that was highlighted in the article was one by the Internet "influencer" Logan Paul who is reported to have around six million "followers" on Twitter. He told his followers about his enthusiasm for a new cryptocurrency named "Dink Doink." This was supposed to earn purchasers a portion of the income attributed to an animated cartoon character that was going to appear in movies and cartoons. Mr. Paul's promotion was made in June of 2021, and it is reported that by mid-July of that year the market price of Dink Doink had crashed to a fraction of a cent. It is reported that in making his promotion, Mr. Paul had not revealed that he and the creator of this crypto were friends and that he had received a large allocation of those crypto coins when the product was launched. In a subsequent interview, Mr. Paul is quoted as saying:

> I don't know what went absurdly wrong. That's the project from hell, and I just wiped my hands of that.[916]

Do celebrities and influencers who promote crypto have any legal liability for their activities if those who are influenced to invest in crypto by promotions they participate in lose a significant amount of money after being influenced by them? This

913. Tiffany Hsu, "All Those Celebrities Pushing Crypto Are Not So Vocal Now: Crypto Boosters Such as Matt Damon, Reese Witherspoon and Gwyneth Paltrow Have Been Criticized for Hyping Virtual Currency Without Highlighting the Risks." The New York Times, online, May 17, 2022.
914. *Ibid.*
915. David Yaffe-Bellany, "How Influencers Hype Crypto, Without Disclosing Their Financial Ties: Logan Paul, Paul Pierce and Other Celebrities Have Promoted Risky and Obscure Digital Currencies, Sometimes Failing to Mention Their Conflicts of Interest.," The New York Times, online, May 27, 2022.
916. *Ibid.*

is something that these celebrities and influencers may need to discuss with their legal advisors in light of the nature of the promotions or advertisements that they participated in.

However, it is worth looking at U.S. Securities laws and regulations on investment advertising. In particular, one might consider the Investment Advisors Act of 1940 Rule 206(4)-1(a)(1), which states that an investment advertisement may not:

> Include any untrue statement of a material fact, or omit to state a material fact necessary in order to make the statement made, in light of the circumstances under which it was made, not misleading.[917]

The *NY Times* article recounts that in a Super Bowl commercial for The FTX crypto exchange, "the comedian Larry David denigrated important inventions such as the wheel and the lightbulb before rejecting crypto. The ad winkingly urged viewers: 'Don't be like Larry'":[918]

> Jeff Shaffer, the director of that Super Bowl spot, said in an email that he and Mr. David did not have a comment on the market collapse.
>
> "Unfortunately, I don't think we'd have anything to add as we have no idea how cryptocurrency works (even after having it explained to us repeatedly), don't own it and don't follow its market," he said. "We just set out to make a funny commercial!"[919]

2022 has experienced a number of dramatic crashes in the value of cryptocurrencies that were once extremely popular and considered to be worthwhile investments. For example, a Korean entrepreneur, Do Kwon, created a cryptocurrency called "Luna" that he described as "my greatest invention." He reportedly attracted significant investment from several venture capitalists, and at one point the total market value of Luna exceeded US$ 40 billion. When people challenged him on the wisdom of investing in his cryptocurrencies, Mr. Kwon reportedly said, "I don't debate with the poor."

However, in May of 2022, Luna experienced a spectacular crash with the price falling to almost zero.[920]

These dramatic rises and falls in the prices of cryptocurrencies underline the basic truth that cryptocurrency is totally dependent on what purchasers think someone else will be willing to pay for it in the future.

So, are we able to predict whether crypto is going to continue to expand as an investment and as a substitute currency or whether the negative issues connected with

---

917. Electronic Code of Federal Regulations, Title 17—Commodity and Securities Exchanges, Chapter II-SEC—Part 275—Rules and Regulations, Investment Advisers Act of 1940, section 275.206(4)-1 Investment adviser marketing, online, Cornell Law School, Legal Information Institute, accessed May 18, 2022.
918. Tiffany Hsu, *supra*.
919. *Ibid.*
920. David Yaffe-Bellany and Erin Griffith, "How a Trash-Talking Crypto Founder Caused a $40 Billion Crash," The New York Times, online, May 18, 2022.

it (such as the FTX collapse) cause people to lose interest and regulators to make it harder to own and trade crypto?

That is difficult to predict and involves many factors and a wide range of issues.

The world of cryptocurrency has been changing so rapidly it is difficult to speculate about what the future of cryptocurrency will be.

It is reported that the Bank of England Director for Financial Stability has pointed out that the cryptocurrency business had, by the beginning of 2022, grown to ten times the size it had been two years before. She urged financial institutions to be cautious about getting involved with crypto, given their volatility and their unfortunate relationship to criminal activities. This appears to be good advice not only for financial institutions but for anyone considering becoming involved in cryptocurrencies.[921]

However, there are some trends and some issues that do still need to be resolved, and the Director offers some suggestions about how these might be resolved in the future.

She has had years of experience dealing with complex financial services products such as derivatives, private payment systems, interest rate swaps, currency markets and others. Many of these provide complicated problems. However, few financial products are as convoluted as the cryptocurrency markets. Trying to see what is actually going on with them is to truly travel down the rabbit hole.

In the first place, there seems to be no resolution either by the creators and users of cryptocurrency or governments of the jurisdictions within which cryptocurrencies are being used as to whether these are money, investments or commodities or some complex combination of all three. What makes this difficult to resolve is that these currencies largely exist in a virtual, digital as opposed to material or concrete state. Are these things merely exist in the imagination of the cloud or in the imaginations of their creators or do they have any concrete reality? When one owns cryptocurrency, exactly what does one own? In fact, the value of these things is largely dependent on what third parties think of them. Do they consider them useful or valuable enough to accept them in exchange for goods or services or not? That test is what determines whether or not they are indeed "currency" or merely a fairy tale from someone who is selling air.

One of the things that has happened with the rise of the value of digital currencies is that they have been touted by some as a "store of value" as a rival to gold.[922] It has been reported that the investment bank Goldman Sachs has been one of the boosters of this idea expressing the view that Bitcoin possessed "inflation proof" qualities that put it in competition with gold as a store of value.[923] Indeed, Goldman was reported to have expressed the view that cryptocurrency "already accounted for 20% of what is called the 'store of value' market, comprising gold and Bitcoin … ."[924]

921. Greg Cameron, "Tread Carefully with Crypto, Says Bank Official," The Times, online, January 21, 2022.
922. Simon Nixon, "Hopes of Bitcoin Becoming Credible Have Slumped Along with Its Price," The Times, online, February 3, 2022.
923. *Ibid.*
924. *Ibid.*

The financial markets' enthusiasm for cryptocurrency deflated significantly after November of 2021 when Bitcoin's value fell by about 40%, while the price of gold did not change significantly.[925] If it is not already, it should be clear to everyone by now that investing in cryptocurrency is a gamble that can result in significant losses to anyone who owns it.

Of course, some of the enthusiasm of investment banks for cryptocurrency is understandable. For them, it is another product to sell and trade. Regardless of whether they are inclined to invest their own funds in this product, they can earn significant fees from the purchases and trading in cryptocurrency engaged in by their clients. To this end, it is reported that Goldman Sachs has set up a cryptocurrency trading desk and that Morgan Stanley has launched crypto funds. Bitcoin futures contracts are also now being traded on the Chicago Mercantile Exchange.[926]

The opinions of third parties about the value of these digital currencies are also what determines whether or not they work as an investment. The number of cryptocurrencies that exist makes it clear that most of them are not being used as "money." Most are being bought and sold in the hope that their value will increase over time, thereby earning those who purchased them a profit. Those cryptocurrencies that are reasonably well known such as Bitcoin or Ethereum have themselves been extremely volatile, with their market value rising and falling by significant amounts in a relatively short period of time depending upon what is said about them by well-known people, regulators or others.

Their value seems to be entirely independent of their "purchasing power" in the markets for goods and services. This seems to confirm that all cryptocurrencies function primarily as investments and not as "money."

Also, the number of persons who sell goods and services that will accept cryptocurrencies in payment also seems to fluctuate over time. An example is the industrial group of Elon Musk which sometimes indicates it will accept Bitcoin for its products and other times indicates it will accept a crypto called Dogecoin. Of course, Mr. Musk's pronouncements on these things can change at anytime, and that will severely affect the usefulness of these cryptocurrencies as mediums of exchange. In conclusion, the evidence seems to be that cryptocurrencies are being created, offered, bought and sold primarily as investment products rather than as "money"

This should affect how cryptocurrencies will be treated by regulators. There are three principal types of regulators that need to consider how to respond to cryptocurrencies. The first are controllers of money on behalf of governments. Do cryptocurrencies represent a useful tool to supplement the existence and liquidity of fiat currency? Or are they competitor or distraction that needs to be suppressed?

The second are investment regulators. As discussed above, the uncertainty that cryptocurrencies exhibit as mediums of exchange is a strong argument for regulating them as investments.

925. *Ibid.*
926. *Ibid.*

Finally, there are the law enforcement authorities dealing with criminal behavior such as money laundering, fraud and theft. Here is the question of theft. As discussed in previous chapters, criminals have been finding increasingly clever ways to get access to cryptocurrency that does not belong to them.

In 2022, the size of cryptocurrency thefts has been increasing. In February of 2022 it was reported that U.S. officials had arrested two people in connection with the theft (and attempted money laundering) of approximately 120,000 Bitcoin worth about 5 billion dollars. The currency had originally been stolen by a hacker from the Bitfinex currency exchange. Reportedly, the hacker was able to break into the exchange and engage in thousands of unauthorized transactions that funneled money to the hacker's digital wallet. In order to counter this kind of crime, the U.S. Justice Department had established a National Cryptocurrency Enforcement Team (NCET).[927] This does go to show that US is taking the growing world of cryptocurrency very seriously.

But how many more thefts will there be, how big will they be, and can the stolen currency be recovered? These things remain unknown.

The U.S. government, along with governments of other major market centers, has expressed the view that investors should be cautious when investing in cryptocurrency because of their demonstrated volatility. In particular, U.S. government officials have suggested that retirement plan trustees should "exercise extreme care" before putting any of the assets under their control into cryptocurrencies.

Nevertheless, in April of 2022, it was reported that the biggest provider of retirement plans in the US, Fidelity Investments, which administers over US$ 11 trillion in U.S. assets, was going to allow their clients to include Bitcoin in their retirement plans. That such a highly respected organization would accept this change is a reflection of how strong the demand is among Fidelity clients to be allowed to include cryptocurrencies as part of their retirement plans.[928]

It is not yet clear whether Fidelity Investments' concession on this issue will be imitated by other pension providers, but it is certainly an indication of how popular cryptocurrencies are becoming.

[B] Visa, Mastercard and Cryptocurrency

There is evidence that other major financial institutions are beginning to take cryptocurrency more seriously, despite the problems that these digital assets have been experiencing in the financial markets.

In March of 2021, Visa published an online announcement entitled:

> Digital currency comes to Visa's settlement platform: With the direct acceptance of payments in USD coin, Visa forges new connections between digital and traditional currencies.[929]

927. *BBC News*, online, "Record-high Seizure of $5bn in Stolen Bitcoin," February 9, 2022.
928. Callum Jones, "Fidelity Investments Investors Can Add Bitcoin to Pension Savings," The Times, online, April 27, 2022.
929. Visa, online at: usa.visa.com, March 29, 2021.

Visa offers the following explanation for its decision:

> The implications of our work with stablecoins are potentially far reaching—enabling our ability to one day support new Central Bank Digital Currencies (CBDCs) as they become available, central banks are ramping up CBDCs, with 80% reporting that they are engaging in some CBDC-related effort, according to research from the BIS[930] [Bank for International Settlements]. "We are committed to supporting these initiatives so they can be integrated into existing payments ecosystem. At Visa, we are on a mission to connect the world through the most innovative, reliable and secure digital payment network—and we're continuing to push the boundaries of that network by connecting to public blockchains and new forms of money. Where proud of the work we've done so far, and excited about what the future holds."[931]

[C] Crypto Winter?

The viability of cryptocurrency as a popular investment came into question by June of 2022 when the dramatic price fall from the record high of November 2021 had prompted many owners of cryptocurrency to sell their holdings. The sell-off was so dramatic that Coinbase global, a large cryptocurrency trading exchange, said that a looming economic recession in the US could lead to such a dramatic decline in crypto ownership and trading that crypto would in effect enter a "crypto winter."[932] Fear of this market change led Coinbase to make about 20% of its workforce redundant. About 1,100 of its workforce found themselves discharged, and Coinbase has said it expects more layoffs.[933] This concern was prompted by the fact that Bitcoin, the most popular best-known cryptocurrency, had lost about 60% of its value from its market price in November of 2021. If confidence in this well-known cryptocurrency had fallen so dramatically, there was little doubt that the many other cryptocurrencies that had been created suffered similar or even worse declines in value. It is reported that the CEO of Coinbase, Brian Armstrong wrote the following email to Coinbase staff:

> We appear to be entering a recession after a 10-plus year economic boom. A recession could lead to another crypto winter and could last for an extended period.[934]

Mr. Armstrong appeared to be correct that winter is coming. In early August of 2022, it was reported that Coinbase global suffered the loss for the second quarter of 2022. Coinbase said it suffered a loss of 1.09 billion dollars in the quarter that ended in June of 2022. This is dramatically different than the profit of over US$ 1.6 billion it made a year earlier. Trading volumes were nearly cut in half, down from over US$ 450

930. BIS Papers No. 107, "Impending Arrival—A Sequel to the Survey on Central Bank Digital Currency," January 2020.
931. *Supra*, Visa, above.
932. Russell Hotten, "Coinbase Cuts 1,100 Jobs as Chief Warns 'Crypto Winter' Is Coming," The Times, online, June 13, 2022.
933. Martin Strydom, "Crypto's Fall Will Cost More Jobs At Coinbase, Says Bank," The Times, online, June 28, 2022.
934. *Ibid*.

billion to just over US$ 215 billion. Coinbase is a major cryptocurrency exchange. It is reported it has over 90 million users in more than 100 countries and is a listed company on the NASDAQ Index. In response to this bad news, Coinbase shares suffered price declines.[935]

It is thought that the retreat from cryptocurrency ownership was in response to a general fear among the public that a possible economic recession in the U.S. would leave them with less disposable income, and consequently, many people decided to end their exposure to what are considered to be risky investments.[936]

[1] Is There Any Thaw?

At the end of September 2022, an article appeared on CNN business asking the question of whether "Bitcoin winter [was] beginning to thaw out."[937]

The conclusion of the article was that signs of improvement were beginning to appear in the cryptocurrency market. The positive signs included rises in the comparative value of cryptocurrencies such as Bitcoin against traditional fiat currencies such as the British pound and others. This was touted by crypto supporters as evidence that cryptocurrencies might be coming to be regarded as a financial "safe haven." However, one has to keep in mind that this was occurring because the U.S. dollar was at the time increasing in strength against other national currencies. So of course it could be a sign that the dollar was being considered the real safe haven.[938]

At that time, cryptocurrencies were still worth about 60% less than they had been the previous year. A number of crypto businesses went bankrupt.[939]

From comments he reportedly expressed at the same time, it was clear that chairman of the U.S. Federal Reserve Jerome Powell did not regard cryptocurrencies as any sort of "safe haven." He is reported to have said, "There's a real need for more appropriate regulation."

Powell also reportedly stated that he did not believe the US was going to issue a "Digital Dollar" anytime soon. He is reported to have said:

> We see this as a process of at least a couple of years, where we're doing work and building public confidence in our analysis and in our ultimate conclusions, which as I say, we certainly haven't reached yet.[940]

Other central bankers also failed to express positive feelings about cryptocurrencies. Ravi Menon of the Singapore Monetary Authority reportedly said:

> I don't see any redeeming value [in cryptocurrencies]. Their time for reckoning has come.[941]

935. Robert Miller, "Crypto Winter Comes Early for Coinbase," The Times, online, August 10, 2022.
936. *Ibid.* and Matin Strydom, *supra.*
937. Nicole Goodkind, "Is the Bitcoin Winter Beginning to Thaw Out," CNN Business, September 28, 2022, online at: edition.cnn.com.
938. *Ibid.*
939. *Ibid.*
940. *Ibid.*
941. *Ibid.*

[2] Voyager Digital Bankruptcy

Another symptom of growing problems in the digital currency business was the July 2022 bankruptcy filing of Voyager Digital, the American crypto lender/broker. This was said to be a result of the dramatic fall of cryptocurrency values in the spring and summer of 2022.[942] A crypto brokerage house, Voyager Digital, allowed customers to trade a number of cryptocurrencies on its platform. Its filing for bankruptcy in the U.S. Bankruptcy Court for the Southern District of New York listed liabilities in the billions of dollars and assets of between 1 billion and 10 billion dollars. It listed over a billion of crypto on its trading platform and over 300 million in customers' cash on deposit in a New York commercial bank. A major problem for Voyager was the default on a loan of over US$ 600 million from Voyager by a crypto hedge fund called Three Arrows Capital.[943]

Voyager is a publicly traded company listed on the Toronto Stock Exchange. Its shares lost 90% of their value since the beginning of 2022. The dramatic fall during the crypto crisis in the spring and summer of 2022 caused severe liquidity problems for crypto businesses triggered by a large number of customer withdrawals over concerns of crypto value declines.

Voyager said it hoped that its bankruptcy would allow it to undertake restructuring that would permit them to reimburse customers.

Voyager is not the only crypto business to have so far suffered severe reversals in 2022.

[D] FTX's Involvement

As discussed above, in several places in this book, FTX ran into many serious problems that resulted in bankruptcy and criminal investigations. Head of FTX, Sam Bankman-Fried, extended loans to Voyager and other crypto firms in an attempt to prevent their collapse. Bankman-Fried had made FTX a lender of last resort for the troubled industry. Some compared Bankman-Fried's efforts to the role played by famous banker John Pierpont, or JP, Morgan in rescuing Wall Street lenders from collapse after a series of bank runs known as the Panic of 1907 which preceded the establishment of the Fed. However, as discussed above, FTX itself filed for bankruptcy in November of 2022, and Bankman-Fried was arrested for fraud and other criminal offenses.

[E] Crypto Going Green

In September of 2022, Vitalik Buterin, the cofounder of Ethereum, the second most popular cryptocurrency in the world, made a public announcement that Ethereum was going to change its business model to one that used almost 100% less energy.[944]

942. "Voyager Digital Files for Bankruptcy Protection in Crypto Fall," The Times, online, July 7, 2022.
943. Ryan Brown, "Crypto Brokerage Voyager Digital Files for Chapter 11 Bankruptcy Protection."
944. Joe Tidy, "Ethereum Merge: How One Big Cryptocurrency Is Going Green," *BBC News*, online, September 14, 2022.

That is a significant announcement because Ethereum has said that in June of 2022, Ethereum used as much electricity as the Netherlands to power its crypto mining operations. "Crypto mining" is well known to be the way that major cryptocurrencies such as Bitcoin and Ethereum were created. They were issued as "proof of work" for having used an enormous amount of computing power on large arrays of expensive powerful computers called graphics processing units to perform complicated mathematical transactions. In return for this "work" the "mining" organization, in this case Ethereum, would be issued a unit of cryptocurrency. The existence and any subsequent transactions involving this unit of cryptocurrency would be recorded in a universally accessible digital action record called a "block chain." The blockchain record verified for anyone who accessed it the existence and ownership changes of any cyber currency unit.

Ethereum maintains a well-known blockchain to verify ownership and movement of its cryptocurrency. Other major cryptocurrencies such as Bitcoin, Dogecoin and Litecoin also maintain blockchains to support their cryptocurrency systems. They rely on the "proof of work" systems to legitimize their existence. This method is believed to give buyers and sellers of cryptocurrency a level of confidence in the legitimacy of the cryptocurrency they are dealing in.

However, the fact that crypto mining requires so much electricity to power so many powerful computing arrays around the world has led to criticism that using this much electricity does significant damage to the environment by requiring electricity suppliers to release carbon dioxide when generating the electricity required for these operations.

From the point of view of a large cryptocurrency issuer, such as Ethereum, the "proof of work" system is very costly. They have to pay for the computers, pay for the electricity to run them, and pay for the staff and the premises needed to conduct these complex operations. This has caused a number of crypto mining operations to move to more remote areas to reduce the costs of their crypto mining operations. For example, it is reported that by January of 2022, Kazakhstan was the second biggest crypto mining country in the world. In the desert near the city of Ekibastuz, *there* is a mine there using 50,000 computers operating around the clock with staff working twelve hour shifts. The electricity needed to power this operation is provided by high polluting coal-fired power stations. This concentration is not necessarily always a positive thing for the crypto mining industry. It was reported that for several days, the Kazakh crypto mining operations were cut off from the Internet, causing cryptocurrency transactions around the world to be disrupted.[945]

What is one to make of Ethereum's announcement? Is that the case that the large crypto miners are suddenly overcome with guilt about the damage they could be doing to the environment? Or is this an indication that recent volatility in the crypto coin markets have endangered the revenue streams of the major cryptocurrency issuers and they are looking hard for ways to reduce their costs? Moving away from crypto mining in order to produce and support the issuing of cryptocurrencies could significantly

945. Joe Tidy, "Inside Kazakhstan's Giant Crypto-mine," *BBC News*, online, January 31, 2022.

reduce the costs of operations for major cryptocurrency companies such as Ethereum, Bitcoin and others because they will not need to spend as much money on computer arrays, staff, premises and electricity costs, etc. However, this does raise the question of whether public confidence in cryptocurrencies will not be significantly reduced if they are no longer supported by "proof of work."

[F] Will Digital Assets Last?

The volatility of digital assets, the number of them that have flooded the market, their use by criminals to perpetrate various cybercrimes and the skepticism of some government regulators as to the legitimacy and value all raise questions as to whether digital assets will continue to have a viable market.

However, despite these problems, interest in digital assets has remained strong. In response to this strong interest, government regulators, around the world, are now adjusting their financial regulatory systems to take account of and control the growing use of digital assets by financial institutions and individuals. In addition, many governments are considering either adopting or recognizing existing digital assets (such as Bitcoin) as legitimate mediums of exchange or issuing their own digital currencies to replace or complement existing national fiat currencies.

[G] Support from Young Investors

Another factor that supports the likelihood that digital asset markets will continue to exist is the strong interest in digital assets by younger investors. In September of 2022, an article in *The Times* reported that:

> Youthful investors ... are increasingly turning to the bright lights of Bitcoin and meme stocks.[946]

The article said that during the pandemic, there was a rise and interest in nontraditional investments, such as cryptocurrencies, among investors who are under 35. Statistical evidence of the interest in these volatile investments is indicated by the fact that during the tax year that ended on April 21, 2021, the amount of capital gains tax paid had nearly doubled. This was attributed by some to the fact that digital investments, such as Bitcoin, that rose to a value of more than US$ 44,000 created big capital gains for investors who had cashed out when the market was high.[947]

In June of 2021, it was reported in the *New York Post* that:

> Young investors are abandoning stocks for crypto – and making millions.[948]

946. Dominic Walsh, "Young Investors Cash in with Risky Crypto Bets," The Times, online, September 19, 2022.
947. *Ibid.*
948. Brooke Kato, "Young Investors Are Abandoning Stocks for Crypto—and Making Millions," New York Post, online, June 30, 2022.

The article goes on to say that many Gen Z and millennial investors are buying crypto coins such as Bitcoin, hoping to win big in those volatile markets. David Yermack, a Professor of Finance and Business Transformation at New York University, said:

> The volatility attracts people who like gambling, excitement and so forth. They're not so interested in underlying economics, but [rather] the chance of a very rapid, high gain, or a very rapid sharp loss. ... [During the pandemic] people had a lot of free time on their hands and were locked in their apartments. ... [Investing in volatile markets fill] a gap that had been created by the lack of entertainment and the lack of recreation that the pandemic caused. Young people seem to enjoy taking what we would call 'contrarian positions' that bet against the wisdom of Wall Street.[949]

One successful 26-year-old crypto investor who lives in Los Angeles said that someday alternative currencies will be completely "mainstream." He said:

> Regardless of where the price goes in the next couple of months, this industry is here to stay.[950]

It is also a factor that social media, which has attracted billions of followers in recent years, has a huge audience among younger people. On social media, some users give information about investments such as cryptocurrency and other digital media that their "followers" pay attention to. As a result, a "passionate community" of young people has developed that shares investment information and advice that can have a significant impact on investments.[951]

It seems likely that these factors, and the growth of electronic commerce generally, will continue to provide enough support for digital assets for the markets to continue and grow. This makes it inevitable that financial regulators will increasingly believe that it will be necessary to carefully regulate the creation and use of these assets. There is no doubt that the years to come are going to see a tremendous growth in digital asset regulation. It is wise for those whose business is connected to the financial and digital markets to understand the principles of this regulation and to be aware of the changes that are likely to occur.

[H] Financial Services Sandbox

One thing that is bound to encourage expansion of the digital asset offerings around the world is the establishment of "regulatory sandbox" regimes in many countries, such as explained above in chapters about the U.S. and U.K. regulatory regimes.

Regulatory sandbox regimes permit the introduction and sale of innovative financial products such as cyber currencies and other digital assets on a limited "test" basis within a lighter regulatory regime if the offeror reaches a relatively informal

949. *Ibid.*
950. *Ibid.*
951. *Ibid.*

agreement with the relevant financial regulator regarding the nature and scope of a test marketing effort of a new and perhaps innovative financial product.

It is not within the scope of this book to provide details on all of the sandbox regimes that have been introduced in countries around the world. However, it may be useful for the reader to know that, as of the writing of this chapter, it has been reported that the following countries have instituted sandbox regimes within their jurisdictions.

Details about how these sandbox regimes are regulated can be obtained from qualified advisors in those jurisdictions.

By the beginning of November 2020, the World Bank reported the existence of seventy-three sandbox regimes in fifty-seven jurisdictions.[952] Around 20% of the sandboxes have been established in what the World Bank considers advanced economies, and about 70% are found in what are considered emerging markets and developing economies.[953]

The introduction of sandbox regimes has been reported by the World Bank in the following countries:

- Australia
- Bahrain
- Barbados
- Bermuda
- Brazil
- Brunei
- Bulgaria
- Canada
- China
- Columbia
- Denmark
- Egypt
- Eswatini
- Fiji
- Georgia
- Hong Kong (China)
- Hungary
- India
- Indonesia
- Isle of Man
- Jamaica
- Japan
- Jordan
- Kazakhstan
- Kenya

952. The World Bank, "Key Data from Regulatory Sandboxes Across the Globe," Brief, November 1, 2020, online at: worldbank.org.
953. *Ibid.*

- Korea
- Kuwait
- Kirghizstan
- Lithuania
- Malaysia
- Malta
- Mauritius
- Mexico
- Mozambique
- The Netherlands
- Nigeria
- Norway
- Pakistan
- The Philippines
- Poland
- Russia
- Rwanda
- Saudi Arabia
- Serbia
- Sierra Leone
- Singapore
- South Africa
- Spain
- Sri Lanka
- Switzerland
- Taiwan
- Thailand
- Tunisia
- Turkey
- UAE
- UK
- USA.

[I] Conclusions

The existence of these more informal regulatory arrangements will undoubtedly encourage the introduction of new financial products into the foreseeable future. Consequently, it is unlikely that cyber currencies and digital asset products will disappear from the international financial markets despite their risks and volatility.

This is a new world of financial market products and financial regulation. It exists for a number of reasons, including the fact that there is significant competition between legal jurisdictions for the benefits and taxes that financial markets can bring. The ability to create valuable assets from digital code offers the opportunity for people anywhere to compete in these markets. That opportunity is likely to encourage a growing number of people and firms to encourage computer coding to make money. Only a limited collection of digital equipment is necessary to compete for a share of the world's wealth. Consequently, it is likely that more and more people will seek to take advantage of this new opportunity to get rich. Financial regulation may limit or eliminate that opportunity in some jurisdictions. But it seems unlikely that all jurisdictions will reject digital assets, and the strictness of the regulations will vary. Computers and the Internet offer financial marketers access to the world. It is unrealistic to think they will not continue to take advantage of that.

In conclusion: digital assets (including digital currencies, tokens and NFTS) are here to stay.

Index

B

E

M

V

W

X

Y

Z